Illicit and Illegal
Sex, regulation and social control

Joanna Phoenix
and Sarah Oerton

WILLAN
PUBLISHING

Published by

Willan Publishing
Culmcott House
Mill Street, Uffculme
Cullompton, Devon
EX15 3AT, UK
Tel: +44(0)1884 840337
Fax: +44(0)1884 840251
e-mail: info@willanpublishing.co.uk
website: www.willanpublishing.co.uk

Published simultaneously in the USA and Canada by

Willan Publishing
c/o ISBS, 920 NE 58th Ave, Suite 300,
Portland, Oregon 97213-3786, USA
Tel: +001(0)503 287 3093
Fax: +001(0)503 280 8832
e-mail: info@isbs.com
website: www.isbs.com

© 2005 Joanna Phoenix and Sarah Oerton

The rights of the authors to be identified as the authors of this book have been
asserted by them in accordance with the Copyright, Designs and Patents Act of 1988.

All rights reserved; no part of this publication may be reproduced, stored in a retrieval
system, or transmitted in any form or by any means, electronic, mechanical,
photocopying, recording or otherwise without the prior written permission of the
Publishers or a licence permitting copying in the UK issued by the Copyright Licensing
Agency Ltd, 90 Tottenham Court Road, London W1P 9HE.

First published 2005

ISBN 1-84392-080-8 (paperback)
     1-84392-081-6 (hardback)

British Library Cataloguing-in-Publication Data

A catalogue record for this book is available from the British Library

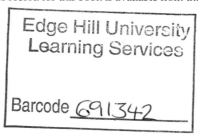

Edge Hill University
Learning Services

Barcode 691342

Typeset by GCS, Leighton Buzzard, Bedfordshire, LU7 1AR
Project managed by Deer Park Productions, Tavistock, Devon
Printed and bound by T.J. International Ltd, Trecerus Industrial Estate, Padstow,
Cornwall

Contents

This book is dedicated to all those who have been,
and are victims of sexual violence and abuse

Acknowledgements

We should like to thank a number of people, who in their own ways, helped and contributed to the production of this book. Earlier drafts of many of the chapters were read and commented upon by a number of individuals. We would like to thank, in particular: Henrice Altink, Catrin Forster, Jude English, Susan Hutson, Emma Carmel and Jenny Pearce. The University of Glamorgan provided financial assistance at varying stages in the research undertaken as well as throughout the writing up process and for that we are very grateful. We would also like to thank Brian Willan for his patience and professionalism. Joanna Phoenix would especially like to thank Sandy. She has been unfailing in her support of and interest in this and many other projects. Sarah Oerton would like to thank Jenny Kitzinger for her help at the eleventh hour.

Chapter 1

Introduction
moral authoritarianism and official and quasi-official discourses of sex

Sexuality must not be described as a stubborn drive, by nature alien and of necessity disobedient to a power which exhausts itself trying to subdue it and often fails to control it entirely. It appears rather an especially dense transfer point for relations of power; between men and women, young people and old people, parents and offspring, teachers and students, priests and laity, an administration and a population. Sexuality is not the most intractable element in power relations, but rather one of those endowed with the greatest instrumentality; useful for the greatest number of manoeuvres and capable of serving as a point of support, as a linchpin, for the most varied strategies.

(Foucault 1978:103)

Introduction

It would appear that contemporary British society is, perhaps more than ever before, obsessed with sex; or more specifically with curtailing, constraining, limiting, regulating and specifying what should or should not be done in the name of sex. Day after day, popular media carry stories of sexual crimes, rape, assault, child sexual abuse as well as sexual scandals between the supposedly 'upright', 'respectable' and the 'vulnerable' or exploitable. Film plots abound in which sexually dangerous acts, behaviours and liaisons rebound on the characters, destroying family lives, careers and communities. Popular magazines tell women and men just how to enjoy sex, with whom, where, how often and when. During the summer of 2004, women were told by both broadsheet and tabloid newspapers not to bemoan turning 50 because being in their 50s: 'is the new 30s', a time when women can truly enjoy sex without the constraints of either concern for birth control or self-consciousness. In short, sex can and should be 're-discovered' upon turning 50. To aid this process, a range of different television programmes now specialize in giving advice on sexual performance to the novice or the initiated. Furthermore and whilst not without its problems, the visibility of lesbian, gay, bisexual and transsexual people in public spaces, not least in various media, has reached new heights. In this, it is held, we have reached a time when we are truly sexually liberated, open and free.

It would also seem that the current obsession with sex is not limited to the realm of popular culture. Religious organizations have had to encounter the history of sexual abuse from clergy to young parishioners. Social care organizations have also had to do so. As a result, there are few if any large scale organizations that have not discussed or formally adopted policies and protocols about 'appropriate' sexual behaviour. In the arena of private business, human resource and personnel departments have been busily drafting sexual harassment policies that specify who can do what with whom, where and when. The concern for excluding sex from organizations has led to policies in which employees can be dismissed for having sexual relationships with other employees. During the same period, social science research has truly opened the realm of 'sex' to scrutiny such that it is possible to talk about a corpus of work that might be called 'the sociology of sex'. Feminist scholars have written extensively about sexual violence, its prevalence, its regulation and its punishment (or lack thereof). Organizational sociologists have examined sex and sexuality in the context of work, employment and organizations. The list is endless, and the story of sexual predation, violence and infractions of what are considered 'appropriate' ways of conducting sex are not confined to research and policy. Popular culture has plentiful references to the 'new bogey man' – the sexual abuser. Indeed, UK society in the early twenty-first century is thought to abound with shadowy and unknown sexual 'predators' of all types, and our streets and homes are held to be no longer safe (if they ever were) from sexual 'excesses' of every kind. Suffice at this point to say that there remains virtually no aspect of social life that has not been touched by some concern for sex, or more particularly, the 'problem' of sex.

This book started as an exploration and explication of this 'problem', as made manifest in the proliferation of regulations that arose in the context of a growing 'noise' about sex across a range of different social arenas. It ended up as a deconstruction of formal and informal regulations concerned with sexual violence and sexual infractions. The shift of focus came because in the early days of this project, we observed that, at their heart, these wide-ranging regulations appeared to be an attempt to keep sex under wraps, to constrain and control what was perceived as its potentially threatening and dangerous aspects. In the early stages of analysis, it became clear that a variety of institutions were engaging in a process of publicly claiming, amongst other things, that the 'sex-which-threatens-us' is not here, that the 'dangers' of sex are not on 'our' doorstep. What also became clear, however, was that accompanying this recent obsession with sex and since about 1999, there has been a tremendous outpouring of official and quasi-official 'utterances': consultation documents, guidance statements, codes of ethics, human resource and personnel policies, best practice guides, white and green papers and new laws concerning many aspects of what might be called 'sex'. Many of these documents and statements have been authored by state agencies (Department of Health, Home Office) and others come from far less formal quarters, such as professional associations, private businesses and organizations and local authorities. As a mass these 'utterances' about sex are, quite simply, too many to count. But, taken together they represent a 'system', a collection of knowledge about what the 'problem' of sex is and how to deal with it across a wide variety of settings from private, intimate relationships to formal, public settings. This 'system' of knowledge is not neutral: its impact and effect is to shape (governmental, company or citizen) practice, to set limits on how sex is done. The knowledge speaks of what cannot or should not (ever) be done in the name of sex. Thus, most 'utterances' or publications are concerned with specifying what adults and children, men and women and individual adults should not do without incurring some type of punishment or censure. In this book, we have not concerned ourselves with whether and to what extent this knowledge translates into actual lived and embodied practices either at the level of individual sexual encounters or at the level of the policing and punishment of any infractions of these laws and policies. Instead, we have attempted to both understand the conditions of existence of these 'utterances' as well as provide some (albeit limited) analysis of their content through the deconstruction of key texts produced since the turn of the millennium and in relation to specific types of 'sex'.

In relation to understanding their conditions of existence, we have borrowed heavily from the work of Burton and Carlen (1979) in which they examine and analyze documents which pertained to governmental investigative committees that focused on perceived law and order problems of the day. Using a bricolage of concepts from Foucault,

Bachelard and Lacan, Burton and Carlen (1979) construct an analytical framework in which it is possible to displace the authorial subject as the originator of meaning and in so doing relocate and reconceptualize the writers and speakers of official discourse as having only limited control over the texts' connotative effects. In other words, the meanings of the texts in question are not wholly derived from the intentions and motivations of the specific authors. More, Burton and Carlen's (1979) framework opens the theoretical space for an analysis of documents focused on deconstructing the key terms of reference within any particular discourse and the 'syntax' deployed if only because it is the syntax that enables 'meaning to exist beyond … at a place where the signifiers are absent' (Burton and Carlen 1979: 31).

But more than this, Burton's and Carlen's (1979) argument about how Official Discourse operates in relation to 'law and order' crises seemed to have a particular relevance and resonance with much of what is happening today in relation to the voluminous utterances about what to do about sex. Specifically, Burton and Carlen (1979) argued that:

> Official Discourse on law and order confronts legitimation deficits and seeks discursively to redeem them by denial of their material geneses. Such denial establishes an absence in the discourse. This absence, the Other, is the silence of a world constituted by social relations the reality of which cannot be appropriated by a mode of normative argument which speaks to and from its own self-image via an idealised conception of justice.
>
> (Burton and Carlen 1979: 138).

In other words, one characteristic of official discourse on law and order is that it is necessarily engaged in a symbolic erasure of the very material realities that generated the 'problem' to which official discourse addressed itself.

In this book, we start with the assumption that there has been, in the last two or three decades, a similar 'legitimation deficit' in regards to regulations around sex and particularly in relation to what might be termed sexual violence or abusive sex. Specifically, and beginning with the second wave of feminism in the 1960s and 1970s, there has been a critical examination of virtually all aspects of sexual relations between men and women. This has included interpersonal and intimate relationships as much as governmental practice and policy in the shape of civil legislation and criminal law as well as the enforcement and punishment of infractions of both. Subsequent to this examination have been three specific arguments:

(i) Sexual abuse of and violence against women and children (and less frequently, men) by men is regular, routine and commonplace.

(ii) Policies purporting to 'protect' women and children from sexual abuse from men often do not, in practice, offer protection, mainly because of the discriminatory ways in which they are implemented. Key examples include the ways in which rape and sexual assault victims were assumed to have contributed to their victimization in some fashion and the necessity felt by the police to 'disprove' allegations of sexual violence when they took statements from victims.

(iii) The various ways in which men who sexually abuse women and/or children are dealt with within criminal justice, civil legislation and private organizations are understood to be inadequate, problematic and offering little to help the victims. So, for example, there has been a continual debate within feminist circles about the social and political efficacy of invoking stronger and stronger punishments against men who rape. This debate has been driven by the recognition that simply locking these men in prison does little or nothing to help women. This debate has also been mirrored in the discussions around mandatory prosecution policies in regards to domestic violence.

Combined, these three arguments (and the research that supported them) amount to a sustained critique of both the lived realities of sex and sexual relationships for women (and children), and a devastating assessment of the policies and guidelines that are contemporarily in place to deal with these problems.

Subsequent to this critique, there have also been sustained campaigns for 'something to be done' about the problems outlined above. Calls for reform have come from many different quarters, both within and outwith feminism. Often these calls dovetailed with the media coverage of scandals and systematic abuses. So for instance, in the 1980s and 1990s Cleveland, the Orkneys and various children's homes within Wales and the southwest of England all made media headlines when systematic child sexual abuse was uncovered. Coupled with this were the *exposés* of cover-ups of abuse within the Catholic Church in both Ireland and the United States. By 2002, Operation Awe hit the media and the public were told that over 7500 individuals from across a variety of western states were downloading child pornography. By the early part of the millennium, increasing media coverage was also given to the rising rate of reporting rape as the conviction rate was haemorrhaging.

One result of these calls has been the reform of all sexual offences within England and Wales (a critique of this forms the first part of this book). More importantly for the second part of this book, one other result has been to put the issue of sexual 'impropriety' on the agenda for other organizations such as professional bodies, private businesses and increasingly anything and everything connected with the internet. And, whilst the less-than-state responses to this perceived heightened awareness of 'the problem of sex' have been uneven, there has nevertheless been an increased volume of policies and guidances that companies, professionals and employees are now expected to adhere to.

Let us be clear, in this book we are *not* arguing that the contemporary 'problem' of sex is all about perceptions. We are not arguing that the legitimation deficit is merely and only a question of 'moral panic'. Instead, we start with the premise that these calls for reform are part and parcel of the legitimation deficit; that women and children are experiencing sexual victimization of one variety or another in ways that cannot be and have not been encompassed by contemporary laws and informal guidances. We use the term 'the problem of men' in this book to refer to this legitimation deficit. Our argument, in keeping with Burton's and Carlen's insight about how official discourse works, is that contemporary discourse and regulation of sex necessarily denies the very embedded and real lived experiences of sexual predation, violence and abuse (i.e. 'the problem of men') by syntactically and symbolically shifting the meanings of the key terms of reference (i.e. 'victim' and 'perpetrator') as well as other more context-specific terms of reference such as 'family', 'community', 'professional'. It denies the realities of the social relations that it seeks to describe because the discourse is constituted via the deployment of a symbolic landscape which 'speaks to and from its own self-image via an idealised conception of justice' (Burton and Carlen 1979: 143). In other words, the very structures and meanings of the discourses that we examine in this book foreclose the possibility of recognizing the lived realities of intimate relations between men and women and children in which violence and the threat of it are all too routine, despite an official social 'rhetoric' that claims that these episodes are rare.

We trace these erasures through what we are calling both official and quasi-official discourses on sex. Official discourse pertains to all those utterances that are more or less state authored. In relation to this book, the key documents include the Sexual Offences Act (2003) and all the consultation documents and official statements leading up to it, such as the green papers *Setting the Boundaries* (Home Office 2000) and *Protecting the Public* (Home Office 2002), as well as other consultation and guidance documents such as *Safeguarding Children in Prostitution* (Department of Health/Home Office 2000) and *Paying the Price* (Home Office 2004). Each of these consultation documents or official guidances refers to other papers and documents. It is the full range of these which we refer to as official discourse. They all have in common the site of authorship (namely, one or other of the many state agencies, usually the Department of Health or Home Office). They all define what is to be seen as the 'problem' of sex. They all specify the 'solution' to the 'problem' of sex. They all act in ways that impact upon the practices of statutory and voluntary agencies that work with people and as such, they shape sexual conduct. A note should be made, however, of the fact that this book was written on the cusp of change. It started as the reforming process began and its completion came within months of the implementation of the Sexual Offences Act 2003 in May 2004. Therefore, at the time of writing there has been no established case law or further guidance 'testing' the new provisions.

But, we also trace and analyse 'quasi-official' discourse on sex. We use this term to denote a much looser and wider variety of documents and guidance that, in line with official discourse, share a similar site of authorship (organizational personnel departments, professional associations and the like). Moreover, quasi-official, like official discourse on sex, details how the 'problem' of sex should be conceptualized and understood and what the 'solution' to the 'problem' is. However, unlike official discourse, quasi-official discourse does not have the same type and level of impact on the practices of others. Infractions are usually sanctioned, but through a variety of informal means such as censure from the professional body, disconnection of services provided, discontinuance of employment and so on. In short, quasi-official discourse is comprised of 'utterances' which pertain to more informal 'guides' on the conduct of sex.

In the course of the book, we also refer to 'regulatory frameworks'. It is helpful at this stage to clarify what is meant by this term. We use the term to denote a more specific context than the broader terms official and quasi-official discourse. Regulatory frameworks are, simply, the collection of rules that specify what should and should not be done. In the case, for instance, of prostitution, the regulatory framework is the formal criminal law, coupled with specific guidance documents that delimit what private citizens can and cannot do (namely, solicit in public for prostitution) and what professionals should and should not do (namely, treat young people in prostitution as offenders).

By way of further clarification as to what the book is not about, we are not attempting simply, solely or comprehensively to provide a descriptive overview of the trends, patterns, occurrences or events of sexual offending. Moreover, whilst not incidental, cultural, normative and uncodified 'rules' (unwritten norms, values, taboos and so on) are also not the focus of this book. Neither do we treat media reportage as a form of 'official utterance', although that is not to say that we do not draw upon media output as data from which to illustrate our arguments. We do make mention of the successes and failures of political campaigning moves, but this is only insofar as they have contributed to the shaping of particular 'turns' in the contemporary rules of engagement surrounding sex. Finally, we are also not concerned with how regulatory frameworks produce 'sexed subjects', namely, what the impact of regulation is upon how the sex that is done is understood or integrated into people's sexual lives. Not only is it not possible to read off identity, micro-practices and experience from what is codified and institutionalized, but that would be the subject of an altogether different book. It is also important to make clear that we are not simply depicting the regulatory frameworks we outline here as repressive 'arms' or apparatuses of state control. It can be suggested that enshrined in the laws, policies and guidelines governing sex are stipulations that uphold rights and responsibilities in terms of individuals, families, communities and networks of people (such as employees or patients, for example). In that sense, regulatory frameworks can be seen as productive and protective of the power and status of certain individuals and groups, as well as prescriptive, or even exploitative, of others' relative lack of power and status. However, as will become clearer in the course of our analysis, we see sex as not only the site of its own construction but also a site through which other issues (protection, safety, propriety and so on) can be highlighted and defined. Hence we are not particularly concerned with which regulations can be regarded as sexually progressive or repressive; we are concerned not so much with evaluations of those regulations as with explanations of the their underlying workings, and as such then, this book is more about the contemporary concerns that shape sex, than about sex itself. The next section outlines some of the varying ways in which sex has been conceptualized in contemporary thinking.

Competing constructions of sex and sexuality

Sex is often a slippery and indeterminate category or concept. It has been conceptualized in a myriad of different and sometimes competing ways. Drawing upon such diverse writings as those of sexologists and psychoanalysts, feminists and libertarians, it is clear that there is not (and never has been) any agreed definition of sex. Yet this does not mean that sex as such cannot be interrogated and indeed, many academics, particularly in the last 30 years or so, have attempted to do so. In the process and even in its supposedly 'normal' and 'natural' manifestations, it is clear that sex is a highly complex and multi-layered phenomenon. Sex is traditionally thought of as taking place between adult, heterosexual couples in intimate settings such as bedrooms, and is constituted as being not only personal and private, but also legal and acceptable. Of late, however, concepts of sex have resisted such limited categorization; sex has broken out to become a site of conflict and debate, gaining public attention through being formulated in a vast array of different guises, including appearing in terms of new phenomena such as 'date rape' and other recent inventions like sexual 'grooming', both of which were unheard of only a few years ago. In its many new and different guises then, sex has become increasingly ambiguous, contested and difficult to pin down.

This is not to argue that there have not been numerous theoretical attempts to specify precisely what sex is. However, by refusing to hold sex in place or pin it down, we want to highlight the basic point that sex can be opened up to a wide range of interpretive possibilities, which may or may not on the face of it, appear to have anything to do with conventional understandings of sex. In this way, we are of the view that sex has no pre-discursive, foundational location. In other words, we can never really 'know' what it is we are dealing with when we speak (or write) about sex. As Plummer (2004) maintains: 'Sexuality ... has no reality sui generis, and any concern with "it" must always harbour wider social issues: human sexualities have to be socially produced (no human can ever just do it). Socially organised, socially maintained and socially transformed, human sexuality is always conducted at an angle: it is never just sex' (Plummer 2004:32). Nonetheless, whilst we eschew any attempts to pin sex down in any definitive way, it is important that we acknowledge the various theoretical attempts that have gone before to explain and understand what sex is, for it is in the constitution of 'sex-as-(in)determinate' that the symbolic landscapes underpinning contemporary sex regulation and control can be glimpsed. At this juncture then, we want to highlight that in terms of the vast array of different understandings of sex on offer, it is possible to identify a range of traditions, stretching from the production of pseudo-scientific typologies and taxonomies to more recent postmodern writing which posits the diversity of sexual styles, personas, activities and so on. It is not necessary to provide a linear historical chronology of these various

9

traditions here, nor is it desirable to order them hierarchically. At this point, these traditions are briefly outlined in order to identify the various approaches taken by those who adopt different theoretical positions with regard to sex. We begin with some of the most early and basic understandings of sex, based upon biological and medical models.

Biological and psychological models tend to medicalize sex, highlighting its more mechanistic, performance-orientated and reproductive aspects. In these theoretical schema, sex tends to be seen not only as fixed and immutable but also based upon a sub-structure or bedrock, itself founded upon 'common sense', natural and even instinctual understandings about what sex is, how to 'do it' and so on. At its most limited, this idea of sex being 'normal' and 'natural' is firmly linked to gender identities, romantic love and family relationships. In this way, it is held that 'normal' and 'natural' sex takes place between a man and a woman who are involved in a stable, long-term (ideally marital) relationship; it is a private activity that takes place only at certain times and in certain places; and it is an activity that involves only certain kinds of physical acts largely focused upon the genitals of both partners. Built into these biological and psychological ideas about what sex is are powerful assumptions concerning male and female sex drives; conscious and unconscious sexual desires and proclivities; 'active' and 'passive' sexual roles and so on. But in these attempts to classify and categorize 'normal' and 'natural' sex are also buried assumptions concerning the need to define and rein in the unorthodox, the aberrations, the pathological, the perverse, the disabling and the diseased. As a result, many attempts at regulation and control which drew (and still draw) upon biological and psychological understandings of sex have been concerned with controlling the corporeal bodies and behaviours of those deemed sexually 'abnormal', 'unfit' or simply 'unsettling'. In that sense, these early biological and psychological approaches are often considered to be reductionist and even oppressive. Even so, and although they are extensively criticized because of their reliance upon understandings of sex as having a 'natural' bedrock, it should also be acknowledged that such theoretical understandings do pay some attention to the cultural, social and historical forces at work in producing sex. These biological and psychological models are often acknowledged, often by those that subscribe to them, as a product of time and place – Freudian psychoanalysis being a case in point. Hence it is also fair to say that it has not all been a case of 'nature' at the expense of 'nurture'. However, in terms of placing more emphasis upon the latter, it is to other, more sociological theories that we now turn.

Social constructionists have gone much further and argued the basic point that sex is always socially controlled, context-dependent and subject to historical and cultural variation. They argue that it is in the context of everything from individual activity to institutional power relations that ideas about sex are shaped at any given moment. These ideas then operate under the rubric of social controls delimiting what is 'essential', 'biological' or 'god-given' (or not, as the case may be). In this way, sex is no more 'natural' than 'unnatural', for it is always subject to social construction (and re-construction). For social constructionists then, sex depends for its existence upon socio-sexual scripts, temporal and spatial props and arrangements, and so on. Social constructionists have thus maintained that sex (and sexuality) cannot be named unless it is embedded in social contexts and conditions. How we 'do' sex makes it sexual, and the doing of it makes it sex, as opposed to something else which may or may not be seen as 'sex' (such as 'medical treatment', 'income-generation', 'leisure pursuit', 'high art' or 'spiritual quest' to name but a few other possibilities). In short, social constructionists argue that sex has to be invented and invested with social meaning in order to become 'sex' at all. In the process, that which is officially spoken about sex creates the categories and concepts by which sex is con-stituted. This raises important questions about how, when and by whom sex is so defined, since such inquiry will be fundamental in constituting 'legitimate' and 'licit' sex across a multiplicity of different contexts. Social constructionists may appear to offer a comprehensive 'corrective' to the shortcomings of biological and psychological understandings of sex. This is because they have usually been positioned as occupying the other end of the spectrum from biological and psychological models. But rather than positing the idea of a continuum, we want to argue that it is more useful to draw upon the idea of an increasingly crowded playing field, with players shifting positions as the goalposts change. It is to these other, related but different theoretical understandings of sex that we next turn.

Bearing these competing allegiances in mind, it can be argued that social constructionism shares some common ground with another major theoretical perspective on sex and sexuality, that of feminism. As Jackson (1999) has pointed out: 'the forms of sexuality existing in any given society at any one time are products of a particular history and culture, particular institutionalised and habitual ways of doing sex' (Jackson 1999: 5). But social orders, their histories and cultures, are not gender-neutral, and feminists have been concerned to illuminate the ways in which sex-as-gender informs the dynamics, relations and practices of sex. Feminists have interrogated the contingent categorizations of sex, focusing in particular upon unpacking and problematizing heterosex and its relationship to hierarchies of gender (and age, class, race/ethnicity and so on). Feminism has engaged with gendered heterosexuality as an organizing institution of heterosex, not only in terms of how hegemonic forms of heterosexuality delimit appropriate categorizations of masculinity and femininity, but also in terms of how heterosex is enacted and re-enacted in everyday situations. The privileged status of heterosexuality has been unmasked by feminists as being about more than, as social constructionists might have it, sexual scripts, social meanings and interpersonal conduct. For many feminists, heterosexual sex has been central to men's humiliation, objectification and possession of women. In this way, the coercive and predatory aspects of men's heterosexuality, the equating of sex primarily with penetration and male orgasm, the idea of men's sexual desire as an unstoppable force and so on, have all been subject to scrutiny by feminists. In other words, the power and inequality that constitute gendered heterosexual relations, together with the con- trolling practices that constrain or force women into sexual subordination (some have called it slavery) at the hands of men, have been the main focus of feminist inquiry. But this is not to say that all feminists have adopted a 'sexual oppression' view of gender power relations, and some have highlighted the possibilities for empowerment and resistance to heterosexual orthodoxies (Vance 1989). This has been taken further by postmodernist and queer theorists.

Whereas social constructionists and feminists have tended to concentrate upon the social contexts of everyday sexual experience, the material conditions in which sex is organized and the ways in which power (and for many feminists, dominance and oppression) is structured, postmodernists have tended to concentrate on texts, discourses and cultural practices. Postmodernists, and in particular queer theorists, have sought to deconstruct and destabilize all rigid conceptualizations of sex, especially the notion of 'real' sex as quintessentially heterosexual. Instead, all sex is seen as highly malleable and plastic, fashioned from the erotic, desiring possibilities of different, subjectively constituted, bodies/selves. Furthermore, queer theorists challenge not only the supposed inevitability and normality of heterosexuality but also that of all disciplinary regimes of the 'normal' and 'natural', particularly with regard to how the heteronormativity of sex constitutes its social acceptability (and legality) with regard to particular behaviours, activities and identities. Queer theory has also highlighted the extent to and ways in which perverse or dissident sex, sexualities and sexual practices have been regulated and positioned as marginal and/or 'other'. It is the destabilizing potential of this 'otherness' which has preoccupied queer theorists. Queer theory has thus developed as a political critique of the binary categorization of sex as normal or deviant; masculine or feminine; straight or lesbian and/or gay. Queer theory further constitutes sex carrying with it certain kinds of social meanings which prescribe 'outlaw' status and standing. This is clearly the case for much of the illegal and illicit sex codified and contained within 'official' pronouncements. By virtue of it being officially 'outlawed', queer theorists argue, sex regulation illuminates what it is about 'sex-as-threat' that is so destabilizing and disturbing.

As stated earlier, it is not our task here to make claim to a particular theoretical approach. What we are attempting to do here is point to the different ways in which sex has been conceptualized by various theoretical traditions in order to provide a backdrop for what follows. At this juncture, however, it is important to reiterate that from all this, apparent paradoxes emerge. It would seem that just at the historical moment when sex appears to have become ever more subject to 'free' choice, greater openness and pluralism, there is a simultaneous proliferation of laws, policies and guidelines which seek to define the complex, vast and ever-changing 'rules of engagement' surrounding sex. In effect, it would seem that the more sex becomes a 'special' category of human behaviour, the more it is seen as requiring formal and official containment. It is possible to argue therefore that accompanying such liberalization and proliferation, there is a growing desire or will to lock sex, hold it down and contain it, whilst at the same time many people simply carry on doing more and more sex without critically reflecting on so doing and moreover, without ever turning to any 'rule book' concerning sex before they do it. It is important to note that we are not arguing that the 'rules of engagement' concerning sex are thus only of interest to researchers, policymakers and activists. Nonetheless, it can be argued that sex regulation and control in the past, and in the current climate, appears to have suffered from paradoxical muddle, confusion and sometimes sheer incomprehensibility. It is not (nor ever has been) a stable and completed project, but a project in the making.

But despite and perhaps even because of the supposed liberalism and permissiveness of the late modern era, if not the doing of then at least the talking about sex has become more of a confessional *modus operandi*, in both private and public contexts. As argued earlier, there are many publicly voiced concerns about the 'problems' of sex. To the extent that sex has been constituted by legislatures, courts, 'experts' in the field, various social institutions like professional associations and so on, it is now more 'known' about and understood. For example, terms like 'consenting adults', 'penetrative sex' and 'minors' are common currency nowadays, and have been so for some considerable time. But sex is still constantly being re-drawn and re-invented. In the next section we outline the contours of the symbolic landscape underpinning and making possible the current, particular and paradoxical re-drawing of sex regulation, highlighting especially the ways in which we will be using these contours to expose the controlling impulses governing the regulation of illegal and illicit sex.

The symbolic landscape of sex regulation

One of the central arguments in this book is that there is a new moral authoritarianism regarding sex in contemporary British society that allows sex regulation and control to 'make sense'. This is despite a powerful discourse which posits that contemporary society 'does sex better' than ever before. Underpinning and making possible this moral authoritarianism is a symbolic landscape comprised of various con-tours. In this respect, we have identified five main underpinning discursive contours, or sets of assumptions, which run as follows:

1. The precise character, shape and form of sex (as 'threat', 'danger', 'problem', 'harm', 'wrongdoing' and so on) need never be precisely specified as such. It is always possible to collapse and elide 'sex-as-threat' into something else other than sex (such as 'exploitation', 'misconduct', 'humiliation', 'offence', 'obscenity', 'malpractice', 'immodesty' and so on). This means that whilst there is huge weight given to the 'wrongfulness' of much illegal and illicit sexual conduct, neither the 'wrongs' themselves, nor the 'wronged' and/or 'wrong-doers', have to be precisely specified. This permits particular discursive constructions of 'victims' and 'perpetrators' to come into play and further permits 'solutions' (to the 'problem' of sex) to be offered with little direct reference to whose interests are being served here, or whether these 'solutions' (as opposed to any others) are in the best interest of the public or any of the 'injured parties'.

2. There has been an emergence of particular kinds of sexual 'victims', subject to certain discursive constructions of 'victimhood'. This has not only gathered momentum of late but has also been used in an uncritical fashion to constitute 'victims' as always and already blameless, weak, vulnerable, passive, and crucially, in need of the

kinds of protections the regulatory frameworks offer. Moreover, this particular construction of 'victims' relies heavily on very specific understandings of coercion, force and consent in which consent is understood as being about the capacity to make and effect choices, and coercion and force are understood as being the absence on the part of the victim of any capacity to act otherwise. In effect, coercion, force and consent are all collapsed into simplistic and asocial notions of individualism, free will and voluntarism, which can be (all too easily) compromised should 'victims' not adhere to particular constructions of their 'victimhood'. What we mean by this is that within this symbolic landscape, 'victimhood' is an unstable and contingent category. In varying contexts, it is possible to simultaneously position 'victims' as 'wrong-doers', subjecting their 'perpetrators' to malicious and false claims, or occupying a paradoxical 'perpetrator-victim' position by virtue of lying on the cusp of the lines drawn between the two.

3. There has also been an emergence of a new 'perpetrator' rhetoric in which the alleged 'offender' is constituted as a shadowy but ever-present figure, often driven by base, ordinary and sometimes 'natural' and 'normal' desires, but largely unknown and unknowable (even sometimes to themselves). This means that safety and security from this unknowable but ever-present sexual 'threat' is never assured, if only because of the unknowable, and ever-present 'dangers' posed. Moreover, the perpetration/perpetrators of sexual 'wrong-doings' have in the past supposedly suffered from a lack of scientific, rational templates for understanding their 'problems', but it is now held this has can be rectified by newer, expanding and better methods; more accurate and 'expert' knowledge of the extent of sexual 'abuse' and 'injury', better inter-agency communication, 'truer' knowledge about sexual pathologies and so on. Perpetrators have thus come to be regarded as something of a technological 'problem' requiring pseudo-scientific, rational 'solutions' (sex offenders' registers, tagging, therapeutic interventions, rehabilitation programmes and so on).

4. Simultaneously, there has been a re-inscription of particular political discourses regarding that which constitutes the 'backbone' or 'bedrock' of society. This relates in particular to the invocation of notions of righteous, responsible, good, up-standing citizenry, new 'moral guardians' and so on. Within this are particular discursive re-constructions of categories such as the family, the community,

professionals, politicians, 'respectable' business enterprises/ organizations and so on. All such personages/bodies are constituted as self-evidently reasonable, rational 'adult figures', capable of providing an unquestionably accurate yardstick or temperature gauge against which infractions of sexual laws, policies, guidelines and so on can be measured. Moreover, such personages/bodies are also sometimes constituted as 'caring parents' who act not in their own self-interests but for the welfare and protection of the weak and vulnerable. All this has occurred against the backdrop of a political climate in which it is held that society has changed to such an extent that traditional sites of moral authority and control (such as schools, conjugal families, religious orders and institutions) are no longer able either to contain the 'problem' of sex or indeed to regulate its more destructive manifestations.

5. Finally, there has been a notable assimilation and silencing of particular 'voices', such that the counter-discourses regarding sex that emerged throughout much of the 1960s and 1970s have been accommodated and incorporated into this new dominant discourse of 'dodgy' sex, so that it now has a particular political 'hold'. Witness the ways in which earlier proclamations, for example that sex 'play' between adults and young people/children were a part of the moves towards greater sexual freedom, have now become silenced in the outpouring of widespread public vitriol against paedophilia. Such an assimilation project has increasingly and successfully been taken up as part of New Labour's political agenda, insofar as they have castigated the 'swinging sixties', make widespread use of feminist notions of sexual 'exploitation', 'abuse' and so on, at the same time as drawing upon liberal notions of the integrity of 'personhood' and individual expression of 'selfhood' through personal sexual practices.

We want to highlight that the object of control of this new moral authoritarianism about sex is not sex *per se*, or specific practices, but rather broader sexual relationships between men and women, adults and children. To be clear, the proliferation of regulations may appear to have as their object the rare, the 'abnormal', the 'marginal' and the 'deviant'. In contrast, however, they act to regulate the commonplace, the 'natural', the 'normal', the mundane and the routine, everyday sexual relationships in which we all engage. As will become apparent from our examination of both formal and informal regulations and controls, what many of these regulations have as their 'fallback', is the acceptability and legitimacy of only one type of (impossible to define but often articulated) sexual relationship – namely, what is referred to in these 'official utterances' as the '*genuine* relationship'. Indeed, it might now appear that all other sexual relationships, besides that of the 'genuine relationship', are suspect and potentially 'wrong', if not downright dangerous. However, we also want to argue that in its very constitution, this moral authoritarianism is always an unstable enterprise, for within such a symbolic landscape, there must be a necessary admission of the possibility that the normal itself is abnormal, and this is of course, deeply problematic. For, as noted above, the great silence at the heart of official and quasi-official discourse of sex is that there 'really' is a persistent and intransigent 'problem', maybe not with sex *per se*, nor with sexual relations between adults, or even adults and children, but with men, and what men do.

The book's argument

Earlier we stated that official and quasi-official discourses on sex deny the social realities of their own origins. One of the ways this occurs is through the erasure of gender. In this respect what is, by and large, sexual violence by men against women and children is translated into sexual violence by people (adults or children, men or women) against other people (again, adults or children, men or women). But the erasure of gender, ironically and paradoxically, permits a greater degree of control and regulation of the lives and relationships of women and children. More than this, however, it is through sliding and shifting meanings of both 'victims' and 'perpetrators' in conjunction with the symbolic and syntactic denial of gender that we begin to see a moral authoritarianism asserting itself. Fundamental to this new sexual enterprise is a growth in the willingness and capacity of various groups, such as professional associations, companies and businesses alongside government, to be empowered to regulate individual sexual relationships. In this respect, despite a rhetoric of equality and progression, more and more relationships and activities are being brought within a net of formal control and punishment that has a thinner and thinner mesh and weave. Put another way, a net widening of formal control has occurred in which more and more sexual behaviours and conducts are now included as objects of legal regulation as well as more and more types of relationships being defined as in need of intervention and regulation. Wider organizational controls have also been affected, with all manner of private companies and public organizations (including professional associations) authoring policies that delimit certain sexual conduct, particularly that which involves 'consenting' adults and occurs within public contexts and settings.

Part and parcel of this new sexual moral authoritarianism is a powerful voice which posits that in recent times, something has gone dreadfully wrong with sex. Outside of specific parameters, sex appears to have spilled out, gone awry, run amok. It is often held that sex has broken free of its traditional constraints, supposedly leading to greater individual and social satisfactions, but in so doing its increasing lack of boundaries, its growing looseness and licentiousness, is now threatening the very fabric of contemporary society. Fears about the uncontrollability of sex are not new, and indeed have a long historical tail, but what are new are the multiple interfaces between the different sites of authority that are now seeking to regulate sex. Or to put this argument another way, the official and quasi-official discourses on sex (or more precisely, sexual infractions) are a response to both the perception of increasing risks *vis à vis* sex and sexual relations, as well as the critique of gendered sexual relations. On the face of it, these discourses acknowledge the 'realities' (of abuse and so on) and attempt to deal with them better by, for instance, plugging any gaps in existing legislation (such as creating a law against the sexual violation of corpses where no law previously existed) or policies, or further clarifying and refining existing policies and laws.

There are two different but interlinked sets of arguments that we make in this book. The first pertains to these observations about official and quasi-official discourses on sex; the second to the changing nature and content of those discourses. So, the key arguments about the conditions of existence regarding official and quasi-official discourses on sex are outlined as follows. Firstly, the last two decades have witnessed a legitimation deficit in regards to the 'problem' of sex and of sexual infractions that has recognized the routineness of sexual victimization of women and children by men and the inability of structures and institutions of governance (i.e. criminal justice, professional associations, business and so on) to deal adequately with this 'problem'. Secondly, contemporary official and quasi-official discourses, whilst attempting to address this 'problem' of sex, necessarily deny the social realities (the problem of 'men'). This is achieved via an erasure of gender and through shifting meanings for some of the key terms of reference deployed. Thirdly, one impact of the above has been a new sexual enterprise that extends formal control and regulation (and punishment) to a greater number and more concentrated set of relationships. It is this that we refer to as moral authoritarianism.

Whilst the above argument addresses the conditions of existence for contemporary official and quasi-official discourses on sex, it does not address the characteristics of those discourses and the manner in which they act to regulate sex more generally. Our more specific arguments about the formal and informal regulation of sex are as follows:

1. **'Sex' and its regulation can be seen in terms of a vacuum or vortex, which draws more and more into itself, in order to secure its own moral project.** This 'vortexing' of sex and sex regulation acts to serve particular political interests, not least that of establishing and securing powerful notions or formations, including governments, employing organizations, professions and communities. All of these social formations are constituted as major political players in the arena of both formal and informal sex regulation, particularly as these particular social formations are constituted herein as nothing more nor less than powerful, all-knowing and benign 'protectors' of those deemed to be endangered. In the process of regulating and controlling sex, all of the regulatory institutions/bodies we discuss in this book are thereby shaped in particular ways, constituting themselves as standing for (and often standing in for) the 'righteous' when it comes to regulating and controlling the 'threats' posed by unrestrained sex.

2. **By marking out more and more sex for containment, the regulations themselves both create and re-create the ever-present 'threat' of sex.** To some extent, this 'threat' is managed by being deployed and displaced upon particular constructions of 'victims' (and 'perpetrators'). 'Victims' (and 'perpetrators') are absolutely crucial to the current constitution of sex and sex regulation. But there are also, we argue, further 'threats' (often publicly unacknowledged) to the social formations of government, employing organizations, professions and communities, for these too can all too easily become 'victims' in the context of the ever-widening vacuum or vortex that is unbridled sex. Such all-encompassing notions of 'victimization' (namely, that anyone and everyone can be a 'victim') means that sex cannot ever be allowed to 'run amok' for that would, and does, threaten the very fabric of the social order. The 'dangerousness' of sex is that it is now so very necessary and needed in terms of securing wider moral projects. Sex is necessary and needed because sexual 'victims' (and 'perpetrators') are necessary and needed. And sexual 'victims' (and 'perpetrators') are necessary and needed

because sex regulation is always about power relations, and particularly about power (by definition) exercised over and on behalf of those positioned as 'vulnerable', 'weak', 'in need of protection' and so on. This makes contemporary sex regulation and control a highly moral project, a project about the constitution of morality itself, for morality is always and already at the heart of the social order.

3. **The contemporary project of moral authoritarianism is not so much about distinguishing 'good' from 'bad' sex (although it is in part ostensibly about that) but is more about positioning sex as being that unique social activity which has the potential to be the 'glue', 'cement' or momentum which ultimately holds the social fabric together (despite its simultaneous and paradoxical inscription as that which threatens).** As 'old' collectivities (conjugal families, religious orders and so on) disappear, there has been a widespread casualization of intimate relations. Sex now has an added *frissance* because it has become the primary – perhaps the only – means whereby individuals succeed (at least as an ideal) in achieving inter-connection, co-dependence and reciprocity in a rapidly changing social order. At the beginning of the twenty-first century, it is not our sexual identities that define and shape who we are, individually and collectively, but it is now in the very doing of sex that we 'find' ourselves. This means that, as a society, we increasingly experience ourselves as unable to 'get together' unless and until we 'get it together'. In other words, we can have no shared, collective lives, unless and until we 'do' sex. And from this it follows that everybody and anybody (including children, animals and the dead) have to be 'guarded' for and against, for all of us have now been opened up to the possibility that we have to constantly 'do' sex anywhere, anytime, anyhow in order to live otherwise unlivable lives. This of course, is very, very dangerous. Because ultimately, sex is always a 'glue' that can very easily come unstuck – a 'cement' that can also fracture and tear us apart. Indeed, our contemporary obsessions are nearly all about how we 'do' or don't 'do' sex safely, not individually or even in couples but as collectivities. Hence in the final analysis, the contemporary atomization of individual lives (Giddens 1992) that appears to make our sexual experiences more and more 'freely' chosen, has also produced that which threatens and endangers us. And in such a climate of fear and uncertainty, the search for any moral authority (above and beyond oneself), to which to make discursive appeal concerning the 'rules of engagement' of

sex, will inevitably reach new heights. Hence the widening of the net, the increasing search for regulations, policies and guidelines to act as frameworks encompassing agreed standards for deploying sex as a means of living connected lives. Indeed in all this, sex has now become the most pivotal and paramount means for living any kind of life at all, for without it there would, at this moment in history, be nothing else to hold us all together.

Content and structure

The internal logic of this book is to move from an analysis of illegal, formally regulated sex (namely, that which constitutes a criminal offence), via an analysis of illicit, deviant or troublesome sex which is subject to far less formal regulation and control, through to sex which is almost impossible to regulate in that it is at the 'outer limits' of what are the possibilities of sex regulation and control. In some respects then, the six main chapters in this book are organized so that we move from discussion of the formal regulation of serious sexual offending, through the less formal regulation of 'troublesome' sex to the *ad hoc*, informal and nigh on non-regulation of the 'outer edges'. But this is not to suggest that we take a 'hierarchy of seriousness' approach to sex regulation (Thomas 2000: 4), for the issue of what constitutes the 'dangerousness' or 'wrongness' that is being regulated cannot be measured in this categorical way. Neither – and this is a key point – do we take a linear, historical view of the 'progress' that has been made in this area, in terms of reining in and controlling that sex which is *de facto* dangerous or harmful. Indeed, we reject any progressive, linear view of sex regulation and control. In so doing, we challenge any simple 'march of progress' reading which supports the idea that as we enter the twenty-first century, UK society is increasingly becoming sexually 'liberated', free and open. Instead, we are arguing that this very 'opening up' of sex provides the conditions in which more sex has become subject to greater attempts to regulate and control it. In short, the more sex opens up, the more regulation proliferates; the more 'liberated' sex becomes, the more it is deemed necessary to subject it to tighter controls. This on the face of it, may appear to be a 'reading against the grain' for it is often supposed that we are far less regulated and controlled when it comes to doing sex than in the past. But the regulation and control of sex has never been (nor is still) a simple or straightforward process. It certainly cannot be read as a matter of movements in the direction of the 'greater good' of sexual freedoms overcoming out-dated and repressive controls. So we are not attempting to come down on one 'side' or another in this way – either in favour of greater liberalization or in favour of greater constraints. Moreover, we would emphasize that debates about sexual values and ethics have often been driven by complex combinations of right-wing 'moral' agendas, liberal and libertarian impulses and no little feminist campaigning. In short, we are arguing that there is much greater complexity to the regulation and control of illegal and illicit sex than binaries of 'left' and 'right', 'good' and 'bad' permit.

In terms of structure, the book is divided into two parts, each containing three discrete chapters. Following this Introduction, Chapters 2, 3 and 4 (written by Joanna Phoenix) deal with formally regulated illegal sexual activities whilst Chapters 5, 6 and 7 (written by Sarah Oerton) deal with informally regulated, illicit sexual activities. Each of these substantive chapters has been written so that they can be read independently of the other chapters and in a way that outlines both formal and informal regulation as well as offers our deeper analysis of sex regulation. Three points need to be reiterated at this juncture: firstly, we maintain throughout the book that both illegal and illicit forms of sex have no meaning outside the contexts in which they are embedded. Hence in taking the regulation and control of both illegal and illicit sex as our subject matter, our chapters may appear to be somewhat unconnected inasmuch as we draw upon phenomena which may or may not ordinarily be deemed 'sex'. This is possible because we maintain that all sex – especially in its illegal and illicit manifestations – is an empty centre or vacuum into which all manner of multiple, diverse and ostensibly bizarre 'sex' – including what may appear to be non-sexual activities, behaviours, relationships and so on – can be written. Secondly, it is important to make clear that we do not attempt to cover all permutations of phenomena which might be deemed 'sex' in the six chapters which follow. We do maintain that sex has no *a priori* existence and as such, is incapable of being pinned down or contained within designated boundaries which delineate the sexual from the non-sexual, or the illegal and illicit from the legal and licit. Sex is always and already fluid, unstable and subject to changing interpretations, much of which we treat as our business to uncover and subject to scrutiny in terms of how it is regulated and controlled. Thirdly, we do argue that because illegal and illicit sex has to be bounded by regulatory frameworks in order to have any meaning at all, then it is possible to subject to particular consideration that sex which is considered so 'wrongful' as to be incorporated into formal and informal codifications. We need to make it clear that we do not devote specific chapters to regulations pertaining, for example, to heterosex and homosex, or to sex regulations governing specific groups or categories of people such as 'adults with learning disabilities', 'prisoners' or other incarcerated populations. All such social identifications, where important, will be woven into our wider analysis of what it is that lies behind official and quasi-official discourses of sex. It is also important to bear in mind that the persons addressed in the regulations (and by extension, our analysis) are already and always socially situated; they are 'adults' or 'children', 'men' and 'women' as much as they are an undifferentiated mass or totality of 'persons', despite what the regulations may actually say.

To turn now to the content of the six main chapters of the book. Following on from this Introduction, Chapter 2 (entitled 'Destructive Sex: Sexual Autonomy, Victimhood and the "Problem of Men" ') focuses on the recent history of legislation concerning rape and sexual assault. We use this as the starting point for the book as the deconstruction of official discourse on rape and sexual assault exemplifies how official discourse confronts the legitimation deficit by erasing the 'problem of men'. Chapter 3 (entitled 'Threatening Sex: Protection, Communities and Childhood') focuses on recent reforms to laws concerning child sexual abuse. This chapter establishes how in erasing the 'problem of men', official discourse provides the bedrock for a moral authoritarianism. Chapter 4 (entitled 'Commercial Sex: Consent, Coercion and Sexual Exploitation') focuses on current reforms to the regulation of prostitution. This chapter provides details of the new sexual enterprise by showing how the combination of erasing the material origins of the legitimation crisis confronting sex regulation and shifting notions of 'victimhood' produces the conditions for greater levels and depth of regulation of individual relationships. Chapter 5 (entitled 'Nuisance Sex: Harassment, Collusion and Decency') includes that sex which is sometimes but not necessarily deemed to be illegal, but which is often regarded as 'wrongful'. The main focus here is on the propriety of 'sex' in public places, including workplaces. The focus will partly be upon discussion of regulations pertaining to nudity, including what has colloquially been referred to as 'flashing' or 'streaking'. Such 'nuisance sex' can be deemed illicit because, when conducted in public places or inflicted upon 'innocent by-standers', it is considered to be unwanted, unwelcome, unacceptable, inappropriate, or simply in 'bad taste'. This chapter also focuses upon anti-harassment and bullying policies in a cross-section of privately-owned businesses, local authorities and voluntary sector organizations as well as recent changes in the law regarding indecent exposure and voyeurism. Chapter 6 (entitled 'Professional Sex: Ethics, Trust and Moral Guardianship') refers to the contexts in which particular occupational or work-based sexual relations, particularly in health-care and allied medical occupations, are conducted. In seeking to explore the regulations that operate in professional settings, we identify particular constructions, codes of ethics and so on, that uphold notions of professionals as moral guardians. Many professional associations have guidelines relating to sexual 'misconduct' or 'malpractice', where it is suggested that a professional may be behaving in a sexually inappropriate or irresponsible manner, even if the sex or sexual relations that form the object of concern are between adults and are consensual. Chapter 7 (entitled 'Transgressive and Digital Sex: Margins, Edges and Limitless Victims') deals with sex which might be considered to be at the borders or edges, largely because it is often regarded as so bizarre or fantastic as to be almost completely 'off limits'. The focus here then is upon that sex which is (arguably) adult, 'consensual' and 'freely chosen', but which is nonetheless deemed to require regulation and control because it is seen as harmful or injurious to the parties involved, even when there are no 'obvious' or apparent 'victims' (because for example, they do not exist as living 'persons'). Finally, in Chapter 8 (entitled 'Conclusion: Victims, Perpetrators and the New Sexual Enterprise') we offer some concluding thoughts.

Part I

Deconstructing official discourse of sexual violence

Chapter 2

Destructive sex: sexual autonomy, victimhood and the 'problem of men'

'Sexuality' today has been discovered, opened up and made accessible to the development of varying life-styles. It is something each of us 'has', or cultivates, no longer a natural condition which an individual accepts as a preordained state of affairs. Somehow, in a way that has to be investigated, sexuality functions as a malleable feature of self, a prime connecting point between body, self-identity and social norms.

(Giddens 1992:14)

It is through sex ... that each individual has to pass in order to have access to his own intelligibility (seeing that it is both the hidden aspect and the generative principle of meaning), to the whole of his body (since it is a real and threatened part of it, while symbolically constituting the whole), to his identity (since it joins the force of a drive to the singularity of a history). ... Hence the fact that over the centuries it has become more important than our soul, more important almost than our life; and so it is that all the world's enigmas appear frivolous to us compared to this secret, miniscule in each of us, but of a density that made it more serious than any other. The Faustian pact, whose temptation has been instilled in us by the deployment of sexuality, is now as follows: to exchange life in its entirety for sex itself, for the truth and the sovereignty of sex.

(Foucault 1978: 156)

Introduction

In the final three decades of the twentieth century, the way in which rape and sexual assaults were constituted, discussed and reported changed considerably. The success of a particular type of narrative about rape transformed thinking and practice in most western countries (or at least countries within which there was a visible feminist presence). In just over 20 years not only have laws and criminal justice practice been significantly altered in the UK, the USA, Canada, New Zealand and Australia, a new approach to rape has emerged. Evidence of this is noted in the mushrooming of rape crisis centres throughout the world. In the USA, Canada, throughout Europe, Australia, New Zealand, and the African continent, rape crisis centres expanded rapidly such that by the turn of the millennium the list of countries without specific counselling and advice services for rape victims was small.

Plummer (1995) noted that in the nineteenth and throughout most of the twentieth centuries, rape was not one of the defining issues of feminism. Instead, feminist campaigning both in Britain and abroad focused on political rights of citizenship and suffrage, rights at work and in the family and rights of access to a variety of public services and amenities (such as health, education and so on). When rape was discussed, it was in the context of broader sexual purity campaigns about men's sexuality, prostitution or in relation to extreme and unusual sexual violence (such as the Jack the Ripper murders). Plummer (1995) claims that throughout this time period, the dominant narrative of rape was a 'male-constructed' medical and legal narrative in which (i) rape was first and foremost about sex; (ii) rape was a rare event; (iii) women's sexuality was constituted as passive; (iv) and men's as aggressive. In short, good women sexually submitted to their husbands. Bad, pathological women actively sought sex. In a similar fashion, good men were sexually active – a fact which, occasionally and regrettably found expression outside the confines of marriage with mistresses and prostitutes. Bad men, rapists, were sexual fiends and monsters. They were men with excessive or perverted sexual desires. Hence, rape was both sexual and unusual.

However, by 2004, rape has assumed an altogether different symbolic position. Rape and other forms of sexual violation and violence are seen as alarmingly routine, a daily act of violence, power and aggression and not about sex *per se*. Such a re-conceptualization of rape as a routine act of power and domination, rather than a rare act driven by sexual pathology, opened the space in which feminist campaigns could deploy rape as the central metaphor. In this way, by the early 1980s, rape was seen as being both a practice and ideology which keeps all women in a state of fear and in so doing, acts as a form of social control and regulation (Brownmillar 1975, Russell 1984, Kappeler 1988). As we will demonstrate in what follows, this newer feminist-inspired narrative is one that underpins much of the contemporary official discourse on rape and sexual assaults.

Like all the chapters in this book, this chapter does not challenge the veracity or truth of contemporary stories about rape, the 'fit' between such stories and formal legal regulation or whether contemporary regulatory frameworks are 'correct'. Rather, like subsequent chapters, this chapter deconstructs official discourse on rape and sexual assaults as made manifest in the documents which constitute the formal regulatory framework. In regards to rape, key to this is an examination about the dominance of a specific notions of victimhood, changing conceptions of the relationship between sex and the law and shifting boundaries between sex activity, sex identity and notions of the self.

In this chapter we argue that there has been a legitimation deficit in relation to the governmental response to rape and sexual assault. The basis of this legitimation deficit lies in the recognition that women and children regularly experienced sexual violation and that law and criminal justice processes were at best incapable of dealing with the abuses of men, and at worst collusive in the ways in which women and children victims were treated. This legitimation deficit led to the reforms encompassed by the Sexual Offences Act 2003. However, we also argue that contemporary official discourse on rape and sexual assault has erased its own material origins of the legitimation deficit. These origins lie in the relationship between the complex social realities and relationships that condition the sexual victimization of women and children by men, and the law and criminal justice. This occurs through: (i) symbolically decontextualizing rape and sexual assault by, paradoxically, recognizing 'gender' and victims' experiences of sexual violation and criminal justice; and, (ii) invoking a particular notion of 'victimhood' that positions 'victims' of sexual violation as undergoing 'social death'. Combined, this symbolic landscape also has the effect of generating the imperative to action which makes increased levels of punishment possible and forecloses the possibility of the law being used to ameliorate the sexual victimization of women. In so doing, the contemporary official discourse on rape and sexual assault provides the bedrock for a moral authoritarianism. For, as we shall argue below, if rape and sexual assaults are 'a fate worse than death', then it is incumbent upon the government to intervene into the lives of individuals so as to prevent the social death of its citizenry. This chapter, therefore, whilst not directly critiquing the reforms of sex regulation in regards to rape and sexual assault, raises some of the issues and themes that will be explored in subsequent chapters.

This chapter is divided into four main sections. In the first section we outline the main critique of regulations *vis à vis* rape and sexual assault prior to the reforming process. In the second section, we briefly discuss the innovations and changes to the regulatory framework put in place with the Sexual Offences Act 2003. We do not discuss the actual provisions within the Act in any great depth as these can be found adequately outlined elsewhere. Instead we focus on the changes to the way in which the 'problem' of rape and sexual assault is framed. In the third section we address the question of conditions of possibility for these changes and in particular we examine the symbolic landscape underpinning these changes and ask what the impact of this is. Here, we raise the issue of how contemporary official discourse on rape and sexual assault constitutes 'discrimination' and 'victimhood'. In the concluding section of this chapter, we broaden the discussion by highlighting the themes raised in a deconstruction of official discourse on rape and sexual assault that are relevant to the rest of the book.

The case for reform

In 1987, Temkin wrote: 'For over a decade public disquiet has been intermittently but vehemently expressed about rape and the way it is handled by the criminal justice system' (Temkin 1987:1). It would seem that such disquiet gathered momentum and became a loud voice for reform of practice and law in the interceding two decades in the UK. In this chapter we do not provide a full description of the critique of law and criminal justice practice in Britain that led to the Sexual Offences Act (2003). Rather we highlight some of the key issues that gained attention throughout the last three decades of the twentieth century. The critique focused on three main issues: the paucity of the legal definition of rape; the regularity of sexual violation; and the treatment meted out to women in the criminal justice process.

It has only been in the recent past that rape has been defined in statute. Prior to the Sexual Offences (Amendment) Act 1976, the common law definition of rape was 'unlawful sexual intercourse with a woman without her consent, by force, fear or fraud'. With the Sexual Offences (Amendment) Act 1976, rape was defined as having five constitutive elements. There needed to have been sexual intercourse, with a woman, which was unlawful, which knowingly or recklessly took place without her consent. Throughout the 1970s and 1980s feminists challenged this definition because, firstly, it focused on one particular sexual activity (a penis penetrating a vagina) to the exclusion of all other sexual activities (such as forced oral sex or penetration by other objects). Secondly, the manner in which the legal definition centred on the question of consent placed the burden of proof upon the victim in that in practice, she had to prove that consent did not take place. Thirdly, until the early 1990s, it excluded married partners. In an often cited but very early judgment, Sir Matthew Hale CJ claimed in 1736 that a husband could not be guilty of rape because 'by their mutual matrimonial consent and contract, the wife hath given up herself in this kind unto her husband, which she cannot retract'. Fourthly, the narrowness of this definition simply did not, campaigners claimed, resonate with women's experiences of forced oral or anal sex, of being penetrated by objects and of rape within marriage. Fifthly, in implementing such a narrow definition, Kelly and Radford (1996) argue criminal justice practice distinguishes between 'real rapes' and other 'rapes' with 'real' rapes being seen as more serious. 'Real' rapes are those that correspond most closely to legal definition, i.e. they take place at night, in a public place, by a stranger who uses force against an elderly woman or child. Lastly, the manner in which the adjudication of rape focuses on 'consent' belies the social realities for women between submission and force and between pressurised, forced or coerced sex. Kelly (1988) argued that these distinctions and the complex social relationships that shape them were not capable of being reflected in the narrowness of the legal definition subsequent to the Sexual Offences (Amendment) Act 1976.

The issue of the legal definition of rape has been a particularly important one, especially in light of the sheer numbers of women that experience some form of sexual violence. Contrary to earlier understandings (and indeed official statistics) that posited that rape and sexual violation were rare and unusual events, contemporary statistics show that sexual violence is widely experienced by women. Thus, in 2002, the British Crime Survey suggested that 1 in 20 women reported being raped at some point since they had turned 16 years old and that during 1999, some 61,000 had been raped. The Home Office official statistics reported that in the year 2002/3, there were 12,293 recorded cases of rape. For 2003/4, this figure had increased to 13,247, although the percentage which was against women remained the same. Throughout the 1980s and 1990s, a series of studies in both the United States and Britain attempted to quantify the prevalence of rape and other acts of sexual vicitimization. Hall's prevalence study in the UK reported that 1 in 6 had experienced rape and 1 in 3 had been sexually assaulted at some point in their life. Both Russell (1990) and Painter (1991) reported a prevalence figure of 1 in 7 women experiencing rape in marriage.

At the same time as the prevalence and incidence studies were carried out other qualitative studies were beginning to explore the experiences victims had in the criminal justice process. The conviction rate for recorded rapes is notoriously low. Whilst there is some disagreement about the actual rate, most studies place it well below 10 per cent. So, for instance, Harris and Grace (1999) found that only 6 per cent of cases originally reported as rape resulted in a conviction for rape. Specifically, 64 per cent were discontinued by the Crown Prosecution Service or the police (who either 'no-crimed' them or took no further action against the suspect). Others have noted that whilst the numbers of women coming forward to report rape dramatically increased in the last quarter of the twentieth century, the attrition rate has increased. Thus, in 1977 the conviction rate for rape was 32 per cent whereas by 1994, this figure had fallen to 8 per cent (Griffiths 1999).

Such statistics are, indeed, disturbing but not particularly illuminating as to the social processes that make rape and sexual assaults one of the crimes with the lowest reporting rate and highest attrition rates. It is qualitative, more in-depth studies that shed some light on the factors and issues that created the legitimacy crisis in the late 1990s. These studies have confirmed that the prosecution of rape and other sexual assaults hinges on 'extra-legal' factors such as the extent to which the victims conform to very limited stereotypes of appropriate womanhood (Temkin 1995, Lees 2002), or the degree to which the Crown Prosecution Service feels that a case is 'winnable' – winnable being defined as closely conforming to notions of 'stranger rape', i.e. a sudden attack by a stranger rather than an assault by an individual known to or intimately involved with the victim (Harris and Grace 1999). In addition to these criticisms, there had also been long and heated debates about what had come to be known as the *Morgan ruling.* The Morgan ruling referred to the case of DPP *v* Morgan [1976] AC 182 wherein it was ruled that it was an adequate defence against a charge of rape to show that the accused had a genuine but mistaken belief that the victim had consented to sex. The point of contention about the Morgan ruling was that there was no test of 'reasonableness' introduced. In other words, it did not matter whether the belief in consent was unreasonable as long as the defendant genuinely believed that the woman consented. Combined, the high attrition rate, the insights offered by in-depth studies and specific issue campaigns have produced an impetus for changing both the procedures for dealing with rape and sexual assaults as well as the law itself. As a result, there have also been year-on-year reforms to practice. So for instance, specially trained police officers and rape suites are now regularly deployed throughout the police constabularies in England and Wales; the purpose of which has been to create a less intimidating and daunting atmosphere in which victims can give evidence and be examined for forensic evidence.

Hence, by the end of the 1990s, laws and criminal justice practice surrounding rape and sexual assault were perceived to be in crisis. In an attempt to deal with the mounting pressure, the New Labour government announced its plans to reform the law on sexual offences. *Setting the Boundaries*, the government's consultation paper on the reform of sexual offences, was published in 1999. This was followed by *Protecting the Public* in 2003 and finally the new Sexual Offences Act 2003, which was implemented in May 2004.

The rest of this chapter focuses on contemporary official discourse on rape. The next section specifically outlines the changes to legislation that have been made before moving on to deconstruction of these changes.

'Tough, fair, modern – sex laws for the twenty-first century'

The Sexual Offences Act 2003 (SOA 2003) extensively alters the legal regulatory framework concerning both rape and sexual assault. It does this in three ways: firstly, the SOA 2003 is underpinned by a more 'subjectivist' or 'constructionist' approach to sexual offending that moves away from defining sexual offences as particular *acts*; secondly, the SOA 2003 'gender neutralizes' sexual offences; thirdly, it dramatically increases the levels of punishment for sexual offences almost across the board[1]; and, fourthly, it changes the way in which the law is to be implemented in the courts by shifting the notion of harm that underpins sexual offences as well as defining 'consent'. In terms of more particular matters, the SOA 2003 consolidates all possible sexual offences under a rubric of three main offences[2]. Each one of these claims will be taken in turn before outlining the relevant sections of the SOA 2003.

Whereas once sexual offence laws focused on clearly specified, particular acts and behaviours, the Sexual Offences Act 2003 moves away from defining the offence in terms of activity or behaviours. Thus, as mentioned above, prior to SOA 2003, the sexual act that constituted rape had been defined as, specifically, penile penetration of a woman's (i.e. not transsexual's) vagina or anus. Most other sexual offences were similarly mechanistically and 'objectively' defined and, importantly, gender specific. Hence there were old offences of indecent assault on a woman, indecent assault on a man, assault with intent to commit buggery and so on. With the SOA 2003, rape is still defined as penile penetration, but not just of the vagina and anus. So, rape now includes penetration of any orifice (including mouth and anus) of anyone. A new offence of assault by penetration has also been created to cover penetration of body orifices by anything other than a penis and can be committed by men *and* women. Similarly, whereas sexual assaults were very specifically defined around particular sexual acts (buggery, sexual intercourse and so on), sexual assault is now any form of non-consensual touching that is sexual in nature. This 'subjectivist' or 'constructionist' approach is noted in the definition of what 'sexual' means. 'Sexual' is defined as that which any reasonable person would consider sexual or that which is done with a sexual intent.

Prior to the SOA 2003, the regulatory framework limited what could or could not be done to specific categories of people. Thus rape happened to women. Unlawful sexual intercourse happened (mainly) to children. Buggery happened (mainly) to men. In complete contrast, the SOA 2003 focuses on what people can and cannot do to generalized others. The only category of offence that remains gender specific is rape, as the definition of rape remains 'penile penetration'. All other offences have removed any reference to the sex of either the victim or offender. The point we are making here is that the object of regulation has shifted from being what (mainly) men should not do to women and children (largely), to what individuals should not do to others. That the previous regulatory framework was so heavily bounded by gender is evidenced in the history of the Sexual Offences (Amendment) Act 1885, which raised the age of consent to 16 years old. This Act referred only to when it was legal for a man to have sexual intercourse with a woman. It did not set the age at which all individuals were deemed capable of consenting to sex.

Finally, whereas the regulatory framework prior to the SOA 2003 was an attempt to specify a (more or less) exhaustive list of all the different sexual acts which could be defined as illegal (rape, attempted rape, rape and burglary, indecent assault, buggery, unlawful sexual intercourse and so on), there are now only three primary offences: rape, assault by penetration and sexual assault. There is also provision to make any other offence (such as kidnapping or burglary) which includes a sexual element or the intent to commit a sexual offence, a sexual offence.

In relation to how these new offences are to be implemented, there are also significant changes. Firstly, SOA 2003 introduces a test of 'reasonableness' in relation to the defendant's belief in the complainant's consent. The Act reads:

(1) A person (A) commits an offence if –
    (a) he intentionally penetrates the vagina, anus or mouth of another person (B) with his penis,
    (b) B does not consent to the penetration, and
    (c) A does not reasonably believe that B consents.

(2) Whether a belief is reasonable is to be determined having regard to all the circumstances, including any steps A has taken to ascertain whether B consents.

Section (2) above not only supercedes the Morgan decision – thus rendering a defence of mistaken but honest belief inadequate – but frames the issue of lack of consent very differently from previously. The Morgan decision has had the impact of giving legitimacy to the notion that there could be two contradictory, mutually exclusive under-standings of a singular event. In doing this, it allowed a defendant to exploit this disjuncture between the woman's experience of not consenting and the man's 'mistaken' perceptions of the same event. In contrast, SOA 2003 goes some way to closing this gap. Through specifying that the defendant's belief must be 'reasonable' and that part of the test of 'reasonableness' is an inquiry into how the defendant demonstrated that he sought consent, SOA 2003 constitutes the event as having only one reasonable interpretation. Of course it is interesting to speculate at this point – at the cusp of implementation – whether and to what extent the test of 'reasonableness' will change either the process or outcome of specific trials. It has long since been noted such tests can allow myths, ideologies and prejudices to flourish. If all 'reasonable' men think that 'no' means 'yes', then introducing this test will not fundamentally alter practice. Notwithstanding this, the importance of this test of reasonableness is precisely in the way in which it attempts to interrupt the notion that there can be two possible but mutually exclusive understandings of the facts of consent concerning an event of rape.

Earlier we mentioned that the notion of 'harm' that underpins the legislation has also been altered. In terms of common law, the harm that rape and other sexual assaults was perceived to cause was harm not to the woman, but to her husband or father. She became 'damaged goods' (Toner 1977). In contrast, rape and other sexual assaults have now been constituted as threatening, damaging or harming the sexual autonomy or choice of an individual. SOA 2003 also relocates the harm of rape and other sexual assaults *vis à vis* other types of offences. So, if punishment becomes a yardstick by which it is possible to measure the perceived relative damage of a crime (Ashworth 2000), sexual offences have become much more serious in the new millennium. Although rape has always carried a maximum penalty of life imprisonment, the punish-ment for the old indecent assault (now replaced with sexual assault by penetration) has been increased from 10 years to life; sexual assault (a lesser offence) is punishable by up to 10 years' imprisonment; the maximum punishment for burglary with intent to commit rape (now replaced with trespass with intent to commit a serious sexual offence) has also been increased from 14 years to life imprisonment; and the maximum tariff for procurement of sexual intercourse by threat or intimidation (now replaced with obtaining sexual penetration by threats or deception in any part of the world) is 10 as opposed to two years' imprisonment. Ashworth (1995) notes that:

> There is much to suggest that the attitudes of society towards sexual offences, particularly the attitudes of many men (who hold most of the leading posts in the making of policy and law), have tended to undervalue the seriousness of sexual assaults.
>
> (Ashworth 1995: 336)

It would now seem, on the face of it, that this is no longer the case. For it is possible to interpret the significant extensions to the maximum penalties associated with the range of sexual offences as being an attempt to redress this, to increase the 'value' of the seriousness. This is a claim we shall return to later, for it is also possible to conceptualize the increased punitiveness of the SOA 2003 within a different type of discussion about the law's role in consolidating what we refer to as the new sexual enterprise of moral authoritarianism.

The next section moves this chapter in a slightly different direction. It examines the underpinning symbolic landscape that makes it possible to 'gender neutralize' rape and sexual assaults. This is despite the empirical evidence that over 90 per cent of reported victims of sexual assault and rape are women and girls (Research Development and Statistics 2003). At the same time the levels of punishment have been increased across the board. In particular, we focus on the manner in which official discourse on rape and sexual assault shapes the 'problem' as a legal technical problem to be resolved by 'better' law that recognizes both victims' experiences *and* gender.

From vicitimization to victim-identity

One interpretation of the reforming process signified by the introduction and implementation of the Sexual Offences Act 2003 is that it marks the triumph of year-on-year feminist campaigns and scholarship. The argument could run that feminists have successfully highlighted the phallocentric orientation of laws on sexual violence (Smart 1990) and generated a climate in which it is possible to recognize both women's experience and the gravity of sexual violation (i.e. that the harm of rape does not necessarily inhere only in the effects of penetration of a vagina by a penis). Whilst this may well be the case, it is our contention that this is a limited interpretation of the process of reform, for it portrays the reforms as a simple linear progression from lack of enlightenment to enlightenment as inspired by feminist political ideals (Bevacqua 2000). Instead, we offer an analysis that highlights the ways in which the recognition of gender and of victims' experiences paradoxically decontextualizes rape and other sexual assaults and operates to deny and erase the complex material relationships shaping men's sexual violence against women. And, as will be shown, the recognition of gender and 'victims' also provides the symbolic conditions for a greater moral authoritarianism in sexual relationships more generally.

Framing the problem: technical solutions to technical problems

Throughout all official publications concerning the reform of laws on rape and sexual assault, there was a repeated refrain that the older regulatory framework of statute and case law was a 'problem' in that it did not provide justice for the victims. This refrain resonated with the (largely feminist) critique of the ways in which criminal justice dealt with rape and other sexual assaults (as noted above), which detailed that: the extent of sexual violence is much greater than that portrayed in official statistics; when reported, the rate of attrition on rape cases is particularly high; the law itself contained a number of anomalies that were not fully able to capture the experiences of victims; and victims often felt highly dissatisfied with both the process of criminal justice intervention and specifically the types of sentences that convicted sexual offenders received.

Research published in USA, Canada, Europe and the UK has explained many of the failings outlined above as being attributable, to varying extents, to the social context in which law operates and especially the relationship between patriarchal ideologies (or discourses) of heterosexual relationships and dichotomous ideologies of good and bad womanhood (MacKinnon 1987, Smart 1990, Ashworth 1995, Edwards 1996, Temkin 1999, Temkin 2000, Lees 2002). More radical interpretations claim that the police, the law or the criminal justice system does not 'control' male sexual violence. Rather, in patriarchal, capitalist societies the 'law' functions to protect dominant male interests. In this way Kelly and Radford (1996) argue that the protection afforded clients is made visible at several stages throughout the adjudication of a case (perhaps most clearly in what was the acceptable defence of mistaken belief in consent). For the purposes of our argument in this chapter, it is not necessary to discuss the intricacies or relative merits of these various explanations – we wish merely to demonstrate that for many years researchers have been drawing links between broader social contexts and the very specific problems associated with the formal legal framework pertaining to rape and sexual assault.

In contrast, contemporary official discourse on rape and sexual assault has constituted these 'problems' as being merely and only technical problems. It does this by denuding the process of legal method and the creation of law of its social context. The law is located outside any social processes, as occupying an autonomous, privileged position untainted by the ideologies and structures of the social world[3]. In *Setting the Boundaries* (STB), it is claimed that the law:

> … set[s] out the parameters not just for what society considers to be acceptable and unacceptable behaviour, but designate[s] behaviour that is so unacceptable as to be criminal … The criminal law sets the boundaries for what is culpable and deserving of punishment including sexual activity.
>
> (Home Office 2000: 1)

In relation to rape and sexual assaults, therefore, the 'problem' was that the boundaries that had been set by previous statute and case laws were flawed.

> Some behaviour that should be covered by the criminal law is not at present. We know far more now about the insidious ways in which sexual abuse takes place and we have listened to the voices of victims about the profound and long-lasting effects of abuse. Our new framework of offences will *plug existing gaps* and seek to protect society from rape and sexual assault at one end of the spectrum and from voyeurism at the other.
>
> (Home Office 2002: 8, emphasis added)

> The nature and effect of sexual assaults of all kinds on the victim, both men and women, were not sufficiently understood by the law, despite the significant advances in understanding made in recent years; this impacted throughout the criminal justice system, including sentencing.
>
> (Home Office 2000: 11)

Put simply, it was held that ignorance of the 'realities' of sexual violence did not allow the experiences of victims to be heard. The solution, therefore, was presented as a technical one in which through the acquisition of better knowledge about victims of sexual violence and sexual vicitimization, a more comprehensive legal framework could be woven which permitted no gaps. In constituting the 'problem' and the 'solution' as a technical one, the space is foreclosed to recognize the relationship of the law to the wider social relationships and material realities which condition men's sexual violence and women's sexual victimization. Hence, the power of law remains unchallenged, as does the social context that makes sexual violation routine.

Victims' experiences: voices from beyond the grave

Earlier we claimed that one of the key symbolic shifts that has made it possible to erase the material origins of the legitimation deficit present in contemporary official discourse on rape and sexual assault has been to recognize and open the space for victims' experiences to be incorporated into the reforming process. Cynically, it could be argued that the strategy of claiming to incorporate the experiences of victims into statute proffers the reforming process a degree of legitimacy. It gives the reforms a 'common sense' rationale (i.e. reforms appear to be based on the inadequacies of the current system identified by victims who have first-hand experience). Framing the reforms as 'victim-centred' also means it becomes very difficult to critique the proposals, as any such critique becomes reframed as being unsympathetic to sexual victims. But not all victims' experiences have been incorporated into official discourse – the focus has only been on particular narratives. As indicated in the above section, victims who experienced the policing or adjudication of the rape as being as traumatic as the rape or sexual assault itself have been silenced in the face of a construction of the problem as a technical one.

The types of victims' narratives that have been given space can be seen through the ways in which contemporary official discourse has constituted the nature and harm of the victimization experienced. 'Victims' are portrayed as being victims of extreme trauma brought on by their sexual violations as well as being victims of injustice caused by a system that 'did not hear them'. Indeed, as we shall see in the following section, the level of trauma is so great as to disable any other social role possessed by the individual. 'Victims' are constituted as being individuals whose totality of life has imploded around her/his status as a victim of sexual violence.

These are all extremely serious violations of victims which leave them physically and psychologically damaged for many years.

(Home Office 2000: 15)

As part of our policy of increasing protection we also identified a number of gaps and mismatches in the present law which may result in a degree of injustice to victims. The review also identified areas of the law which, in the light of their impact on victims, should be regarded much more seriously.

(Home Office 2000:14)

The trauma is thus constituted as a totalizing version of victimhood. Individuals are not merely victimized; they are victims in their very person. This is a subtle and nuanced construction of the victim as undergoing a social death. In sociological literature, social death often refers to the process an individual undergoes towards the end of their life when other individuals within their social sphere treat the dying as though they are already dead. So, for example, individuals suffering from Alzheimer's disease are understood as dying long before their actual bodies die. Social death is also understood as being a concept that permits an understanding of what it means to be 'alive' and to be a 'social actor'. Hence, one reason that the individual with Alzheimer's disease is perceived as dead before their biological death, is that they can no longer perform the variety of social roles (i.e. mother, lover, friend, employee) that they once performed (Howarth and Leaman 2002).

Earlier we commented that it is only particular narratives of rape and sexual violation that have found expression in contemporary official discourse on rape and sexual assault. In short, it is precisely the stories of sexual violation as being a form of social death that predominate. Narratives in which rape and sexual assault are not fundamentally dissimilar to other acts of violence and/or in which victims overcome and survive their experiences are effectively silenced. Fundamental to excluding these other narratives is the way in which official discourse constitutes rape and sexual assault as being an act of violation of the sexual 'integrity' and 'autonomy' of the individual as opposed to being merely acts of violence. And, in violating the autonomy and freedom of individuals, their ability to act as full social actors is called into question and the spectre of their social death is raised.

The most common feature of all these offences [dealt with in STB] are that they are acts of sexual violation (whether or not they include any physical violence or force) which take place without the consent of the victim. Consent is the crucial issue for these offences because the lack of consent is the essence of the criminal behaviour. It is one individual forcing another to undergo an experience against their will. *It is a violation of the victim's autonomy and freedom to decide.*

(Home Office 2000: 9, emphasis added)

We thought that rape and sexual assault are primarily crimes against the sexual autonomy of others. Every adult has the right and the responsibility to make decisions about their sexual conduct and to respect the rights of others. No other approach is viable in a society that values equality and respect for the rights of each individual.

(Home Office 2000: 14)

Hence, contemporary official discourse 'blurs the edges' of rape and sexual assault, reconstituting it as a metaphor encapsulating a cautionary tale for the modern age. We are told that rape and other sexual assaults can be a 'fate worse than death'. We are not calling into question the devastation that sexual violence can cause to the lives of those who experience it. Rather we are highlighting that if rape and sexual assault are symbolically deployed in such a way, the specificity of those experiences is lost in the face of a totalizing narrative which situates sexual violence as the worse thing that can happen to a person. This is seen in the discussion within STB about whether to create a lesser rape offence for instances of 'date rape' and victim submission.

A more serious question is whether there are genuinely lesser rapes. Victim/survivor organisations told us that although all victims/survivors were deeply affected by rape, there was often greater victimisation in rapes that were seen as lesser than the traditional model of stranger rape … The crime of rape is so serious that it needs to be considered in its totality rather than being constrained by any relationship between the parties.

(Home Office 2000: 16)

The essential common element of many of these situations was that there may be submission by the victim. Submission may reflect reluctant acquiescence, but it may also reflect a lack of consent and/ or ability to resist. The fact of submission does not imply consent – it may well be better to suffer 'a fate worse than death' than to be killed or grievously wounded.

(Home Office 2000: 18)

Significantly, rape or sexual assault does not actually need to take place for a social death to occur. Indeed, there only needs to be the *threat* of attack. This can be seen in discussions drawing lines of demarcation between attempted rapes and sexual assaults and violent and sexual offences.

> The intent of the assault may however be quite clear to the victim who, even if no rape has occurred, is left deeply affected ... The victim suffers far greater fear and trauma than for a non-sexual assault because the intent to rape was clear and the terror and trauma suffered is related to that. It may be comparable to an actual rape.
>
> (Home Office 2000: 28)

> Even if no rape occurs, the trauma of being seriously threatened with rape by an intruder in your own bedroom or workplace, where you think you are safe, is profound ... We concluded that the essence of the crime was the sexual intent rather than the burglary, and that hence it should be regarded as a sex offence [i.e. burglary with intent to rape].
>
> (Home Office 2000: 28)

Thus, to experience the social death of rape, an individual does not actually need to be raped. One reason that such a nuanced construction is significant is that within these symbolic landscapes, the actual, lived experiences and traumas of rape get conflated with the metaphor of dying and the specificity of the actual experience is lost.

That official discourse posits sexual assault and rape as 'a fate worse than death' in which the trauma is so severe as to warrant the types of punishments meted out for murder is not wholly surprising. Observing contemporary society, both Giddens (1992) and Foucault (1978) have made specific comments regarding the privileged position of sex and sexuality in permitting an individual to both experience and express their 'selfhood'. Giddens (1999) argues that in a context of the profound social changes that have taken place in the way in which men and women conduct their intimate lives, sex and sexuality assume a new position. He argues:

> Among all the changes going on today, none are more important than those happening in our personal lives – in sexuality, emotional life, marriage and the family. *There is a global revolution going on in how we think of ourselves and how we form ties and connections with others.*
>
> (Giddens 1999, emphasis added)

Specifically, he argues that within late modernity, sexual activities become uniquely placed as ways in which individuals are able to 'actualize' and express their identities (Giddens 1992: 76). Of course, this is not a new argument for Foucault had made a similar argument nearly two decades earlier[4]. Foucault (1978) argued that it is through sex that an individual is able to both comprehend and express 'the truth' about him/her self. In short, sex produces subjectivities. Regardless of the specific limitations of the arguments put forward by Giddens (1992) and Foucault (1976), both theorists are pointing to the way in which sex, as an activity, is constituted in contemporary society as having a privileged position regarding the 'self'. Without sexuality, the 'self' will struggle to be expressed. In short, without sexual autonomy, the social self is jeopardized. In this way, contemporary official discourse on rape speaks to some of the profound social changes that have occurred in relation to how individuals 'do' sex, the way in which 'sex' is located in relation to other aspects of our social selves, and by extension, to *all* our relationships as well as to the social fabric itself.

However, the point that we are making here is that by positing rape and sexual assaults as a 'fate worse than death' and constituting sexual victims as socially dead, an imperative to action is created. This imperative then forms part of the conditions of possibility for the new sexual enterprise that also finds much, much broader expression in quasi-official discourse, as will be discussed in Chapters 4–7. In the next section, we describe how such notions of victimhood dovetail with a particular version of 'justice' as increasing the level of punishment.

Justice as punishment: protection through imprisonment

Through the articulation of the construction of sexual victimhood as being a form of social death with the 'autonomous', privileged way in which 'the law' is positioned, official discourse creates and draws upon a symbolic landscape which makes a rhetoric of protection and 'justice for victims' not only plausible but imperative. For, if the harms of rape and sexual assault are constituted as being so traumatic as to reduce the totality of individuals' lives to that of social death, then the law and more specifically government, must act to protect those who are either so victimized or vulnerable. We discuss the issue of protectionism and who is constituted as 'the threat' from which protection is needed more thoroughly in Chapter 3. In that chapter, we show how 'the threat' is constituted as being the rapid changes undergone by society which make sexual messages more complex to read, as well as create a climate in which sexual 'predators' are much more commonplace. For our purposes here, however, it is important to note that generating an imperative to action begs the question of what action is necessary. In this instance, the message is clear – tougher and greater levels of punishment[5].

> In July 2002 we published an action plan of practical measures to … make improvements across the whole of the criminal justice system. Through these improvements, we want to give victims of rape more confidence in the system and encourage them to report offences of rape.
>
> (Home Office 2002: 9)

> It is important that penalties for sex offences enable abusers to be properly punished. Existing penalties in some cases are too low and do not take into account the better understanding there now is of the long-term harm caused by sexual abuse.
>
> (Home Office 2002: 9)

> In many cases, we are recommending increased penalties. This reflects in part the fact that many sex offences have comparatively low penalties that are now out of step with our, and the public's, understanding of the nature and seriousness of sex offending.
>
> (Home Office 2000: 129)

We are not challenging whether rape and sexual assaults warrant deeper and increased punishments. At this point, we are merely raising the issue that in so framing 'justice', the possibility of structuring governmental responses and interventions not based on punitive justice is foreclosed.

> The message to victims is clear – you do not have to suffer in silence, help is available and the police, courts and other agencies are on your side. Offenders should know they face tough sentences and stringent controls when they commit their crimes.
>
> (Goggins, Home Office Minister, Home Office Press Release, 30th April 2004)

So, to recap, official discourse on rape and sexual assault is underpinned by a symbolic landscape which both generates an imperative to intervene and shapes that intervention as being the development of 'better' law founded upon 'better' knowledge of the 'realities'. That the law and criminal justice interventions may be part of the problem is erased. More, by situating justice as harsher punishments, official discourse constitutes rape and sexual assault as a problem of individuals who damage others. David Blunkett, then Home Secretary, summarized this as follows: 'We are getting tough in order to protect the public by clamping down on *those who destroy the lives of others'* (Blunkett, 2004, emphasis added). But we argue that whatever imprisonment may do to individual offenders and for individual victims, it is incapable of intervening to alter the complex material relations of gender which enable and condition men's sexual violence against women.

Ending discrimination, recognizing gender and erasing the 'problem of men'

Earlier we argued that the regulatory framework dealing with rape and sexual assault faced a legitimation deficit in the 1980s and 1990s which led to an 'overhaul' of the system and specifically to the introduction of a new regulatory framework and official discourse of rape and sexual assault. We also claimed that one way in which official discourse subverts and displaces the legitimation deficits that periodically occur, is through erasing the material realities which give rise to the crisis in legitimation. In the case of rape and sexual assault, one of the fundamental critiques that generated the legitimation crisis was the (campaigning and research) recognition of the types and expression of 'gender discrimination' that were present in the processing of rape and sexual assault cases. Quite simply, not only was it the empirical case that most sexual offending was against women and committed by men, but cases often hinged on the degree to which women victims were able to demonstrate their compliance to very limited notions of 'good' womanhood. However, although a recognition of gender and discrimination were claimed to be central precepts throughout the reforming process, the type and manner of this recognition not only did not correspond with that contained in the critique, but shifted the meanings of the critique such that the strength of the critique was displaced. Specifically, discrimination was understood as *differentiation on the grounds of gender* both in relation to the types of offences that could, in principle, be committed as well as differential criminal liability on the grounds of sexual orientation.

> Sex offences are an important part of the criminal law. They are concerned with behaviour that society recognises as both unacceptable and criminally culpable … We recognise that it is possible for both men and women to perpetrate sexual crimes on others.
>
> (Home Office 2000: 97)

The review considered whether there was any justification for treating men and women differently in the criminal law, or for making different provision for those of differing sexual orientation. We could find no justification for doing so.

(Home Office 2000: 100)

Recognition of discrimination leads to the question of equality. Official discourse of rape and sexual assault is set in a symbolic landscape in which equality is understood as sameness. In short, men and women should be treated *the same*. In this way, official discourse on rape and sexual assault posits that men and women commit *the same* offences and as such should be liable in the same way. Witness the following:

Sexual offences are for the most part gender specific. Our law is cast in terms of men committing certain offences and women committing others … This leads to anomalies and inconsistencies in the way offenders are dealt with for what is *essentially similar behaviour*. It was strongly argued that this kind of differential treatment was not justified unless there was a specific reason, offences should be couched in gender-neutral terms.

(Home Office 2000: 97)

Whilst this sentiment is difficult to critique, it displaces recognition that women and men *do not* commit the same sexual offences at the same rate or in the same way. In so doing, the space is foreclosed in which the law can be capable of understanding and dealing with the gendered material social relations of sexual violence.

Fundamental to the way in which recognizing discrimination and gender operates to erase the gendered realities of rape and sexual assault is the manner that discrimination against women is translated into a problem of discrimination against gay men. Indeed in the chapter entitled, 'Issues in Gender and Discrimination' in *Setting the Boundaries*, all examples of policy in other jurisdictions related only to differential ages of consent for same-sex sexual activities and heterosexual sexual activities.

Our role was to consider the rights and responsibilities of individuals to make their own decisions about consensual sexual behaviour and the controls that society needs to impose in order to protect its more vulnerable members. In addition, the law needs to ensure that protection is offered to everyone regardless of gender, race, sexual orientation or any other factor and that it operates fairly and equitably. The basic set of assumptions underlying the work of the review which are of most relevance to issues of gender and discrimination were that: any application of the criminal law must be fair, necessary and proportionate; the criminal law should not discriminate unnecessarily between men and women nor between those of different sexual orientation.

(Home Office 2000: 97)

The theme of the extent and nature of the discrimination in the law was a significant element in the responses to our initial consultation exercise ... We were given a consistent message that the law discriminates against certain sections of our society, most notably homosexual men. This message was supported by the research commissioned by the review, the views expressed at conferences and seminars, views of legal professionals, academics, social commentators and the personal experience of members of the review groups themselves.

(Home Office 2000: 97)

Hence, recognizing discrimination against women in relation to treatment of both offenders and victims creates the space in which it is possible to deny gender, to erase the empirical realities that rape and sexual assaults are primarily committed by men against women. Gender discrimination in relation to either the treatment of victims or understandings of the realities of sexual violence is simply expunged in the favour of 'clear' and 'better' law.

If we define offences as those where there is no consent (or where particular protection is required e.g. for children and vulnerable people, or to deal with offensive behaviour in public) then it makes sense for offences to apply to victims and perpetrators of either sex wherever possible. In some instances we have thought it necessary and proportionate to identify some gender-specific offences, but for the most part it is easier and clearer to provide gender-neutral offences that apply to all kinds of sexual penetration or sexual activity. In all our proposals sexual penetration applies to any anal or genital penetration, or penile penetration of the mouth ... We think this approach is simpler and clearer.

(Home Office 2000:101)

The Act repeals existing discriminatory laws so that, with the exception of rape which must involve penile penetration, all sexual offences now apply equally to males and females of any sexual orientation.

(Home Office 2004b: 8)

Conclusion

It is very difficult to critique the current reform of laws on rape and sexual assault, especially when the new regulatory framework that is put in place is ostensibly based on a more thorough and 'accurate' understanding of the realities of sexual victimization of adults. We have not mentioned the more subtle and sophisticated understanding of 'consent' in relation to rape and sexual assault. This is partly because our object of analysis throughout the book is not the law on rape and sexual assault *per se* but rather the conditions of possibility for the regulation of sex more generally, as manifest in official and quasi-official discourses. In this respect, a deconstruction of the new regulatory framework for rape and sexual assault serves as an excellent starting point as it raises a number of the key themes and issues that are pursued in the rest of the book. Namely, we have seen that it was in relation to rape specifically that the legitimation crisis arose. As we stated at the beginning of the chapter, the bulk of campaigning and research in the 1980s and 1990s which critiqued the law on sexual violence generally was, in fact, geared to the gendered realities of the incidence and prevalence of rape as well as the experience of victims at the hands of the criminal justice system. But we have also seen how it was that official discourse was able to shift recognition of these material realities. We argued that this shift was possible through the construction of the 'problem' as being a technical problem and thus the 'solution' also became a technical solution. Put simply, the 'problem' was constituted as one in which older regulations were 'outdated' and did not understand what it meant to be a 'victim'. The 'solution' thereby was drafting new regulations based on a more 'accurate' vision of the experiences of victims. But we have demonstrated that recognition of victims' experiences also operates to decontextualize rape and sexual violence. Specifically we argue that not all victims' experiences are recognized in official discourse: narratives which situate 'victims' as undergoing a social death are the narratives used to constitute a totalizing version of 'victimhood'. Such a version excluded the possibility of recognizing the narratives of victims in which the criminal justice process was *as traumatic* as the assault or in which *sexual* violence was little different from other forms of violence.

We also argue that, paradoxically, recognition of gender and discrimination creates the very conditions to deny and erase the gendered realities of sexual violence in the form of rape and sexual assault of adults. Underpinning official discourse is a construction of gendered discrimination as being the *differential* treatment of men and women in terms of criminal liability as well as the differential treatment of gay men. The solution, therefore, is to 'gender-neutralize' offences so that women and men are equally liable for the same offences as well as equalizing gay and heterosexual ages of consent. Moreover, and in keeping with the changing place of 'sex' in contemporary society, a totalizing version of 'victimhood' provides the space for the assertion of a new moral authoritarianism, for if nothing else, it creates an imperative to action on the part of the government. This is a theme that we return to in the next chapter. The construction of particular types of 'threats' and the necessity of particular types of regulations are made much more manifest in the case of child sexual abuse than in relation to rape and sexual assault. They also dovetail with the construction of sexual 'victims' as experiencing social death that underpin discourse on rape. In the next chapter we pick up this thread and demonstrate, in relation to child sexual abuse, how official discourse also creates the conditions of possibility which underpin the new sexual enterprise we unpack in this book.

Notes

1 See especially the Home Office's website on sexual offending in which a table comparing older provisions and punishments with the new framework is included (www.homeoffice.gov.uk/justice/sentencing/sexualoffencesbill/whatschanged.html).
2 Having said that, it is important to note that there are many more offences than three contained within the SOA 2003. Our point here is that in regards to rape and sexual assault, some eight different offences have been concentrated into only three new offences. Each of these new offences, however, does make distinctions on the grounds of the age of the victim. But this chapter focuses specifically on sexual violations against adults who are not defined as 'defectives' or 'persons with a mental disorder impeding choice'.
3 This critique of the way in which the law positions itself as 'autonomous' and neutral is a long-standing one made by, *inter alia*, Foucault (1977) and Smart (1990). Our claim here therefore is certainly not original, but designed merely to show how locating the law in this fashion has a particular impact on the construction of both the 'problem' of older rape and sexual assault laws and its subsequent solutions.

4 It is worth noting that whereas Giddens' version of the relocation of sex *vis à vis* self is that it has occurred within a growing social egalitarianism in gender relationships, Foucault was much less optimistic and positioned the relocation of sex *vis à vis* identity as part of the technologies of the self that permit 'effective' governmentality. Thus, whilst both theorists argue that sex is capable of producing subjectivities and identities, they differ greatly on the extent to which this occurs as part of the social control of individual, or is a manifestation of greater individual, autonomy.

5 Such a symbolic elision between tough punishment and justice for victims is not unique to official discourse surrounding sexual offending. It has a long history in discourses on punishment and has re-emerged in the twenty-first century across a range of countries.

Chapter 3

Threatening sex: protection, communities and childhood

When we first spoke out, ten years ago, on the subject of incest, of our abuse as children, by fathers and stepfathers, of our childhood rape by older brothers, stepbrothers, funny uncles, grandfathers – there was, for all the pain, sometimes humour …

In these last ten years, things have become unimaginably worse – for child victims, now, and for the women, their mothers, who try to protect these children. And for survivors, who now find the very stuff of their trauma, their degradation, their violation as children, the common currency of talk show guest 'experts' and 'professionals'; find their courageous speaking-out transformed into no more than a new plot option for ongoing dramatic series.

People say to me: 'Well, at least we're talking about it now.'

Yes, but it was not our intention to start a long conversation.

In breaking the silence, we hoped to raise hell. Instead, we have raised for the issue a certain normalcy. We hoped to raise a passion for change. Instead, what we raised was a discourse – and a sizeable problem-management industry.

(Louise Armstrong in Plummer 1995: 78–9)

Introduction

In the preceding chapter, we examined the legitimation deficit facing contemporary regulations *vis à vis* sex. This chapter picks up a number of these earlier themes. It addresses the question of how 'sexual threat' is constituted in official discourses of sex as well as how 'protection' is framed. We also argue that the particular constellation of shifting meaning for 'sexual threat' and 'protection' opens the space for increasing regulations and thereby provides part of the conditions of possibility for the new moral authoritarianism and new sexual enterprise discussed in Chapter 1. The focus of this chapter is upon threatening sex, namely sex which is constituted as so highly dangerous and damaging as to necessitate both criminal justice interventions and official concern about changing family forms. In particular, child sexual abuse is the object of inquiry in this chapter.

An observer of late twentieth century Britain would be forgiven for concluding that the 1980s heralded the 'discovery' of sexual offending against children. A series of high profile cases seemed to put the issue firmly on the public agenda, where it has remained, more or less in constant discussion, ever since. Public debates, reference texts and research regularly repeat this 'history', claiming that until the 1980s sex offending against children was simply swept under the carpet, not recognized and with rare exceptions not dealt with. This popular history is not wholly accurate. Concern about sexual activity between adults and children has a longer history. Contemporary legislation dates back to the late nineteenth century, with the then concern about children's involvement in prostitution and the sexual proclivities of the wealthy gentry (Walkowitz 1980). Notwithstanding this, in the UK, there has not been a specific offence of sexual abuse against children until now. There has been, however, a framework of laws that delimit sexual activity between adults and children. And, the introduction of the Sexual Offences Act 2003 has seen a battery of new laws supplementing existing laws such that any type of sexual activity with or *between* those under the age of sexual consent is now illegal[1].

The only characteristic that the regulations discussed in this chapter share is that they are all focused on the age of the victim concerned. Unlike other sexual offences, offences against children are offences because of the age of the victim. In this sense, sexual offences against children are those behaviours and activities which might be perfectly legal if those taking part were both over the age of 18 years, but which have become offences within Britain's current legal framework because one party is under the age of 18. That this is the case raises an important question. Why should there be a specific regulatory framework concerned with sex and age? For some, it is '[a]xiomatic that children and young persons require and deserve the protection of the criminal law from sexual acts committed by adults' (Burke and Selfe 2001:136) for three key reasons. Firstly, the law must operate to protect those from what is seen as being socially and ethically unacceptable (i.e. sex with children) if only because children, by definition, are legally unable to offer consent. Secondly, the law has a certain denunciative function. By specifying that certain sexual acts are illegal and punishable, the state is able to send a message about what is socially and morally undesirable. Thirdly, by criminalizing seemingly less serious sexual activities (such as possessing indecent or sexual images of children), the law seeks to prevent much more serious sexual offending against children (Burke and Selfe 2001).

This chapter does not challenge the stock of literature that demonstrates the serious emotional, social and physical damage that sex between adults and children can cause. Nor does it seek to discuss whether or not contemporary approaches are 'correct' (i.e. whether the age of consent should be abolished, lowered or raised). Rather, this chapter deconstructs official discourse of child sexual abuse as made manifest in the regulatory framework present in contemporary Britain. Key to this are discussions about the contradictory meanings of 'the family' and 'children' as well as the dominance of a new discourse of child sexual offenders.

This chapter is divided into two main sections: firstly we outline the current legal framework surrounding sexual activity involving children and secondly, we deconstruct that framework, examining both the process of reform of sexual offences against children as occurred in 2003 and the official discourse surrounding that. The central argument of this chapter is that the variable meanings of 'children' and 'the family', as well as the manner in which the 'source' of danger and harm shifts, create the conditions in which it is possible for an official challenge to be made to the moral authority and capacity of contemporary family forms to regulate the lives of children. Such a challenge, it will be argued, is fundamental to the project of constructing a new sexual enterprise of moral authoritarianism. It is argued that the deconstruction of official discourse concerning children and sex demonstrates that underpinning the desire to protect the vulnerable from sexual abuse and the symbolic separation of children from the world of adults, is a struggle over relations between children, families and other adults, and the wider communities in which they live. We will not be discussing the critique of how child sexual abuse was regulated throughout the twentieth century (see Ashenden (2004) for an excellent critique focused on the public inquiries that occurred in England and Wales from the 1980s). In any case, the main critique is very similar to that outlined in the previous chapter. Suffice to say that the legitimation deficit official discourse confronted was one which recognized the routineness of men's sexual violence against children and within families. Moreover, we will not go into depth about how official discourse is able to erase the material conditions that generated this legitimation deficit and the ways in which the complex social relationships of gender and age that make such violence possible are denied. Notwithstanding this, we do start from the assumption that the shifting meanings of 'children', 'family' and 'danger' enable these complex social realities to be appropriated in ways that displace recognition of those underlying material realities.

Changing regulations: from unlawful sexual intercourse to sexual activities with a child

The first section of this chapter describes the regulatory framework as it existed in England and Wales for the better part of the twentieth century, before charting the changes to be brought forward for the twenty-first century with the passing of the Sexual Offences Act 2003 (SOA 2003). Until the Sexual Offences Act 2003, the legal framework pertaining to sex between adults and children was limited in scope. Section 5 of the Sexual Offences Act 1956 made it a felony for a man to have unlawful sexual intercourse with a girl under the age of 13 years. Section 6(1) of the same act criminalized men having unlawful sexual intercourse with girls under the age of 16 years. Subsection (3) under s 6(1) provided what became known as the 'young man's defence' wherein a man under the age of 24 years would not be committing an offence if he had not been previously charged with a like offence and reasonably believed the girl to be 16 years old or older. The Indecency with Children Act 1960 criminalized any 'act of gross indecency with or towards a child under the age of 14'. Finally, section 1(1) of the Protection of Children Act 1978 (later amended by section 84 of the 1994 Act) criminalized any person taking, making, distributing, showing, possessing or publishing 'indecent photographs or pseudo-photographs' of children.

There are some notable features about the ways in which sex between adults and children was regulated throughout the twentieth century. Firstly, the regulatory framework was overtly gendered. Laws pertaining to sexual intercourse regulated only sexual activity between *men* and *girls*. As seen in the previous chapter, this was not unique to child sexual abuse. Burke and Selfe (2001) suggest that such explicit gendering of child sexual abuse can be traced to the origins of legislation on unlawful sexual intercourse in that the laws were passed in a response to concerns felt throughout the nineteenth century about young girls' involvement in prostitution. Where the victims were young boys, appropriate action under a range of other laws regarding nonconsensual sexual activities was taken. These other laws covered indecent assault, acts of gross indecency, buggery and rape. The distinction, therefore, between regulating sex with girls as opposed to boys is that 'consent' was only taken into account when the victim was a girl. If the victim was a boy below 16 years old, then the question of consent was irrelevant. Furthermore, regardless of the statutorily defined age of consent (i.e. 16 years old), the law created space for the possibility that a girl could give 'valid', if not legal, consent even below the age of consent (i.e. she understood the nature of the act and agreed to take part) and even when she was under the age of 13 years old. Where 'valid' consent was not present (either because the girl was too young to understand what took place or where she did not agree to take part), guidance recommended that a charge of rape was appropriate. Prosecutions for unlawful sexual intercourse tended to be reserved for those activities where a charge of rape, assault or indecency was not supported. In this respect, the line of demarcation drawn in regards to the sex of the victim was precisely the notion that girls could, even when not legally recognized, offer a type of consent, which should be taken into account in the processing of a case. This is most notable in relation to the lesser offence of committing unlawful sexual intercourse with a girl between the age of 14 and 16 years old. Section 6(1) subsection 3 establishes the 'young man's defence' precisely for this reason. The law stated that a man must have 'reasonable cause' to believe that the girl was over the age of 16 and left the adjudication of this to a jury. It permitted the jury to look at all available evidence, including whether an ordinary person would think the girl looked older than 16 years.

Just as there were explicit gendered assumptions about 'victims' so too there were explicit gendered assumptions about 'offenders'. Unlawful sexual intercourse was an offence that could only be committed by a male. It was not possible for a woman to be charged with USI (unlawful sexual intercourse), although it was possible for a woman to be charged with being an accessory to the offence. Of course, this was partly attributable to the biologistic notion of sexual intercourse that operated within the law (i.e. penetration of a vagina with a penis). And so, underpinning the framework of laws regulating sex between adults and children throughout the twentieth century was a differential understanding of victims and offenders on grounds of gender. Regarding the offences of gross indecency (which in practice translated to all sexual activities not covered by indecent assault, rape or buggery laws) or those related to indecent photographs of children, there was no such explicit gendering. Both men and women could be 'offenders'. The sex of the child in question was also irrelevant to the charge. The only determining factor was the age (or appearance of age) of the child.

As much as it is possible to argue that twentieth century legal frameworks regarding adult sexual behaviour towards children sought to regulate particular acts, reforms in the twenty-first century have focused on legally separating sex and sexuality from the world of children[2] – and in particular those children under the age of 16 years. Key to this has been the re-definition of 'the sexual'. As alluded to above and with the exception of the laws concerning indecent photographs of children, the previous legal framework focused on very particular, mechanistic and literal definitions of sexual activity (sexual intercourse being penetration of a vagina by a penis, gross indecency was defined in relation to the actual act committed). In contrast and as explored in Chapter 1, the Sexual Offences Act 2003 adopts a 'constructionist' perspective and defines as 'sexual' *anything that individuals reasonably perceive to be sexual or anything that is done for a sexual purpose*. In so doing it has the effect of criminalizing an increased range of activities and behaviours. Section 78 of SOA 2003 defines 'sexual' as:

> … penetration, touching or *any other activity* is sexual if a reasonable person would consider that –
> (a) whatever its circumstances or any person's purpose in relation to it, it is because of its nature sexual,
> (b) because of its nature it may be sexual and because of its circumstances or the purpose of any person in relation to it (or both) it is sexual. (emphasis added)

In other words, a fetishist's activities whilst not considered sexual by someone not sharing that fetishism would nevertheless be deemed sexual because they were done for a sexual purpose. In a similar vein, if a 'reasonable' person would understand any particular activity as sexual, even though it was not understood as sexual by the person doing it, the courts could deem it as 'sexual'. Just as an additional note, there has been a similar broadening of the definition of photographs or pseudo-photographs of a child to incorporate references to images of *imaginary* persons, i.e. the production of computer generated images of children who never actually existed as 'real' people.

The Sexual Offences Act 2003 represents a significant extension of sexual offences in regards to children. This is partly attributable to the fact that all sexual activities with and between young people under 16 are now illegal. This includes all sexual behaviours (such as kissing between two 'consenting' young people who are 15 years old). The SOA 2003 continues to distinguish between 16 and 13 year olds in that punishments are dramatically increased for sexual activities with or between children aged 12 and younger. Moreover, the SOA 2003 criminalizes adults engaging in sex in the presence of a child as well as causing a child to watch images of sex. Other provisions include criminalizing: grooming; abuse of trust (against those under 18 years old and committed by adults in a caring or trusting role); facilitating the commission of a child sex offence; and purchasing sex from a child under the age of 18 years old. Responding to many feminist criticisms of previous law, the SOA 2003 creates a special category of 'family child sexual offences' covering young people up to the age of 18 years. One noteworthy point to make at this juncture is that unlike the previous regulatory framework, the SOA 2003 constitutes some acts as crimes when involving young people up to 18 years old – regardless of the age of consent being 16. In other words, in SOA 2003, there is an upwards slippage of the age of consent: young people are thereby constituted as only being able to offer consent in certain circumstances. The rationale for the upward creep of the age of consent is that some young people, by virtue of their 'vulnerability' in specific relationships, need an extra layer of protection. This will be a theme explored later in the chapter.

It is very difficult to critique a regulatory framework which (i) claims to be derived from 20 or more years of campaigning on behalf of child sexual victims and (ii) seeks to offer more protection to the vulnerable. The new provisions within the Sexual Offences Act 2003 aimed to do just that. There is an attempt to respond to the many criticism of the previous laws – not least of which was that sexual offences against 14 or 15 year olds were seen as trivial if one measures 'seriousness' by the yardstick of punishment. However, there are questions to be raised. The Sexual Offences Act 2003 represents a significant extension to the law and the punitive capacity of the criminal justice system. As stated earlier, all aspects of sexual behaviour where children are concerned have been made criminal. There have also been important increases in the punitive response of the state to child sex offences, as well as increased opportunities for the state to intrude on individual and family life as well as professional practice. One of the questions to be asked, and which will be addressed in this chapter, is how such significant extensions to the power of law can be seen as self-evidently necessary. In what follows, we trace the often-conflicting meanings of 'community', 'family' and 'children' at the same time as unpacking the ways in which 'sexual threat' to children is constituted in contemporary Britain.

Community

'Community' holds a particular place within the New Labour agenda. Community was seen to be the panacea to the rampant individualism of Thatcherism. Blair and his government asserted that it was through the community that society could be reformed. As Levitas (1998) notes, 'the community' takes many forms within New Labour rhetoric. It is that which has broken down under previous governments. It is that which is threatened by the misdeeds of others; crime is positioned as the greatest threat. It is also the judge, and the instrument by which more 'effective' social control can be brought into play. New Labour politicians by the late 1990s had identified specific community agencies as the medium through which greater social controls on the individual could be brought to bear. These include: the police, schools, local authority services, community safety partnerships and other multi-agency local forums (Levitas 1998). In this way, 'community' became a fundamental symbol for New Labour.

Recognizing that 'community' has such a central role to play within the rhetoric and policies of New Labour is perhaps less important in this chapter than knowing exactly what type of communitarianism is at play at any one time. Driver and Martell (1997) note in an early article analysing New Labour's communitarianism that New Labour political rhetoric is underpinned by the notion of a society of common values, meanings and institutions which structure the lives of individuals. In a Durkheimian twist, individuals are constituted as interdependent beings. Within this construction, 'the community' is presented as being morally superior. The 'good society' is one in which individuals work for the 'social good' rather than pursuing their own ends. Thus interwoven in New Labour's conception of the 'the community' is the idea that it is 'moral values' which transcend the community and unite it. More than this, as Driver and Martell note, New Labour's 'strong socially-shared values' are prescriptively laid down. Individuals are enjoined to subscribe and live by the morals and values of that community 'because they have to' (Driver and Martell 1997: 31). It is the community that through its sense of shared moral values will restore the social cohesion lost by the individualism of the 1980s.

The significance of locating the community as the site of moral authority cannot be underestimated. Such a construction opens the space to collapse the distinction between law, harm and morality that has traditionally framed legislation concerning sex and sexual activities, marriage, family and so on. With that, the moralism of New Labour has the capacity to be buttressed by statute and government policy. Any notion of pluralism of morality within the 'community' is significantly *absent* in New Labour's understanding of society.

> So we are left with a communitarianism which – for good or ill, perhaps by default or design – is prescriptive rather than voluntary in nature. Politicians have defined its moral content. And, in the absence of an alternative agency, it seems it will be politicians who will enact it when in power. A lot of the duties and responsibilities that are said to go with rights are to be defined by government from above and enforced by them.
>
> (Driver and Martell 1997: 40)

As stated in Chapter 1, changing official discourse on sex also constitutes and is constituted by a new moral authoritarianism. It is precisely the articulation of 'community' with specific, but shifting meanings for 'children', 'protection' and 'threat' that provides the conditions of possibility for the extension of regulations at a greater depth and across a greater range of relationships. It is within this context that the new criminal provisions specifying child sexual offences can be read and understood. Specifically, the fundamental feature of the new provisions within the Sexual Offences Act 2003 is not that it has made new activities illegal, but that it has (i) legislated for a much more *fluid* approach to sexual offending generally; (ii) detailed the *exact* activities that are to now be considered offences; (iii) *extended* both the remit of criminal justice as well as deepened the nature of the punitive response; and (iv) fundamentally *challenged* the authority of parents and the family to protect children and police the boundaries of acceptable and un-acceptable forms of sexual behaviour.

In what follows we trace the different ways in which the official discourse constituting child sexual abuse and its new regulatory frame-work constitute the dangerousness of child sexual abuse. To do this, it is necessary to ask such questions as: Who is harmed? What is a child? What is a family? Who is dangerous? In addressing these questions, the variable constructions of 'community', 'children' and 'family' will be discussed.

Dangerousness as harm to individuals and communities

Official discourse has constituted the 'problem' of child sexual offences as being a problem of 'dangerousness' through the threat or actuality of 'harm'. Moreover, as we demonstrate below, those experiencing 'harm' are both individual children and 'the community'. Throughout the green and white papers (*Setting the Boundaries* and *Protecting the Public*), as well as various press releases, Home Office convened conferences and records of Parliamentary Reports (from the Home Affairs Committee or the Select Committee), it was continually stressed that the 'problem' to be addressed was that the existing laws on sexual offences, generally and in specific relation to children, were 'confused', 'complex', 'inefficient', 'not used' and, mostly, not punitive enough. Much of this critique originated in precisely the sort of feminist interventions outlined in Chapter 2. The 1980s and 1990s saw study after study confirming the regularity of men's sexual violence against children (both their own and others'). Anti-pornography and anti-prostitution campaigners and researchers also argued that many of the individuals involved in the sex industry were well below the age of consent (Melrose, Barrett and Brodie 1999, Barrett with Barrett and Mullenger 2000, Phoenix 2002a, 2002b). A series of high profile scandals about systematic child sexual abuse within care homes created a climate in which existing regulations were seen as failing to protect children from the 'dangerous'. However, many of these messages were re-interpreted within the official discourse of child sexual abuse. The 'problem', we were told, was not men's sexual violence but that regulations and laws were not sending a clear enough message about 'basic values' and were written at a time when 'not much was known' about just how many dangerous, sexual predators there were out there. Instead, the new laws were positioned as being clear, comprehensive and helpful.

> Our present structure of offences has been built up over time, and added to piecemeal primarily in order to protect girls and boys from older men. It does not form a coherent code, nor one that reflects what we now know of the patterns of child sexual abuse ... Penalties are generally low and there are anomalies between them.
>
> (Home Office 2000: 33)

> The law on sexual offences, as it stands, is archaic, incoherent and discriminatory. Much of it is contained in the Sexual Offences Act 1956, and most of that was simply a consolidation of nineteenth century law. ... It is widely considered to be inadequate and out of date. The law on sexual offences needs to set out what is unacceptable behaviour and must provide penalties that reflect the seriousness of the crimes committed.
>
> (Home Office 2002: 9)

Protection was the first key theme of this review. It forms part of a wider strategy to enhance protection for children, vulnerable people and victims. Such abuse is one of the great scandals in our society … We want to provide a framework of law that will deter and prevent sexual violence from happening, enable perpetrators to be prosecuted fairly and to provide justice.

(Home Office 2000: 3)

In short, the 'problem' is that the 'old laws' were 'expired laws' that were 'soft' and contained no real deterrence. More importantly, the 'problem' was framed as not just being the victimization of children, but it was also the inadequacies of the old law to contain or diminish the *threat* posed to the *community* by child sexual abuse. For it is not just individual children who are victimized both by individuals who abuse them and then by inadequate legal protection and justice; the 'community' itself is threatened or harmed. As Home Secretary David Blunkett remarked, the problem of sexual crimes against children is that they threaten the very stability and continuance of society (or 'the community').

Public protection, particularly of children and the most vulnerable, is this Government's priority. Crime and the fear of crime has a damaging and dehabilitating [*sic*] effect on all who experience it. *But sex crime, particularly against children, can tear apart the very fabric of our society. It destroys lives and communities and challenges our most basic values.*

(David Blunkett, Home Secretary, foreword to Home Office 2002, emphasis added)

The enemies without: new dangers for a new millennium

Central to the assumption of sexual crimes against children being a potential danger to the stability of the community has been the formal construction of a more amorphous 'danger' or 'threat' than has been present hitherto. Specifically, within official discourse on child sexual offending has been the invocation of the figure of the 'paedophile' and the 'child sexual abuser'. Careful reading of all consultation documents and records of public meetings indicates that official discourse was underpinned by an understanding that the 'threat' of child sexual abuse has somehow changed and, more, that governmental understanding of that 'threat' is somehow 'better' than in previous decades and centuries. Of course on one level, 20 years of research makes this claim literally correct. However, and as we shall see, the manner in which this largely feminist critique was re-interpreted, subsumed the knowledge of *men's* sexual violence against children to a 'better' awareness of a growing problem of threatening 'others'.

> The risks to children of sexual abuse, particularly from people they know, are now better understood that ever before … We know much more about the patterns of child abuse that we did even ten years ago. Public attitudes have changed from disbelief to a horrified recognition of the level of abuse, and a realization that it is both adults and other children who can abuse.
>
> (Home Office 2000: 33)

In common with official discourse of rape, the problem of *men* was re-inscribed as a problem of genderless, sexless others. Throughout most of the nineteenth and twentieth centuries, adults who focus their sexual attention on children have been constituted as easily identifiable, pathological others. Now, however, 'child sexual abusers' are constituted as being anyone, anywhere. In other words, they are portrayed as being 'anonymous' 'the man next door' or indeed even 'the man indoors'. It is precisely this construction which gives shape to the Sexual Offenders' Register as a means to monitor and surveil deviant populations. Fundamental to such a construction is the notion that these more anonymous and ordinary men can 'infiltrate' almost any part of the community in order to gain access to and abuse innocent children. The official documents are replete with comments on 'predatory' child sexual abusers and new, better understanding of how different sexual offending is 'now' than 'before'.

> The extent and nature of abuse that can take place within families, within institutions and within communities is only now coming to be realized in all its complexity and horror.
>
> (Home Office 2000: 5)

Furthermore, increased prevalence and incidence has been partly attributable to the widespread use of information technology and access to the internet.

> I know we cannot hope to provide 100% safeguards and protection … In this paper and in our proposal we have sought to achieve [a] balance. *We are doing this in a world of mass communication where*

access to degrading material is easily available and where our common values can be undermined by the behaviour of a minority.
(Blunkett 2002: 5, emphasis added)

Nonetheless and paradoxically, the 'threat' or 'danger' of this less identifiable 'child sexual abuser' underpins the constant attempt to specify all possible types of relationships that are potentially dangerous. So, for instance, the Sexual Offences Act 2003 creates a special category of sexual offences – abuse of trust – between any 'adults who are in certain positions of trust or authority over a child'. As stated above, this provision covers children up to the age of 18 years. Abuse of trust provisions are constituted as those which:

> … relate in the main to relationships where the child or young person is either in an institution of some sort, or where the adult is in a particular position of influence, such as a teacher.
> (Home Office 2000: 59)

The new SOA 2003 also makes provisions for any adults in the child's own family – including their parent, grandparent, brother, sister, half-brother, half-sister, aunt, uncle, step-parent, cousin, foster carer, aunt's and uncle's spouse or anyone living in the same household who is 'regularly involved in caring for, training, supervising or being in sole charge' of the child. In the provisions against sexual grooming, there is a further extension to the identification of who might possibly be a 'child sexual abuser' to *anyone* who does *anything* that is designed to lead to some type of sexual contact with a child:

> Grooming children for sexual abuse is not new. Sex offenders have always found ways of gaining the trust and confidence of children and some have seen the possibilities of misusing the Internet to befriend children for their own purposes … To tackle grooming both on and off-line, we will be introducing a new offence of **sexual grooming** with a maximum penalty of five years' imprisonment. It will be designed to catch those aged 18 or over who undertake a course of conduct with a child under 16 leading to a meeting where the adult intends to engage in sexual activity with a child.
> (Home Office 2002: 25)

In this way, contemporary official discourse constitutes the 'threat' and 'danger' as being ultimately unknowable. Anyone who comes into contact with any child could potentially be a 'child sexual abuser' – up to and including another child. The importance of such a construction should not be underestimated. For, if a child sexual offender could be anyone – including those who care for children – then *all* interactions between adults and children are possibly dangerous and in need of regulation. Whereas once the pederast or child sexual offender was understood as being a knowable, *abnormal* other whose abnormality was visible and identifiable, now the danger to children (and the community) is constituted as being deeply embedded within the *normal* relationships between adults and children: family, school, training and so on. Ironically, this was precisely the point which much feminist work on child sexual abuse was making. However, in denuding the 'threat' of its social context – especially in relation to gender and age – the conditions of possibility which make child sexual abuse prevalent and increasingly widespread and possible are denied and erased.

For the purposes of this chapter, it is important to note that constituting the 'threat' in such a fashion opens the space for a shift in both extent and nature of regulation. So, given that the ultimate danger of child sexual abuse is that it threatens 'the very fabric of society' and that *normal* relationships are no longer capable of shielding children from sexual abuse or from any potential threat of abuse, the state becomes positioned as having the capacity to provide protection where families and other local level organizations and institutions fail. In so doing, the official discourse of child sexual abuse has displaced the assumed 'normal' moral authority of adults and families *per se*, at the same time as creating the possibility for an extension of regulation into the mundane and 'ordinary' relationships between adults and children.

The dangers within: contradictory children and paradoxical families

The previous sections have outlined how the official discourse of child sexual abuse is underpinned by the figure of an unknowable abuser who could be anyone. Accordingly, the symbolic space is opened in which boundaries between the abnormal (i.e. sexual) and normal (i.e. non-sexual) adult/child relationships are collapsed. In doing so, 'the family' has been reconstituted as not capable of being able to protect children (and the community) from 'danger', if only because it is not possible for any family to regulate such a diverse range of relationships. However, official discourse constitutes particular types of 'children' and particular 'families' as being not just at risk of potential 'danger' from sexual abuse, but also as 'threats' to the community in their own rights. In this context, such constructions reposition the state as, once again, the only capable site of moral authority and regulation for it alone has the capacity to identify and regulate abusive relationships, provide protection to innocent children and families, dispense justice to victims and thereby bolster, save and support the community. As the following section shows, however, it is particular types of 'children' and 'families' that are identified as being sources of potential danger.

Contradictory children

The new regulatory framework circumscribing sexual relationships between children and adults is shaped by a fundamental contradiction in construction of children: children are constituted as both innocent and blameworthy, as both knowing and not knowing; as both a proto-adult and non-adult and as both a danger to the community and the vulnerable within the community. In this section we trace some of these contradictory constructions and argue that it is through their deployment that the current regulatory framework is able to further displace the family as the site of moral authority, regulation and protection, thereby providing the symbolic conditions of possibility for the new sexual enterprise based upon a moral authoritarianism that extends way beyond the state.

Children as (un)/knowing

Fundamental to the positioning of children as both at danger and a danger is the contradictory construction of their being both knowing and knowledgeable about sexual matters and unknowing and innocent. This is not new. Such contradictions have been noted by academics such as Aries (1967) through to Foucault (1978), Weeks (1981) and Evans (1993) and have been politically exploited periodically to justify and make possible different sorts of regulations and interventions into family life, women's lives, working class communities and so on. This contradiction is most clearly seen in the discussions regarding the age of consent and whether there should (or should not) be any changes to (i) the age of consent being set at 16 years old; and (ii) the setting of a second age below which all matters of consent are rendered mute, thereby providing extra protection for younger children.

> Subdividing into age bands could give the impression that abuse is really serious only when it involves very young children, whereas practitioners told us that teenagers could be adversely affected and damaged by under age sex.
>
> (Home Office 2000: 43)

In this first quotation there is the implicit understanding of teenagers (i.e. older young people) being no different from younger young people. The lack of difference inheres in their 'innocence' and capacity to be 'damaged' through sexual activity. Other approaches are, however, possible.

> The Australian Model of Criminal Code Officers' Committee has recently proposed that there should be no possibility of consent below the age of 10. This is the age of criminal responsibility in England and Wales, but we felt it was too low to offer proper protection. We wanted to protect children who were clearly pre-pubertal or entering puberty, but recognised that it was impossible to get a perfect match. The age of the onset of puberty is very variable, and as a result of better general health and nutrition, has reduced over the past century. Children mature at very different rates. After careful thought we decided that the *thirteenth* birthday provided a benchmark that is already established in law and recognised by society as the entry to teenage years. We adopted that as the age below which no consent should be recognised. We also thought that offences of adult sexual abuse of a child under 13 should be of strict liability, and attract no statutory defence such as mistake of age.
>
> (Home Office 2000: 43)

However, by the time recommendations were made, the fundamental construction of 'children' that dominated was one that did distinguish between younger children and older children and accords a very different 'nature' to the two categories. By virtue of physical maturity alone, older children are constituted as having the capacity to understand and consent to sexual activities, however socially unacceptable those practices might be. Such a construction opens the space to encode particular 'children' as being culpable (and thus blameworthy) of engaging in a variety of socially unacceptable sexual practices – as will be seen below.

Children as non-adults

There is a further dualistic construction of young people and 'children' that permits the distinction between the 'truly innocent' and the more knowledgeable. This inheres in the manner in which 'children' are positioned *vis à vis* adults in contemporary official discourse about child sexual abuse. Children are constituted as both 'other-than-adult' and also 'proto-adult'.

In constituting children as 'other-than-adult', they are understood as being that which adults are not: asexual, physically immature, emotionally underdeveloped, essentially incapable of understanding and lacking the capacity to consent. They are understood as being completely separate from the adult world of sex and sexuality. Such constructions are most clearly seen in statements commenting on why there needs to be protection for children from the sexual activities of adults.

> Children need particular protection in the field of sexual relations because they are physically and emotionally dependent and not yet fully physically or psychologically mature. The law has long held that children are not, and should not be, able to consent to any form of sexual activity in the same way as adults.
> (Home Office 2000: 33)

> We would protest against the policy of police and prosecutors to recognise the sexual autonomy of children, which is resulting in an increasing number of cautions rather than prosecution, where unlawful sexual intercourse and indecent assault is involved, probably due to the notion that a child can give his informed consent.
> (Justice For Children cited in Home Office 2000: 37)

> Not sure that children can give 'proper consent'; in many cases they may have been groomed. There should be some form of absolute offence for younger children below the age of 13.
> (Home Office 2000: 327)

Such an understanding of children as 'other-than-adults' serves a vital function of foreclosing the possibility that a child could ever be held responsible for any sexual activities, if only because they are always and already positioned as being outside and separate from the realm of sex and sexuality. Such a construction then forms the basis for understanding children as innocent, weak, powerless and vulnerable 'victims', as well as providing the foundation for the call for protection. Before moving on, it must be pointed out that 'children', here, means anyone under 18 years old. Whilst there may be no debate about the capacities of a 6, 7, or even 11 year old, the issue gets very complex when discussing 15 and 16 year olds, let alone 17 year olds.

However, as much as some children are understood to be always and already 'not-adults', other children are constituted as being always and already 'proto-adults' or 'adults-in-the-making'. This construction is also evident in the (rather ironic) discussions about children's ability and capacity to consent to sexual activities. Within such a construction, children are seen as being not asexual, nearly adult and thus not separated from the realm of sex and sexuality.

> ... one of the most contentious areas of sexual offences legislation ... The law holds that a person below that age of consent is incapable of consent. I believe this is condescending and often offensive and distressing to couples caught up in age of consent offences.
>
> (Submission #59 cited in Home Office 2000: 37)

More often, however, contemporary official discourse constitutes 'children' as 'other-than-adults'. This is evidenced in commentary and justification for the creation of a new category of offences: family sexual abuse. Here, the age at which a child is deemed to be unable to consent and thereby incapable of being culpable has been set at 18 years old, i.e. two years over the age of sexual consent more generally.

> ... current Sexual Offences (Amendment) Act will prohibit sexual activity between adults in certain positions of trust and authority and a child under the age of 18 years old. It draws a distinction between the age at which the law permits a child to consent to a full sexual relationship, and that which may be appropriate to protect a child from exploitation with which their maturity and experience of life at 16 may not equip them to deal.
>
> (Home Office 2000: 41)

The importance here is not that there are contradictory constructions regarding 'children' relative to 'adults' *per se*, but that such contradictions permit both the retention and collapsing of the symbolic boundaries between children and the realm of sex and sexuality. As is noted in the Law Commission's policy paper on consent in sexual offences as presented to the Home Office, to leave these boundaries fluid serves useful political purposes: 'What the age should be is a matter for those expert in child development and those with a wider social policy remit' (The Law Commission 2000: 23). Significantly, such fluid boundaries also open the space in which some children are understood as both sexual and posing a specific 'threat' to other children, to the community and to society.

Children as danger /threat

The understanding of 'children' as being sexual and thereby posing a 'threat' to other children can be seen in discussions about the links between youthful sexual activity and health. Underpinning these discussions is the notion that *any* sexual activity between children is 'dangerous'.

> It is clear that children now mature physically at a much earlier age, and are exposed to sexual images and pressures to engage in sexual activity by media and peer pressure when they are very young. However, society has to protect children from inappropriate sexual activity at too early an age when it has the potential to cause physical, emotional and psychological harm.
>
> (Home Office 2000: 50)

The specific harms that are then elaborated are not the 'harms' discussed concerning sexual abuse, for example, psychological trauma, but rather the more 'social' and community level harms of teenage pregnancy, sexually transmitted infections and greater risks of cervical cancer. These become harms partly through the problems that they generate for the individual young people, but more because of the expense to the public purse (Social Exclusion Report 1999).

The construction of 'children' as not being separated from the realm of sex and sexuality and therefore by virtue of that as posing a 'danger' or 'threat', opens the space in which they can be constituted as both culpable and blameworthy *and* therefore in need of surveillance and regulation.

> Yet we know that as well as teenage experimentation in sex, which may well be mutually agreed, children can and do coerce and abuse each other. Even so-called mutually agreed relationships can be called into question. Sexual relations between children are capable of being exploitative.
>
> (Home Office 2000: 51)

> While we recognise that many young people who sexually abuse may have been abused themselves, and are in need of care and protection, that provides a context for their actions; it certainly does not condone or justify them. Unless treated properly they will continue to be a risk to others, and they need to be held accountable

for their actions. … Most professionals working with children recognise that they need early intervention and specialist treatment to help prevent them from continuing to abuse in adulthood.

(Home Office 2000: 58)

Sexual abusers who are also children are thereby 'proto-adults'. That said, there is some subtlety in that young child sexual abusers are understood to be different from adult sexual offenders, and different again from both children as 'proto-adults' and children as 'other-than adults'. They are positioned as highly problematic 'children who sexually offend'.

> The evidence does seem to show that adolescent sex offenders are as varied as adult offenders. Some abuse much younger children, whilst others relate to their peers. There are some consistent findings that around a third of sex offences committed against children were committed by other children. Although a large proportion of adults who abuse children state that their deviant interests began in adolescence, the vast majority of adolescent offenders do not re-offend as adults.
>
> (Home Office 2000: 60)

The significance of these variable and paradoxical understandings of 'children' is that by situating some as responsible, dangerous and blameworthy, the state further displaces the family as a site of moral authority and regulation. If all relationships that children enter into can be, potentially, dangerous and can threaten 'the very fabric of society', then the space is opened in which the regulation of children inside and outside the ordinary institutions of social life is imperative – both for their own protection and for the protection of the community. And, by definition, the family as a social unit is positioned as not capable of providing that regulation. This is made clear in the way in which the difference between sexual experimentation between children and sexual exploitation is defined.

> The evidence from research and experience of those who worked in the child protection area was that incestuous penetrative sex between siblings was almost certainly exploitative and certainly not exploratory. The victims of such sibling abuse are primarily young and weaker or more compliant.
>
> (Home Office 2000: 95)

In other words, wherever there is a disparity in power, there can be abuse; and in families, there is always and already a disparity in power.

In the next section, we trace the different constructions of 'the family' and in so doing suggest that 'the family' (or more specifically, non-traditional, diverse and changing family forms) not only poses a threat to individuals, but also constitutes a key cornerstone in the construction of the 'problem' of child sexual abuse within contemporary official discourse.

Paradoxical families

Just as there is a fundamental contradiction in relation to the manner in which 'children' are constituted in contemporary official discourse on child sexual abuse, so too 'the family' is understood as both a haven for safety and well-being and an always, already pathological institution that poses an inherent threat to children and society. The construction of the 'family' as a place of safety for children and adults forms an important backdrop to contemporary official discourse. It provides the rationale for understanding abuse within the 'family' as being somehow separate or distinct from other forms of sexual abuse of children. It further resolves the formal contradictions, noted earlier, in creating a category of sexual offences based on an age limit above the age of sexual consent.

> The family unit whether formally established by marriage or not, is for most children the cornerstone of their lives. It should be, and often is, a haven where both children and adults can live in safety and develop to their full potential.
>
> (Home Office 2000: 81)

> The offence of incest sets out in law a fundamental social taboo about sexual relations within the family, reflecting widely held abhorrence. We regard the offence as one of a fundamental breach of trust by one family member against another.
>
> (Home Office 2000: 81)

> With the rise in divorce and the increasingly diverse nature of modern families, the offence of incest which outlaws sexual inter-course within the family should be a crime whether it is committed by a natural father or by a stepfather, by a natural sibling or a step-

sibling with no common genes. It is the protection of children within the family rather than the incestuous nature of the relationship which is important ... There should be an offence which punishes the illegal sexual behaviour within the family and adds an extra penalty for the abuse of trust.

(NSPCC cited in Home Office 2000: 81)

Even within constructions of the 'family' as a safe haven, there is nevertheless the simultaneous understanding of 'family' as a place of danger – especially for children.

It is recognised that the balance of power within the family and the close and trusting relationships that exist make children particularly vulnerable to abuse within its environment.

(Home Office 2002: 26)

Interestingly, in relation to 'consensual', if incestuous adult sexual relationships between family members, the inherent 'danger' of the 'family' remains ever present.

The argument is that such relationships are primarily abusive reflecting a long-term imbalance of power in the family. Ostensibly consensual relationships between adults may have their origins in under age grooming or sex. If a child is brought up to think such behaviour normal she may not realize the true nature of the activity for many years. As an adult she is then culpable.

(Home Office 2000: 83)

The reason, it would seem, is that no family relationship is deemed to be without some type of power differential and the way in which official discourse constitutes child sexual abuse is as an abuse of power within families.

The dynamics of relationships within families are different to those between friends. Adults within families take on rights and responsibilities of protecting and safeguarding the weaker members – in doing so they have a degree of power and authority over younger or weaker members. Any abuse of this power is individually destructive and socially disruptive.

(Home Office 2000: 88)

Thus it is that all family relationships are potentially abusive. At this point, it is clear that official discourse on child sexual abuse is drawing on feminist explanations of child sexual abuse. However, whereas the feminist critique of 'families' focuses on gender, official discourse 'gender-neutralises' child sexual abuse within families. 'Power' and its abuse are merely and only a matter of age with no relation to the wider material realities of who precisely enters families or what we referred to earlier as 'the problem of men'.

Part and parcel of this de-gendering of power relationships in families is the way in which contemporary official discourse highlights the changing nature of family forms as being the more pervasive and malign source of 'danger'. Changes to the 'family' are dangerous if only because non-traditional families defy the state's attempts at definition and thus regulation in the context of family child sexual abuse.

> The present offence is limited to lineal blood relatives and siblings, and so does not include today's looser family structures including step-parents, nor does it encompass the transient nature of some family relationships.
>
> (Home Office 2000: 83)

Such a loose structure is constituted not just as increasingly diverse, but also as creating endless opportunities for the anonymous, unknowable 'child sexual abuser'. However, where they surface, these are never any and all men, but particular men who seek out and are intent upon entering 'vulnerable' families.

> It is widely recognised that new partners may present a risk of physical or sexual abuse to a child … It was put to us very strongly at our consultation conference that some of the greatest risks to children came from people, particularly men, who were in a short term relationship with a parent, or who have sought a position of trust in a family in order to gain access to children.
>
> (Home Office 2000: 92)

This creates complex and paradoxical problems for the governance of child sexual abuse.

> However, if the law is seeking to deal with more fluid modern families where it is not always possible to establish a position based

on marriage or other legally defined relationships, we need to think carefully about how an offence could be defined. It would leave an unacceptable gap in the protection offered in the family if there were no offence for live-in partners, and it would also risk creating a perverse disincentive to marriage.

(Home Office 2000: 93)

The significance of constituting 'the family' as simultaneously 'safe' and 'dangerous' should not be taken too lightly. Contemporary official discourse on child sexual abuse does not explicitly privilege one type of family form as being more able to monitor and regulate adult/child relationships. Rather, what is called into question is the ability of all families to self-regulate and protect children. As a result, it forms the foundation for the will to discipline and regulate both traditional and non-traditional families.

Conclusions

At the beginning of this chapter, we stated that we were not challenging the trauma and damage caused to children from those adults who exploit children's vulnerability and immaturity for their own sexual gratification. Instead, our concern was to lay bare the symbolic under-pinnings of contemporary official discourse on child sexual abuse as made evident in the reforming process leading to the Sexual Offences Act 2003. In the course of the chapter we noted that constituting the official discourse of child sexual abuse are new constructions of child sexual offenders, as well as shifting and contradictory constructions of 'children' and 'the family'. Furthermore, we specified throughout the chapter that these shifting and contradictory constructions open the space for a challenge to be made about the ability of the 'family' to govern and regulate the lives of children and other young people in the name of protecting 'the community'. We would suggest that the significance of this challenge has yet to be felt. The dramatically increased level of punishment for those who sexually abuse children as well as the widening of the sexual offenders register are perhaps only two of the more obvious ways in which the desire to protect the vulnerable can elide with the growth of new disciplinary mechanisms and techniques of governance. What is yet to be seen is how the new governance of children (and especially those 'proto-adults' who remain forever both part of and yet separate from the realm of sex and sexuality) will play out.

In relation to the wider argument of this book, however, deconstructing official discourse on child sexual abuse provides insight into how, by gender-neutralizing sexual violence against children, and by shifting notions of 'family', 'children' and 'community', the conditions are provided for the assertion of a new moral authoritarianism. The importance of this is that such a moral authoritarianism permits the state to increase levels of surveillance and regulation not just of sex, *per se*, but of family relationships as well as adults more generally. In the instance of child sexual abuse, this regulation is accomplished through criminal justice, social services and, importantly, punishment.

Notes

1 At the time of writing, there is some question amongst practitioners as to whether children under 16 years who engage in consensual sexual activities will ever be convicted of a sexual offence under SOA 2003.
2 Children are defined in statute as being under the age of 18 years.

Chapter 4

Commercial sex: consent, coercion and exploitation

Victimhood is a powerful, yet contradictory force. Powerful because, once claimed, it can provide the moral basis for redress, retaliation and even revenge in order to right any given wrong – real or imagined. The defence of everything from the death penalty to affirmative action, Serbian nationalism to equality legislation are all underpinned to some degree by the notion of victimhood. Contradictory because, in order to harness that power, one must first admit weakness. Victims by their very nature have less power than their persecutors: victimhood is a passive state – the result of bad things happening to people who are unable to prevent it.

(Younge 2004: 17)

Introduction

In the two preceding chapters, we have argued that underpinning official discourse of sex is a symbolic landscape that erases the material realities of 'the problem of men' via the deployment of sliding notions of 'victims', 'childhood', 'abuse' and 'communities' as well as through the gender-neutralizing of sexual offences. In this sense, social control of sex is both in crisis and yet able to deny the origin of that crisis. This chapter continues this argument through examining the shifting official understandings of prostitution. In particular, we argue that via very limited conceptions of 'consent' and 'coercion', official discourse of prostitution is able to appear to be doing something about 'the problem of men' (in this case, the problem of their sexual and financial exploitation of women and children). But there is a paradox. Underpinning official discourse of prostitution is the deployment of shifting meanings for 'victimhood'. What we argue in this chapter is that through focusing on women and children's victimization and constituting it in specific ways, official discourse is able to open the space to extend the reach of regulation across *all* relationships with men that women and children who also sell sex might have. In so doing, contemporary official discourse of prostitution thereby consolidates moral authoritarianism (via its use of non-governmental organizations (NGOs)) through the criminalization and 'reform' of women and children in prostitution.

✗ In July 2004, New Labour published a consultation document, *Paying the Price* (PTP), offering the first review of all prostitution-related legislation for over 50 years[1]. Although the review made no specific recommendations for changing the legal framework, it did put forward the notion of a 'coherent strategy' to tackle the 'problem' of prostitution. This coherent strategy is an approach wherein existing formal law is dovetailed with new 'soft law' (i.e. guidance from central government to a variety of local and statutory agencies on approaches to the issue, inter-agency agreements, objectives of intervention and so on)[2]. Regardless of the specific detail contained within *Paying the Price*, the consultation document heralded a significant change in official understandings of prostitution and the commercial sex trade. For nearly five centuries, prostitution in England and Wales has been marked by 'tolerance' regarding the actual exchange of sex for money. Selling and buying sexual services is not, nor has it been, illegal *per se*; instead formal legal reform has focused on what has been perceived to be the negative *effects* of prostitution. In contrast, *Paying the Price* relocates prostitution as a 'problem' in need of intervention.

This chapter charts the changes in official conceptions and understandings of the 'problem' of prostitution. We assert that the 'problem' of prostitution has been, and continues to be, constituted as a problem of 'effects', but that the location and specific articulation of those 'effects' has altered significantly in recent times. Thus whereas once the problem of prostitution was the effects of the 'less than moral' choices of some on others, now it is constituted as the effects of violence and exploitation on both the 'real' victims of prostitution (the women and children involved) and the communities in which they work. Whereas the notion of prostitution as a matter of private morality located it as an individualized act, contemporary understandings of prostitution locate it as part of rampant, at times highly organized, occasionally global hyper-masculine criminality. To make our argument and our observations we both note and deconstruct the regulatory framework that has existed for the better part of the last five decades, as well as explore the proposed changes currently up for consultation.

Turbulent times – reports, recommendations and legislation in the 1950s

The 1950s were a key decade in regards to the legal regulation of sexuality generally and commercial sexual activities in particular. The dominant assumption made by legal absolutists that the law could and should specify thresholds of both public *and* private morality was called into question. There was a growing concern that established laws and legal principles were simply not capable of reflecting or responding to the perceived immense social changes taking place in wider society. Specifically, it was argued that throughout the 1950s and 1960s, society had become more 'open' and more 'plural' and that the law was not able to prescribe the type of private morality that should be adopted by individuals (Weeks 1981). This shifting attitude about the function and role of the law *vis à vis* sexual morality found expression in relation to the formal regulations of prostitution.

Prior to the 1950s the laws pertaining to prostitution tended to be fragmented and seldom evenly enforced. They were mainly underpinned by the notion that it was a correct function of law to declaim certain private acts as immoral or moral. By the end of that decade, the Sexual Offences Act 1956 and the Street Offences Act 1959 provided, at least in theory, a uniform, universal approach and philosophy to the regulation, policing and punishment of prostitution. From then until now, there were a variety of minor amendments which served to 'fine tune' the system (i.e. altering punishments, specifying procedures, keeping step with technological changes and so on) but the official understandings of prostitution underpinning the reformations of the 1950s had remained largely unaltered. In contrast, the early years of the millennium witnessed an increasing willingness to govern morality and sexual relationships generally through the use of formal criminal justice mechanisms. The following section describes both the historical events surrounding the 1950s reformation of prostitution regulation and the symbolic landscape that shaped those reformations.

Prostitution: the Wolfenden Report and the Street Offences Act 1959

In 1954 and amid public concern about the apparent rise in numbers of women involved in prostitution in the capital, the then Home Secretary (Sir David Maxwell Fyfe) appointed a departmental committee to investigate street offences – and particularly homosexual offences and prostitution – and make recommendations for legal reform. The committee was chaired by John Wolfenden and its findings and recommendations have become known as the Wolfenden Report. This Report was to have far-reaching effects in that it: (i) consolidated the official discourse of prostitution; (ii) provided a jurisprudential underpinning and justification for the subsequent liberalization of many laws regarding specific sexual practices[3]; and (iii) created a 'new' statutory framework for the regulation of prostitution[4]. The recommendations contained within the report were to form the basis of the Street Offences Act 1959.

The task that the Wolfenden Committee set itself was to consolidate the law regarding the prohibition and regulation of public prostitution-related activities. The Committee made a number of recommendations which included:

- that the laws relating to street offences by prostitutes should be reformulated so that they were generally applicable across England and Wales;

- that the proof of annoyance in order to proceed with a prosecution or secure a conviction be removed;

- that consideration should be given to the introduction of a formal cautioning system which would mean that the only women who would be brought to court would be those who had been cautioned on two separate and previous occasions;

- and, finally, that the punishment of repeated prostitution-related offences should become progressively more severe in that it should start with a fine and culminate with imprisonment of up to three months.

These recommendations were adopted and formed the basis of the Street Offences Act 1959. This Act made it illegal for a woman (and only a woman) to loiter or solicit for prostitution in a public place and introduced the system of prostitutes' cautions. Wolfenden left untouched the battery of other prostitution-related laws that regulated the less than public aspects of prostitution as the Sexual Offences Act 1956 had already brought these together within one piece of legislation and introduced a clear system of adjudication and punishment. The Sexual Offences Act 1956 prohibited:

⸝ or encouraging prostitution (offences which specified ⸝ely: procuring a woman to become a prostitute; procuring a ⸝an to leave the UK with the intention that she would work in a ⸝hel; and, procuring a woman to leave her home with the intention ⸝t she would work in a brothel within the UK);

- Men from living on the earnings of prostitution (known in common language as 'pimping');

- Women from exercising control over a prostitute for the purposes of gain;

- Keeping a brothel, which is defined in common law as an abode which more than one woman uses 'for the purposes of fornication' and other offences connected with renting premises knowing that they will be used as a brothel.

The next section shows how the problem of prostitution as being a problem of 'nuisance' (understood as being an 'affront' to 'public decency') was constituted by two specific assumptions about (i) the relationship of law, morality and sex and with that the division of social life into public or private realms; (ii) the sorts of problems caused by sexual activities which take place outside the confines of what is deemed 'acceptable'.

Sex, law and morality: the separation of the public from the private

Earlier it was stated that beneath the changes in legislation made concerning prostitution in the 1950s was a challenge to the notion that the law could state what was morally right and wrong in relation to both public and private sexual behaviour. This challenge found its most clear expression in the form of the Wolfenden Report in that it offered a rationale to guide thinking about the relationship between individuals' sexual practices and the state, which relocated law to the realm of 'the public' and excluded private sexuality as an inappropriate object of legal control. In what has now become an often-quoted formulation, the Committee's Report begins with a preamble specifying that the purpose of the criminal law is:

… to preserve public order and decency, to protect the citizen from what is offensive or injurious, and to provide sufficient safeguards against exploitation and corruption of others, particularly those

who are specially vulnerable because the~~
or mind, inexperienced or, in a state of sp~~
economic dependence.

(Ho~~

Here, the Wolfenden Committee is doing little mor~
principle of harm which has guided most legislation i~
that the law should not seek to suppress any conduct or~
and until it can be demonstrated that those activities c~
someone. This principle guiding when and where it is ap~   ~o
create formal sanctions constitutes the law as both the neutra~   ~er in
individuals' disputes as well as the key social mechanism tha~ ensures
the safety of individuals. What marks the rationale offered by Wolfenden
as different, however, from the general guiding principles of law was the
specific guidance Wolfenden gave in relation to behaviours and activities
normally thought of as 'private' and sexual. The Wolfenden Committee
continues:

> It is not in our view, the function of the law to intervene in the
> private lives of citizens, or to seek to enforce any particular pattern
> of behaviour, further than is necessary to carry out the purposes we
> have outlined. It follows that we do not believe it to be a function of
> the law to attempt to cover all the fields of sexual behaviour.
> Certain forms of sexual behaviour are regarded by many as sinful,
> morally wrong, or objectionable for reasons of conscience, or of
> religious or cultural tradition; and such actions may be reprobated
> on these grounds. But the criminal law does not cover all such
> actions at the present time: for instance, adultery and fornication
> are not offences for which a person can be punished by the criminal
> law. Nor indeed is prostitution as such.
>
> (Home Office 1957: 10)

There are a number of ironies that arise as a result of this symbolic
separation of law from matters that were deemed to be of private
morality and the interrelated line of demarcation drawn between that
which is considered 'public' and that which is seen as 'private'. Firstly,
the distinction between public and private in relation to commercialized
sex collapses in the face of empirical realities and practices. The sexual
practice that is exchanged – intimate bodily contact between individuals
– is usually exchanged in 'private', albeit a private space created within a
car, an alleyway or within a flat. In this respect, the separation of sex,
sexual practices and sexual morality (judged by the criteria of offence or

from the realm of 'the public' is one that could never be sustained. Secondly, and as has been pointed out by Selfe (2003), Wolfenden formulation relies on the silencing of the contradiction contained within. Specifically, Wolfenden created a framework which protects the morality of some (understood as 'decent' and 'ordinary') whilst punishing the moral choices of others (women involved in prostitution who are thereby not understood as 'decent' and 'ordinary'). To wit, notions of 'offensiveness' and 'affront' are themselves formed on the bedrock of social, political and ideological evaluations. That prostitute women's notions of offensiveness and affront are excluded from the calculation of what is an affront to a 'decent' citizen is one manifestation of this. Moreover, as nearly three decades of research has shown, such a formulation opened the space in which women's choices and infractions of the law become over-policed and over-punished at the same time that offences and violence against them become under-policed leaving them under-protected (Matthews 1986, Kinnell, Bindel and Lopes 2000, Phoenix 2001). More than this, however, such an understanding also creates the very conditions for what has been described as both discriminatory policing and punishment of women in prostitution (see below) (Phoenix 2001, Edwards 1996). This argument will be elaborated in the next section.

The nature of the problem

Constituting the 'problem' of prostitution as a matter of private morality begs the question of what function and role the law could play in its regulation. The Wolfenden Committee and its associated Acts do not either recommend or structure direct legal regulation of the exchange of sex for money. Instead, regulation of prostitution in England and Wales focuses on activities related to ways in which these commercial exchanges take place. Specifically, those activities that offend 'ordinary' members of society or are deemed as an insult to 'decency' are targeted as appropriate for intervention. In other words, as currently constituted in law, the 'problem' of commercial sex is that it is a 'nuisance', that it acts to corrupt or offend 'ordinary' (not prostitute) individuals.

Throughout the Wolfenden Report it was stressed that prostitution 'affronts' 'ordinary' members of society because the visibility of prostitutes in public places insults 'public decency' (Wolfenden 1957:81). The committee was strident in its assertion that this was the case because:

…those ordinary citizens who live in these areas … cannot, in going about their daily business, avoid the sight of a state of affairs which seems to them to be an affront to public order and decency.

(Home Office 1957: 82).

Such was the strength of the Committee's conviction about the offence caused by the visibility of prostitution that it treated the claims as self-evident.

… the simple fact is that prostitutes do parade themselves more habitually and openly than their prospective customers, and do by the continual presence affront the sense of decency of the ordinary citizen. In doing so they create a nuisance which, in our view, the law is entitled to recognise and deal with.

(Home Office 1957: 87)

In focusing on 'affronts to public decency' and 'nuisance' to 'innocent citizens', official discourse at the time thereby constituted the 'problem' of prostitution as being a 'problem' of *effects*. This has not been unique to the Wolfenden Committee. Sion (1977) asserted that the 'problem' of prostitution inheres in the way in which prostitution creates an environment where property values and business in red light areas decline through the 'bad reputation' of that area; where 'innocent and decent men' are accosted; where road traffic is disrupted by kerb crawlers; where fear of molestation is increased by the presence of men on the streets late at might; where other women may be corrupted because they 'may imitate prostitutes in times of financial distress'; and, where young children are 'continuously exposed to the manifestation of prostitution'. The Criminal Law Revision Committee's Seventeenth Report added to this list of nuisances the nuisance of neighbourhoods acquiring a 'reputation for vice' if off-street prostitution in the form of brothels were to be legalized (Criminal Law Review Committee 1985:14). In more recent work, it has been argued that prostitution is a public nuisance because it increases the fear of crime experienced by individuals, particularly women, in communities where prostitution occurs (Matthews 1993) and neighbourhood decline, in that once certain 'incivilities' such as soliciting and kerb crawling become regular features of a neighbourhood, a dynamic change takes place that both attracts more crime and criminal activities and undermines the stability of that community (Wilson and Kelling 1982, Skogan 1990). More practically and more recently still, it has also been argued that prostitution poses a significant public nuisance because of the way in which the detritus of prostituting (condoms, drug needles, tissues and so on) are left on the streets where women work, the sheer increase in the volume of traffic caused by kerb crawlers and all the attendant noise, pollution and congestion (Matthews 1993).

Conceiving of the 'problem' of prostitution (and thereby regulating it) as though it is little more than a matter of 'public nuisance' re-emerged in the mid 1980s and periodically throughout the 1990s. In 1985, the Sexual Offences Act 1985 introduced an offence of 'persistent kerb crawling'. Throughout the summer of 1994, vigilante movements sprang up across many of Britain's large urban centres, the purpose of which was to remove street prostitution from local neighbourhoods because of the 'nuisance' it supposedly caused. By 2000, the police were given powers of arrest for kerb-crawlers. In each episode, the rationale given was the overwhelming necessity to (i) protect 'innocent' women, children and men from the punters; and (ii) remove the cumulative 'nuisance' of prostitution from neighbourhoods.

Interestingly, identifying the 'problem' of prostitution in the 'harmfulness' or 'nuisance' of its *effects* has underpinned the key critique to official discourse, and in particular, feminist conceptions of both the problem of prostitution and its regulation. Feminists have debated the exact nature of 'harm' or 'effect' prostitution has on women as a 'class' (cf. Barry 1979, MacKinnon 1987, Smart 1990, Edwards 1996, McKeganey and Barnard 1996). Radical feminists especially have located prostitution as an effect of male domination and male sexual violence. So, for example, Hoigard and Finstad (1992) assert that prostitution is the result of men's mass victimization of women and can only exist where women's bodies and their sexuality retain a commodity status. Other less academic constructions have highlighted the discrimination of the law on prostitution as well as the violence that women and young people in prostitution regularly and routinely experience without recourse or protection from criminal justice interventions[5]. Research throughout the 1990s showed the discriminatory nature of the law which (i) in charging only 'common prostitutes' with soliciting or loitering, created a presumption of guilt; and (ii) punished poor women via fining them and thereby creating the conditions for their further involvement in prostitution.

The crucial distinction between feminist and official understandings of prostitution, however, has been over the issue of voluntarism. Whereas feminists have highlighted both the coercion of men and of poverty in women's involvement in prostitution, official constructions dismissed any notion that some women engage in prostitution through force, whether that be the force of necessity, or violence and the threat of violence. So, for instance, Wolfenden commented that 'poncing', i.e. living on the earning of prostitution, is:

> … usually brought about at the instance of the woman, and it seems to stem from a need on the part of the prostitute for some element of stability in the background of her life.
>
> (Home Office 1957: 99)

and that: 'the association between prostitutes and "ponces" is voluntary and operates to mutual advantage' (Home Office 1957: 100).

The importance of the construction of involvement in prostitution as both a matter of individual morality or taste *and* as a matter of individual choice cannot be underestimated. It is a construction that is profoundly non-social wherein the law should only operate to protect 'normal' citizenry from the worst excesses of those making 'less than moral' choices. But prostitution is not merely an example of individual or 'private' tastes or moral choices. Prostitution, albeit usually outwith industrial or occupational organization, is a social institution comprised of a complex variety of roles and individuals stretching from the individual woman soliciting to the client, from the outreach workers supplying sexual health information to the police squad or officer tasked with regulating the trade locally, from national policy guidance and formal legislation to local initiatives. More than this, centuries of research (Finnegan 1979, O'Neill 1999, Phoenix 2001, Lombroso and Ferrero 2004,) has clearly linked women's involvement in prostitution to poverty and men's violence.

By way of summarizing so far, for the greater part of the twentieth century, official discourse on prostitution constituted it as a public nuisance and a matter of private morality. Regulation thereby focused on the visible aspects of prostitution. Underpinning such a symbolic landscape and its attendant regulation is the notion that prostitution is, at heart, a matter of private morality. In the following section, we trace the shifts in the construction of the 'problem' of prostitution that has taken place in recent years.

Changing regulatory frameworks

As stated in the introduction to this chapter, *Paying the Price* marks a fundamental shift in the official conceptions and regulatory framework pertaining to prostitution. By 2004, and in contrast with that which came before, prostitution came to be understood as a *social* problem and not simply a matter of private morality. It was now seen as a 'problem' which destroys individual lives and threatens communities. Prostitution has shifted from being perceived as a 'victimless' crime to one which victimizes women, children, families and societies. That said, the conditions of possibility for this shift are both symbolic and institutional. Throughout the 1980s and 1990s, there were fundamental changes to the institutional regulation of prostitution. Specifically, the dominance of policing and criminal justice interventions and management of prostitution gave way to a burgeoning 'welfarist' constellation of organizations, projects and multi-agency teams that sought to minimize the 'harm' (and thereby the effects) of prostitution through sexual health and drugs education and outreach work. We start the second half of this chapter by detailing these changes to prostitution regulation. Following on from this, we trace the ways in which the 'problem' of prostitution has been re-constituted from one of private morality to one that threatens to destroy individuals, families and communities. We note that the 'problem' has shifted to being *both* a problem of effects *and* a problem in its own right. This shift is evident in the way in which recent official consultation documents blur the boundaries of prostitution, collapse the long existing lines of demarcation between prostitute-women and other supposedly 'moral' and 'decent' citizens and locate prostitution as a conduit to social destruction via community decay and global and organized crime. Lastly, we examine the symbolic underpinning to current proposals and especially the bifurcating meanings of 'victims', the consolidation and dominance of distinct visions of 'masculinity' and 'crime', and special notions of 'community' and 'protection'.

Public sexual health and child abuse:
changing institutional conditions for regulation

As indicated above, women involved in prostitution are in an ambiguous legal position. Although the exchanging of sex for money is not in itself illegal, most of the activities that enable that exchange are (such as soliciting or loitering for prostitution, brothel keeping and so on). Such a legal framework is best described as 'negative regulationism' or an approach in which the object has been to achieve a 'more manageable form of prostitution divested of its disruptive and politically embarrassing characteristics' (Matthews 1986: 188). That said, new conceptions of the 'problem' of prostitution that are currently emerging signify a departure from this framework. Instead, there are indications that, at heart, the new regulatory framework of prostitution is an abolitionist framework. In short, it aims to eventually abolish prostitution. For instance, in *Paying the Price*, there is a discussion about the possibilities of introducing 'managed areas of prostitution' (i.e. designating an area in which prostitution, albeit tightly controlled, can occur). The following is put forward as a reason for not adopting 'managed areas' as a strategy in the future:

> We need to consider how flexible communities are prepared to be and to hear strong and convincing argument of the workability and benefits of managed areas before setting off down a road towards what has so far proved to be a problematic measure. *Such a move normalises the concept of street prostitution and pre-supposes its continuing existence, and these are assumptions we need to challenge strongly.*
>
> (Home Office 2004a: 84, emphasis added)

In keeping with other reforms since 1997, New Labour has adopted what can be called a two-pronged approach to prostitution by using NGOs and other welfare based organizations to deliver more traditional social policy ('soft law') in order to intervene in the lives of individuals involved in prostitution, whilst reserving the full power of the criminal law for two categories of people: those who persistently return to prostitution and those who would 'exploit' individuals in prostitution.

Throughout the 1990s, earlier understandings of prostitution as being also a 'problem' of public sexual health re-emerged. This was not unique to the twentieth century. Mahood (1990) noted that in 1497 the Council in Aberdeen passed an Act that stated that all women in prostitution were to be branded so that the public could identify them as possible carriers of syphilis[6]. In the latter half of the nineteenth century the association between prostitution, sexually transmitted infections and public sexual health was officially consolidated with the passing of the Contagious Diseases Acts of 1864, 1866 and 1869. These Acts enabled police to stop any woman suspected of being a 'common prostitute' and gave the health authorities specific powers to undergo medical inspection. Although these Acts were repealed before the end of the nineteenth century, the measures they created were reapplied at the beginning of the First World War with the Defence of the Realm Act (1914). By the end of the twentieth century and coinciding with the HIV/AIDS pandemic, the construction of prostitution as a 'problem' of public sexual health was given renewed vigour. It is at this point in history that we see the beginnings of the official use of NGOs to regulate prostitution. Through targeting funds to genito-urinary clinics and sexual health outreach services, health oriented interventions: (i) differentiated women in prostitution from other women by means of constructing them as individuals whose behaviours would place the general population at threat of HIV/AIDs because of their promiscuity and drug use; (ii) generated vast, if highly localized, amounts of knowledge about the behaviours, relationships and issues for women involved in prostitution; and (iii) created new styles of intervention into their lives. These new style interventions did not seek to criminalize or remove women from prostitution, but rather to 're-educate' them about their supposedly high-risk behaviours. In short, multi-agency services addressed everything from health concerns to housing, from drugs and alcohol abuse to domestic violence.

Although many of the agencies did not explicitly aim to 'exit' women from prostitution, they provided help and services for anyone who expressed that desire. One other function of the burgeoning sexual health and drugs outreach projects was the manner in which they worked in liaison with the police about community issues or the arrest and prosecution of violent punters. By 1997, most major British cities had at least one such project. The importance of noting the growth of sexual health and multi-agency outreach projects is not, at this juncture to note a new discipline or governance of prostitute-women, *per se*, but to locate the shift in the way in which prostitution was regulated. Instead of relying on more familiar and long-standing techniques of criminal justice such as policing and punishment, by the mid-1990s the institutional conditions were in place which enabled a more 'welfarist' 'regulation', policed through NGOs and other statutory bodies. Criminal justice was slowly vacating the field of regulation in favour of health professionals and the growing dominance of the associated strategies of intervention most commonly known as harm minimization or reduction[7]. This was so much the case that throughout the 1990s there was a noticeable reduction in the numbers of women getting arrested and convicted for prostitution related offences. In 1989 there were 15,739 women cautioned or convicted for soliciting. By 2002, this number had fallen to 4,102 (source: Offending and Criminal Justice Group, Home Office).[8]

By the beginning of the 2000, the dominance of a health agenda was challenged by the issue of children's involvement in prostitution. In May 2000, the Department of Health and the Home Office released joint guidance about young people in prostitution. This guidance enjoined all individuals working with young people in prostitution (i.e. those under the age of 18 years) that such young people are best understood as 'victims' of sexual abuse and exploitation. Accordingly, *Safeguarding Children in Prostitution* recommended that all under 18 year olds should be protected rather than criminalized. The wider impact of this guidance was to bifurcate provision for individuals in prostitution. On the one hand, sexual health and drug outreach projects continued to work with *adults* whereas new projects and multi-agency teams sprang up to meet the needs of *young people*[9]. The multi-agency teams were frequently just new constellations of existing children's services and the police. The new projects were often funded by the big children's charities and tended to work more closely with social services departments than the previous sexual health and drugs outreach projects. So, within the 20 years from the mid 1980s to the early 2000s, the conditions of regulation of prostitution had significantly altered. Not only was the regulation of prostitution activated through welfare-based organizations, but there was a growing plethora of organizations that had distinctively different remits and agendas. So, to sum up, the dominance of policing and criminal justice interventions had decreased in the face of constantly developing and fracturing welfare services that distinguished between sexual health and drug needs, the needs of children as distinct from adults, the needs of young men or young women and so on. And, as will be discussed below, underpinning this fracturing has also been a 'de-gendering' of prostitution. As discussed in earlier chapters, one key aim of the SOA 2003 was to 'gender-neutralize' all sexual offences. This has the result of removing the specificity of women's and girls' victimization. It has also enabled official discourse to confront and appropriate the legitimation deficit caused by more than 20 years of research on the links between *women's* poverty, men's violence and prostitution, all of which have now been subsumed within or silenced by extended constructions of prostitutes as 'victims'.

The re-birth of the prostitute victim

Earlier it was stated that the official conceptions of the 'problem' of prostitution have altered significantly. At the time of writing, this conception found its most explicit official expression in the Home Office consultation on prostitution-related laws, entitled *Paying The Price*. The language within it, the proposals suggested and the exemplars of good practice contained within neatly demarcate the 'problem' of prostitution into two categories: the 'problem' of 'victims' and the 'problem' of 'offenders'. 'Victims' of prostitution are described as women and (occasionally) children who are forced, coerced or trapped in prostitution. They are individuals who are distinguished from other 'ordinary', non-prostitute citizens because their need for affection and/or complex personal problems including drug problems, homelessness, school exclusions and so on make them vulnerable to the predatory, exploitative and abusive behaviour of others[10]. 'Victims' of prostitution are also distinguished from others involved in prostitution. These include: 'abusers' who purchase sex from children; 'exploitative partners' or 'pimps' who force women and children into prostitution and keep them there for their own pecuniary gain; the 'drug dealers' who control women in prostitution through their control of the drug market; and, the 'organized criminals' who traffic people across national borders and within the UK for the purposes of sexual commercial exploitation[11].

There are already provisions in place to ensure that prostitution-related 'victims' are protected and 'offenders' are punished. The Sexual Offences Act 2003 expands the remit of criminal justice by: firstly, re-writing many of the previous offences in ways which no longer make those offences specifically apply to men or women. So, for instance, SOA 2003 criminalized 'causing or inciting prostitution for gain' and 'con-trolling prostitution for gain'. Both offences are gender neutral and replace the older offences of 'living off the immoral earnings of a prosti-tute' (a charge which could only be brought against men) and 'controlling and directing the actions of a prostitute' (a charge which could only be brought against women). Similarly, the SOA 2003 removes reference to gender in the offences of soliciting and loitering (which could only be brought against women) and kerb-crawling (which could only be brought against men). It has also introduced a raft of new offences that apply to young people up to the age of 18, two years beyond the age of sexual consent. Whereas the Wolfenden Committee (1957) was very clear in not distinguishing between adults and children in prostitution, the Sexual Offences Act 2003 now makes it illegal to:

- meet a child following 'sexual grooming';
- pay for the sexual services of a child;
- cause or incite child pornography or prostitution; or,
- arrange or facilitate child pornography or prostitution.

The effect of these new provisions (and in particular the final two) is to criminalize *any* adult who might have some type of involvement in a young person's experience of prostitution[12].

Finally, the SOA 2003 explicitly criminalizes 'trafficking for sexual exploitation'. Not only have these new provisions been put in place, but the SOA 2003 also extends the maximum punishment possible for all the above offences. In this respect, whilst the new official discourse of prostitution claims to offer protection for 'victims', its regulatory framework relies on increasing the range and remit of criminal ju intervention for 'offenders'. And, as will be discussed in what follc unless very specific conditions are met, most individuals involved prostitution are excluded from the category of 'victim', for 'victim' statu is only conferred on those individuals: (i) for whom there is the presence of a third party coercer; (ii) who never return to prostitution after being offered help; and, (iii) who co-operate with the NGOs and authorities.

Protection for whom and against what?

Contemporary official discourse constitutes of the 'problem of prostitution' in a way that supposes that there can be a clear and explicit purpose to regulation. *Paying the Price* claims that the purpose of inter-vention is: to protect the victims in prostitution through (i) prevention; (ii) protection and support; and (iii) punishment of offenders. And although some new offences have been put in place in the passing of the Sexual Offences Act 2004, protection is to be achieved through the 'development of a clear and coherent strategy' coordinating the services offered by all NGOs, community and statutory services that come into contact with those involved in prostitution. Arguably, the most profound impact of the new understanding (and the factor that makes it 'new') is the manner in which it redefines the 'problem' of prostitution from being an issue of private morality, public nuisance or sexual health to being a 'problem' of victims and in so doing, paradoxically constructs prosti-tution as a criminal justice (and not social welfare or justice) issue. *Paying the Price* regularly repeats that the 'problem' that needs addressing is the exploitation of women and children, trafficking of individuals for commercial sexual exploitation, the links between drugs markets and prostitution, the ways in which debt and drug addiction trap individuals in prostitution and the manner in which prostitution can aid the growth of serious and organized crime. Throughout the document are constant references to 'pimps', 'traffickers', 'dealers', 'sexual abusers', 'coercers' and a host of other hyper-masculinized criminals[13].

Contained within these shifting constructions is an understanding of involvement in prostitution that was put forward in a much earlier document (*Safeguarding Children in Prostitution*). This presents a model in which the material and social context is erased; instead prostitution becomes little more than three relationships – between the prostitute and the client, the prostitute and the pimp and the pimp and client. But these are not equal relationships. The relationship between pimps and prostitutes is understood as being a pathological relationship *causing* a person's involvement in prostitution. Simply, 'predators' exploit, abuse, control, coerce and trap vulnerable individuals (adults and children) in prostitution for money and sexual gratification. Erasing the social and material context of prostitution provides the conditions in which 'prostitution' can be re-inscribed as something else. Specifically in regards to children, the new model redefines prostitution as child sexual abuse.

> Similarly there can be no such thing as a punter, or a customer of a kerb crawler when discussing children … a man who winds down his window and asks for sexual services from a child is a … child sexual abuser.
>
> (Barnardos 1998: 20)

> The coercers operate by finding 'clients' … 'clients' who assume that payment buys them agreement of the child and puts them beyond the law are completely wrong – they are child abusers.
>
> (Department of Health/Home Office 2000: 16)

In relation to adults, 'prostitution' is redefined as violence, abuse and exploitation (usually at the hands of clients, pimps/partners, traffickers or drug dealers).

> A common pattern is for men and women to be trapped in street-based prostitution after having been coerced into it at a young age, or to fund their own – and often their partner's – problematic drug use. Those involved in this way rarely benefit, apart from ensuring their drug supply. The profits of the 'trade' go straight into the pockets of drug dealers.
>
> (Home Office 2004a: 12)

> People trafficked from abroad is a known route into prostitution in this country … Primarily young women, but also teenage girls looking for a better life are promised work in the EU, made to pay exorbitant charges for travel and forced into prostitution to pay their debts.
>
> (Home Office 2004a: 75)

To be clear, the 'problem' that official discourse of prostitution addresses is not so much the social and material conditions experienced by individuals that often condition their involvement in prostitution, but rather the presence of individuals who would exploit, force, coerce, abuse and profit from that involvement. At heart then it is a 'problem' of 'criminals' and 'sexual abusers'. And it is their presence that contributes to the understanding of prostitution as causing an even wider level and degree of victimization. Prostitution is thus re-constructed not merely as a nuisance in the community, but a cause of community *destruction*.

> Prostitution undermines public order and creates a climate in which more serious crime can flourish. *Street prostitution is often associated with local drug markets, bringing Class A drugs and gun culture to local communities* ... Dealing effectively with prostitution could have a dramatic effect on reducing more serious crime and help to stifle drug supply.
> (Home Office 2004a: 74, emphasis added)

At the same time as constituting prostitution as 'violence', 'abuse' and 'exploitation', official discourse also constitutes prostitutes as a 'threat' to 'communities'.

> Communities are often seriously concerned about the existence of local street-based prostitution ... This can *also* lead to a decline in public order and an increase in lawlessness. There is also evidence of crime specifically associated with those involved in prostitution and their users. Those involved in prostitution, particularly where this is to fund a serious drug habit, may also be involved in theft and other areas of criminality.
> (Home Office 2004a: 79)

As stated earlier, such an explicit re-inscription of prostitution as detailed above forecloses the space in which it is possible to recognize the poverty and social and material conditions that many individuals in-volved in prostitution experience. In this way, the legitimation deficit faced in the 1990s is accommodated. Fundamental to this process has been the construction of individuals involved in prostitution as having little or no individual agency. They are not individuals actively negotiating their social environment and circumstances. They are victims: passive, entrapped, forced and waiting to be rescued.

The rhetoric of victimhood: coercion and 'the problem of men'

To further elaborate upon our analysis, we argue that contemporary official discourse of prostitution hinges on specific understandings of the terms 'consent', 'coercion' and 'force'. As stated above, adults in prostitution are understood as being involved because of the activities of exploitative, coercive and abusive 'criminals'. Clients of individuals in prostitution who are under 16 years old are 'child sexual offenders' because the young people they purchase sex from have no legal capacity to consent. Even when individuals (especially young women) do have the legal capacity to consent, any consent they may offer is constructed as illusory. So for instance, *Safeguarding Children in Prostitution* makes it quite clear that any expression of voluntarism is not to be treated, *prima facie*, as evidence of consent. Pimps, partners, and other older adults are 'coercers' because they target the vulnerable and crush the young person's ability to consent through violence, intimidation and/or charm. Indeed, voluntary and statutory agencies are told to be wary of expression of voluntarism and claims of love and affection between the young people and the older adults with whom they are involved.

> The fact that outsiders would consider this a delusion does not make it any less real for the individuals concerned … When working with young people all agencies must recognise the strength of this attachment and the time and difficulty there may be in breaking it.
>
> (Department of Health/Home Office 2000: 16)

Paying the Price echoes these sentiments in relation to all adults that prostitute-women come into contact with. Throughout the document are several references to the way in which drug dealers and pimps/partners use violence and drugs to control individuals in prostitution.

> The increase in crack use means increased violence among those involved in prostitution, and between them and their pimps and clients. This is an area of major concern. Violence, including sexual violence is routinely used by pimps as a means of control.
>
> (Home Office 2004a: 44)

> The link between commercial sexual exploitation and Class A drugs is a crucial one … Often those who control prostitution are also closely involved with crack houses and other forms of drug dealing.
>
> (Home Office 2004a: 74)

There is evidence to show that there are shifting patterns in the way in which prostitution is operating. The trend is away from pimps controlling a number of women and towards 'pimp/partner' relationships. In these circumstances, the violence which pimps may use to control their partner is properly classed as *domestic violence* ...

(Home Office 2004a: 46, emphasis added)

'Coercion' and 'control' are constituted within official discourse as having the capacity to defeat and even pervert the voluntarism of the child, young person or adult in prostitution. Thus *Paying the Price* is able to constitute individuals in prostitution as not being able to offer *true* consent: whatever assertion of voluntarism they may make may not be a *true* reflection of their *own* choice – it may only be a reflection of other factors.

Debt and drug addiction play a major part in driving people into prostitution as a survival activity. They are also significant factors, along with the threat of violence from pimps/partners, in making it difficult to leave. Those involved in prostitution can be particularly difficult to reach, claiming that prostitution is their choice and that they don't want to leave – through a combination of fear, the process of normalisation or in an effort to maintain dignity.

(Home Office 2004a: 39)

It is possible to argue that by acknowledging debt, official discourse leaves open the space to recognize the complex social and economic realities of prostitution and that individuals might actively negotiate their choices and be involved in prostitution voluntarily. However, careful reading of *Paying the Price* would indicate otherwise. 'Debt' is used as a short-hand for 'debt-bondage' as opposed to poverty. When discussing the difference between human trafficking and smuggling, the meaning of 'debt' is clearly drawn:

There is often some confusion between the terms trafficking and smuggling. People smuggling is the more common form of organised immigration crime, where organised crime gangs facilitate illegal entry for a fee by means of clandestine passage or using false documentation. Migrants are generally willing participants and the relationship with the facilitator normally ends on arrival at their destination country. Human trafficking is where the intention behind the facilitation is the exploitation of those migrants when they reach their destination ... People trafficking from abroad is a known route into prostitution in this country ... Primarily young women but also teenage girls looking for a better life are promised work in the EU, made to pay exorbitant charges for travel and forced into prostitution *to pay their debts.*

(Home Office 2004a: 75, emphasis added)

It is thus that 'debt' becomes indebtedness to a 'criminal' or 'gang' and not an acknowledgement of poverty or its aggregate effects. And, as such, 'debt' is translated into another instance whereby women's involvement in prostitution is not voluntary, but coerced.

Just as poverty is erased in the service of an all-encompassing construction of individuals in prostitution as being 'victims', so too the relationships between adults in prostitution and their partners have been re-configured in the service of a construction of these relationships as pathological, problematic, exploitative and criminal. *Paying The Price* refers to these relationships as 'pimp/partners', thereby eliding any distinction between those individuals who cynically, violently and intentionally exploit women in prostitution and the 'ordinary' men who, for whatever reason, experience equally chaotic lives of poverty, multiple social deprivations and drug addiction.

> One recent in-depth study included 19 men described as 'classic pimps' as opposed to the new style pimp/partners ... Although the 'classic pimp' continues to exist, increasingly common is the boyfriend with a serious drug addiction who pimps his girlfriend to fund both their drug habits.
>
> (Home Office 2004a: 16)

One impact of such a construction is to foreclose the possibility of recognizing as anything other than pathological the relationships of women in prostitution that are not based on a notional male bread-winner. Specifically, an intimate or domestic relationship that a woman in prostitution might have, wherein her partner or family member financially benefits from her involvement in prostitution, becomes pathologized in ways that were simply not present under Wolfenden. Ironically, one of the criticisms of the framework instituted by the Wolfenden Report was that it did not recognize the exploitation of women at the hands of their intimate partners. But now, the symbolic conflation of intimate partners and domestic/familial relationships with 'pimps' means that all prostitute-women's relationships are subject to potential criminalization and regulation.

Thus underpinning and shaping new official discourse of prostitution is the figure of the 'criminal', 'violent' and 'exploitative' 'offender' who crushes any possibility of resistance from children and adults through the use of force, intimidation and violence. There can be little doubt that many women and young people do experience such relationships and the violence is real, devastating and long-lasting in its impact. Recognizing the victimization of individuals in prostitution at the hands of particular categories of 'offenders' is not the same as basing the regulatory framework and policies on the notion that most, if not all, economic relationships that prostitute-women have are always and already 'pimp/partner' relationships.

The rhetoric of victimhood: consent and the bifurcation of individuals in prostitution

Given that older constructions of the 'problem' of prostitution have had the impact of over-policing and regulating the women involved in prostitution at the same time as under-policing the violences and abuse of them (Matthews 1986), it is possible to argue that the emerging notion of prostitute-as-victim has the potential to impact beneficially on women in prostitution. However, as will be detailed in this section, official discourse of prostitution creates the very conditions for increasing the levels of regulation and, indeed, criminalization of women and children in prostitution. This occurs for two key reasons: (i) the rhetoric of victimhood is reified to a level of explanation (i.e. individuals become involved and stay in prostitution *because* they are 'victims'); and (ii) the rhetoric of victimhood that is deployed relies on an all too literal understanding of 'consent', 'voluntarism' and 'coercion'.

In both *Safeguarding Children in Prostitution* and *Paying the Price*, a lack of voluntarism on the part of the individual involved in prostitution is linked to their status as 'victim'. Adults and young people in prostitution are 'victims' because they are coerced and vice versa. Within such a symbolic landscape, the possibility of a 'voluntary victim' is forever foreclosed. As demonstrated by Walklate (1989) and Smart (1990), one of the defining elements in being recognized as a victim is that the individual does *not* consent to their victimization. Thus, if individuals in prostitution are the victims of 'abusers' and 'exploiters', they have not voluntarily, rationally and actively engaged in prostitution. Put another way, 'voluntarism' is constituted as the capacity to make a *different* choice – to choose not to be involved in prostitution. 'Force' or 'coercion' is constituted as the absence of 'voluntarism', as the absence of choice. Within the new discourse, some other factor (abusive adults, exploiters, drug dealers, human traffickers) removes the individual's ability to make other choices.

These naïve and asocial understandings of choice, voluntarism, consent and coercion have the effect of displacing discussion and recognition of how material and social circumstances operate to funnel the range of choices to which individuals have access and impel them in their decision-making. In short, linking consent to voluntarism in such a fashion erases other forces, such as the forces of necessity. Arguably more important, conceptually erasing the force of necessity effectively bifurcates the recognition of individuals in prostitution into *either* those who are victims *or* those who made the choice and are therefore (i) *not* 'victims'; and, (ii) *not* deserving of protection.

Throughout *Safeguarding Children in Prostitution* and *Paying the Price* are recommendations of what to do with young people and adults who have, for whatever reason, made the choice to be engaged in prostitution. *Safeguarding Children in Prostitution* enjoins local authorities and police constabularies to be alert to the possibility that some young people do freely enter into prostitution.

> The entire emphasis of the Guidance is on diversion using a welfare based approach to children and that it should be adopted *in all cases*. However, it would be wrong to say that a boy or girl under 18 *never* freely chooses to continue to solicit, loiter or importune in a public place for the purposes of prostitution, and does not knowingly and willingly break the law … The criminal justice process should only be considered if the child persistently and voluntarily continues to solicit, loiter or importune…
>
> (Department of Health/Home Office 2000: 27, emphasis in the original)

Put simply, young people who *choose* prostitution are 'criminals' complicit in their own offending behaviour. In relation to adults, there is a slightly more sophisticated bifurcation. Instead of directly discussing adults who *choose* to be involved in prostitution and for whom only traditional methods of criminal justice interventions are appropriate, *Paying the Price* suggests that the criminal law could and should be used 'rigorously to clamp down on unacceptable behaviour and criminality' whilst simultaneously offering 'support to those families and individuals to change their behaviour' (i.e. stop prostituting) (Home Office 2004a: 67). Such an approach is referred to as 'enforcement plus support'. Hence, in discussing the use of the fine (which by 2004 had become the standard punishment for loitering or soliciting for prostitution), *Paying the Price* recommends that 'penalties available to the courts [should] also deliver effective rehabilitation' (Home Office 2004a: 69).

For this to happen, a range of new disposals are suggested. These include:

- Using prostitutes' cautions to 'encourage them to seek help, particularly with problematic drug use';

- Using conditional cautioning which 'provides a further opportunity for an individual to be steered towards drug treatment and other rehabilitative activities';

- Using arrest referral to 'break the cycle of arrest, charge, fine and return to the streets';

- Using community orders to 'allow for a more rehabilitative penalty to be imposed in the case of those who are found to be persistently loitering or soliciting';

- Using Anti-Social Behaviour Orders (which if breached can attract a maximum sentence of five years' imprisonment) backed up with other support services for 'those leading chaotic lives, particularly where there is a serious drug misuse [because] the individual is more likely to adhere to the behavioural boundaries set by the order if it is accompanied by support'.

By using this full range of disposals, it is argued that '… the police and courts, working in partnership with local support agencies, can help direct those involved in prostitution towards the help they need, particularly in terms of appropriate drug treatment' (Home Office 2004a: 71).

What makes this approach both more sophisticated and different from the explicitly bifurcated approach adopted in relation to young people is that it *individualizes and responsibilizes* the adults in prostitution. Criminal justice responses are put in place in an attempt to support women to 'exit' prostitution, and when they fail to do so, the next punishment up the tariff can be imposed. It is important to note at this juncture that the majority of *Paying the Price* documents describe both the vast array of voluntary projects working with individuals with drug problems, housing difficulties, sexually transmitted infections, safety, healthcare and so on, as well as the variety of guidance and exemplars of best practice in relation to multi-agency work with individuals with drug and alcohol problems and so on. In this respect, the 'coherent approach' framed by official discourse on prostitution is an approach in which both welfare and criminal justice work to get women out of prostitution. In the next section, we describe how the official discourse of prostitution denudes individuals in prostitution of their social context in ways that translate what are *social* problems into *individual* problems.

Risks, needs, vulnerability and the responsibilization of adults in prostitution

At first sight it would appear that *Paying the Price* is about dealing with the overwhelming levels of victimization experienced by women and children in prostitution, offering support for individuals struggling with a host of problems from debt to drug addiction and so on and prosecuting those who exploit, force, and abuse (primarily) women and children. However, careful reading reveals that another story of prostitution is all but completely absent: the story of the individuals whose lives have been so violently fractured by the aggregate effects of poverty, by being outwith the traditional disciplines (and benefits) of family, education, employment, by being pilloried by press and communities[14] and by having so few options that involvement in prostitution is a plausible, if risky, choice (see Phoenix 2001, 2002b). Given that over two centuries of research confirm that prostitution is conditioned by social and material deprivation and poverty, the question becomes how the official discourse of prostitution is able to exclude the question of necessity in its attempts to 'support' and 'prevent' individuals from prostitution. This section details the ways in which the new discourse locates individual women as being responsible for the social problems they encounter, thereby justifying a punitive response, when, despite the best efforts of the support agencies around them, they continue with their involvement in prostitution.

In keeping with many other aspects of New Labour thinking on crime and social problems, the language of 'class' and 'sexism' has all but disappeared from official usage. In its place is the language of 'social exclusion' and 'risk factors' (Levitas 1998, Carlen 2002). Prostitution is no exception. *Safeguarding Children in Prostitution* forecloses the possibility of recognizing anything other than *abuse* as conditioning children's involvement in prostitution. Similarly, *Paying the Price* lists the factors which make individuals 'vulnerable' to prostitution as being:

> ... experience of violence or abuse in the home; truancy or exclusion, and poor educational attainment; running away;

experience of living in care; homelessness; problematic drug use, alcohol abuse; and debt.

(Home Office 2004a: 24)

These factors are not seen in any causal connection or indeed even structuring or conditioning young people's or adults' involvement in prostitution. They are, instead, located as 'risk factors'. In discussing each of these, *Paying the Price* suggests that the route 'forward' is to support people in learning how to deal with these difficulties in their lives. So in respect of debt, it is suggested that:

> Debt can be a contributory factor to the vulnerability of men and women to prostitution. Appropriate advice and support can help people to avoid, manage and escape from debt. It is recognised that to be accessible to the most vulnerable groups, debt advice needs to be provided locally, face-to-face and in easy to reach locations.
>
> (Home Office 2004a: 31)

In other words, the 'solution' to the 'problem' of debt lies with the individual and to aid the individual, and *Paying the Price* recommends that they be offered debt counselling. Similarly when discussing training/retraining (for employment), it is recommended in *Paying the Price* that individuals who are at 'high risk of social exclusion' are identified by the appropriate support agency who should ensure that they are 'able to access high quality advice and be supported in addressing their needs'. Therefore, the new construction of the 'problem' of prostitution is shaped in part by an assumption that it is the *individual's* responsibility to change their circumstance after the appropriate 'advice and support' have been given. The material needs (and thereby the force of necessity) are translated into 'risk factors' and 'vulnerabilities' which themselves are further translated into 'problems' that the individual should solve.

Of course this raises the question of what approach is to be taken with those who do not change, who, despite the best efforts of the plethora of agencies, do not address their 'risk factors' and continue to be 'vulnerable' to prostitution and 'exploitation'. On this point, *Safeguarding Children in Prostitution* is very clear. Instead of arresting and fining, young people are to be referred to Youth Offending Teams and can face any of the disposals possible within the Youth Courts (which range from fines to up to two years in Detention and Training Centres). The new approach to prostitution has expanded the punitive reach of the state as regards young people in prostitution. Similarly, in respect of adults, prostitutes' cautions and fines are now supplanted with the range of disposals mentioned above. In both individualizing and responsibilizing the individual's involvement in prostitution, official discourse is able to eject the figure of the woman or young person who chooses (through the force of necessity or for whatever other reason) to become involved in prostitution. Instead, there are only 'vulnerable' 'victims' who are ready and waiting to escape and be rescued by paternalistic support and help. And where those 'vulnerable' 'victims' do not do so, then by definition they are the 'other' of the new discourse. In effect, they become positioned as nothing more nor less than 'criminals' who along with 'pimp/partners' and other adults connected with prostitution threaten communities, increase the lawlessness of areas and create an atmosphere where urban regeneration is not possible (Home Office 2004a: 63) and where serious crime flourishes (Home Office 2004a: 74).

Conclusion

In the introduction to this book, we argued that official discourses of sex regulation have altered in recent years. Specifically we noted that there has been an emergence and consolidation of a new construction of 'victimhood' which constitutes 'victims' as always and already blameless, weak, passive and in need of protection. In this chapter, we have shown that this construction heavily relies on particular understandings of coercion, force and consent which themselves are constituted by and within common-sense and literal notions of capacity and absence of choice. Although this understanding has not displaced earlier understandings of the 'problem' of prostitution being a 'problem' of nuisance, of crime or indeed of public health, it has re-interpreted these understandings through assumptions about the victimization of individual women and children in prostitution.

But an individual's status as a 'victim' is always and already unstable when that status relates something outside or external to any specific incident of victimization (in this case to an individual's capacity to choose or not choose something other than involvement in prostitution). In this way, the recognition of individuals in prostitution as 'victims' is an unstable category because much of the involvement in prostitution is conditioned not so much by a literal lack of choice, but by social and material conditions that funnel choices. This has the impact of creating the very conditions in which prostitutes-as-victims structures an understanding of them as both (i) individually responsible for the social problems that they encounter; and (ii) appropriate subjects for criminal justice punishments and interventions through the expanded range of disposals now available to the courts.

We have also seen how the emergence of a new understanding of prostitution as victimization is conditioned by the simultaneous emergence of new rhetoric about exploitative, abusive perpetrators. And, in a similar way to the construction of individuals in prostitution as 'victims', 'pimp/partners', 'human traffickers', 'exploiters' and so on are also unstable categories, if only because they too are denuded of any social or material context. In this way, and as we have seen above, anyone involved with anyone in prostitution is suspect and potentially criminal. The impact of this is to increase the extent of official regulation of the interpersonal relationships of women and men in prostitution.

In the course of this chapter, we have argued that shifting constructions of prostitution have created a new regulatory framework in which the majority of interventions into the lives of women and children in prostitution are conducted by NGOs and welfare based organizations in a way which does not challenge or displace the power and authority of criminal justice interventions. Arguably, because of the way in which the new understanding individualizes and responsibilizes (especially) women in prostitution for the social problems that they experience and translates those problems into 'risk factors' which themselves are further translated into the need for psychological re-adjustment interventions, this particular constellation of NGO, welfare-based and criminal justice interventions have the capacity to deepen the level of regulation of women's and children's lives.

Finally, we argued in this chapter that the way in which prostitution is currently made sense of in official discourse is part and parcel of the new sexual enterprise around sex whose object of control is not sex *per se* (or in this specific instance, the exchanging of money for sexual activities) but broader social relationships between men and women and between specific groups of people (in this case between 'prostitutes' and 'pimp/partners' or between 'prostitutes' and the 'wider community' who suffers lawlessness, etc.). As with the other exemplars in this book, regulations and constructions of prostitution extend well beyond the specific instance of the victimization of women and children in prostitution and this in part helps to constitute the contemporary moral authoritarian response to sexual risk so dominant in New Labour policies. To explore how this works in extra-statutory settings and contexts beyond but linked to governmental control, we turn our attention in the second half of this book to unpacking the quasi-official discourses that underpin informal sex regulation.

Notes

1 The Criminal Law Revision Committee reviewed the regulation of off-street prostitution in 1986 (Home Office 1986).
2 At the time of writing, *Paying the Price* had only just been published. To avoid an analysis that would necessarily have been a 'best guess' as to the particular direction that policy and law would take, this chapter examines the symbolic framework up to and including *Paying the Price* but brackets off the bigger question of whether and what type of new models of regulating prostitution more generally might be introduced, in the future.
3 Wolfenden is credited with providing the groundwork for the eventual decriminalization of homosexuality in Britain.
4 Self (2003) has challenged many of these claims about Wolfenden and instead argues that the Wolfenden Report was little more than a reflection of general misogynistic attitudes towards women involved in prostitution.
5 Organizations such as the English Collective of Prostitutes (ECP), Call Off Your Tired Old Ethics (COYOTE, San Francisco) and the UK Network of Sex Work Projects (UKNSWP) exist partly to fight these regular and routine discriminations against women in prostitution.
6 Of note is that this Act was passed over a century before there was a medical association between syphilis and sexual intercourse (Spongberg 1997).
7 This is an approach to intervention that has as its objective increasing the level of awareness to the risks involved in particular types of activities, be they drug taking, prostitution or other 'risky' activity.
8 Official statistics on cautions and convictions tell us little more than levels of policing activities. For this reason, we cite these statistics as indications, not of a general fall-off of prostitution related activities, but rather as a decline in traditional criminal justice responses to and regulation of prostitution.
9 With the passing of the Sexual Offences Act 2003, this bifurcation has had devastating consequences in that it has criminalized arranging or facilitating a child to be involved in prostitution (i.e. anyone under the age of 18 years). Arguably this leaves sexual health outreach practitioners vulnerable to such a charge. In the past such vulnerability has resulted not in the criminalization of individuals, but rather in the self-policing of organizations. Simply, many sexual health NGOs just stopped providing services to under 18 year olds (Phoenix 2003).
10 We are not challenging that many individuals in prostitution do, in fact, experience these social and economic problems. Rather, we are asking questions about how the links between these social factors and an individual's involvement in prostitution are drawn.
11 As with other chapters, we are not calling into question the lived realities of violence, exploitation and abuse.
12 Although it is too early to know for certain how and in what ways these provisions in the SOA 2003 will be used, it is possible to argue that such provision could criminalize a foster parent who knows that a young person

(aged 16 years) in their care occasionally prostitutes and helps to secure contraception or sexual health advice for them in an endeavour to ensure their safety and well-being.

13 One of the great difficulties in deconstructing official discourse on sex is that critique of the discourse is often mistaken for not recognizing the victimization that women and children do experience. In this respect, we recognize the real, tangible and often routine victimization and exploitation that women and children in prostitution experience, although we take issue with the manner in which their victimization is reified and translated into a totalizing vision of 'victims'.

14 The summer of 1996 provides an excellent example of how 'communities', in the sense of neighbourhoods, can function to victimize and scapegoat women in prostitution. Throughout that summer, most of England's major cities saw the birth of vigilante organizations whose sole aim was to remove prostitution from their area. Some of the tactics used were fairly mainstream (such as conspicuously taking the registration details of potential kerb-crawlers and thus driving demand from the neighbourhood), others were more violent (including in Birmingham, attacking a number of the women as a warning to other women not to prostitute in that particular neighbourhood).

Part 2

Deconstructing quasi-official discourse of sexual infractions

Chapter 5

Nuisance sex: harassment, collusion and decency

Naked protest over in a flash

An attempted nude protest through central London ended as quickly as it began. A group of men had vowed to highlight the case of Steve Gough, the 'naked rambler', who was arrested during a walk from Land's End to John O'Groats. They planned to take their clothes off in Selfridges department store in Oxford Street and then walk to Hyde Park to highlight their belief that nudity is a basic human right. Five of the men simultaneously disrobed, but after walking through the shop to the main doors they were met by staff and police who told them to get dressed. The case against Mr Gough, 44, who was arrested at the start of a walk from Land's End to John O'Groats was dropped on Thursday. He was seized on 17 June while being interviewed by a television crew near St Ives in Cornwall. Mr Gough, from Eastleigh, Hampshire, was charged with behaviour likely to cause a breach of the peace and bailed to appear before Truro Magistrates' Court. But Simon Jones, prosecuting, asked for the case to be withdrawn because Mr Gough – who did not appear in court – had not committed a criminal offence. Mr Gough is still facing charges in Scotland where he is being held in custody after being arrested near Inverness. Mr Gough planned to undertake the 847-mile trek dressed only in a hat, socks, boots and a rucksack to publicise his campaign for a change in the laws on nudity.

(BBC News UK Edition 6th September 2003)

Introduction

In the next three chapters of this book, we turn our attention towards policies, guidelines and other quasi-official utterances that, whilst not having the same status as the legal regulations discussed in the three previous chapters, nonetheless seek to regulate and control sex in a variety of ways. By way of introducing this chapter, we also offer some thoughts as to the unifying themes of this second half of the book. The emphasis here is upon much less formal rulings governing sexual conduct, but where pertinent, we do draw upon formal regulations, for we do not want to suggest that the demarcations between illicit and illegal sex are absolutely clear-cut. Neither do we want to suggest for the purposes of our analysis, that informal codifications, policy guidelines and so on be regarded less seriously than the laws on sexual offending, for they carry organizational weight as well as reflecting and reproducing many similar (but also some different) concerns regarding the governance of sex as discussed in the three previous chapters. But we are entering new terrain here inasmuch as an analysis of quasi-official discourse extends our arguments in specific ways.

To begin with, we need to make clear that what we deal with in the next three chapters is largely 'consensual' sex involving adults. The informal regulations we discuss in this and the next two chapters then, illustrate the manner in which illicit sex involving 'consenting' adults comes to be constituted in terms of a moral authoritarianism which has as its focus not sex *per se*, but the naming of that which is unacceptable, inappropriate, unwanted, unwelcome, unprofessional or simply unthinkable with regard to sex. What we are focusing upon here then is the issue of how adult sex (and sexual relations) that lies on the cusp in terms of acceptability, is regulated and controlled in any manner of public settings, including on the telephone, in email communication and on the digital 'superhighways'. What (and who) determines how and where such sex crosses the boundaries of public propriety, decency and order and hence becomes a 'problem'? The quasi-official discourses and the informal regulations we examine speak of the 'problem' of illicit sex involving adults, in terms of it being socially troublesome, as causing 'problems' which whilst not sexual offences as such, nonetheless require political attention. This is partly because such sex disturbs and rattles the margins of the 'normal' and 'natural'. But precisely because much illicit sex steers close to what is regarded as 'normal' and 'natural', there is a need to establish what, specifically, is 'wrong' with it. Indeed, in the case of this much less formally regulated sexual conduct, many of the policies and procedures that we examine in this and the next two chapters are underpinned by *ethical* concerns regarding sex. As such, this requires establishing that some adult, 'consensual' sex is 'wrong' because, for example, it is between the 'wrong' people – because it involves adults who occupy different and unequal power positions in public settings.

But at the same time as there are moves to disallow it, there is also a tendency in many of the regulations we examine in this and the next two chapters to treat illicit sex as if it did not need to be named, as if there were no sex at all at stake in this particular political project. This is because the moral authoritarian project we unpack herein rests on the deployment of other key terms of reference such as 'impropriety', 'indecency', 'unacceptability' and so on. In the case of informal regulations then, it is not so much sex *per se* that 'really' matters, but establishing these terms of moral and ethical reference in order that such regulations might secure their wider project of prohibiting the 'unethical' and 'immoral'.

In order to explicate our analysis of this wider project, we take as the subject of our inquiry in this chapter the regulation and control of what we have called nuisance sex, whilst Chapter 6 is devoted to discussion of the regulation of what we have called professional sex. Following on from this, we deal in Chapter 7 with the regulation of transgressive and digital sex. In each of the areas we refer to, we outline, illustrate and critique our arguments with reference to a range of policy guidelines, some typical and some atypical. It is not our intention in this, or the next two chapters to draw upon a systematically representative sample of organizational policies, for that would be an altogether distinct and different task. Neither are we attempting to cite illustrative examples of what might be considered 'best practice', for that has been undertaken by many other academics and policy-makers in the field (Cahill 2001; Collier 1995). What we are attempting to do in the second half of the book is to develop our analysis of the underlying sets of assumptions shaping both illegal and illicit sex by exploring the links between the official discourses surrounding criminalized sexual activities, and the quasi-official discourses that inform and shape various organizational policy guidelines, most of which carry law-like status but have little or no statutory power. We want to suggest that there are both similarities and differences in the symbolic landscapes underlying all sex regulation, whether formal or informal.

To be clear about the ground we are covering in the second half of the book: inasmuch as we are interested in uncovering the sets of assumptions that frame the codification of illicit sex, we take as our starting point the ways in which sex has been subject to regulations of a more informal kind, outside the remit of the law. That is not to say we discount the law, but it is via an examination of less formal regulations that many of the points that illuminate our analysis are made. What this means is that much of the regulation of nuisance sex discussed in this chapter will be in terms of the equal opportunities and anti-harassment and bullying policies put in place by various private companies, public and voluntary sector organizations and so forth. We also take as further illustration of our arguments, informal regulations of illicit sex in 'leisure' arenas such as health/relaxation centres, where facilities such as pools, tubs and saunas are communally used. This will lead into discussion of the regulations surrounding nudity and so on in public places, particularly as this issue has recently had a 'bumpy ride' with regard to its potential inclusion in the Sexual Offences Act (2003). Interestingly, regulations pertaining to the public display of the body (or more particularly certain parts of the body) that are deemed sexual, can be contrasted with the non-regulation of the body in contexts where there is deemed to be a less obvious (even little or no) sexual element, as in health education settings or art installations. Witness, for example, the display of several hundred, live naked bodies on escalators in London's Selfridges store in Oxford Street in 2003. Such mass public nudity may have excited media interest but caused little impact in terms of infringing law or policy. We argue that this was due in no small part to the absence of any clear 'victims' of such supposed 'sexual nuisance'.

But first we turn our attention to the issue of what constitutes nuisance sex. In the last 20 to 30 years, and notwithstanding of the issue of prostitution, the notion of sex as a publicly constituted nuisance has risen in prominence, increasingly coming to dominate political agendas in terms of being seen as a legitimate target for reform. In particular, the issue of what has popularly come to be known as sexual harassment has gained greater currency, making its appearance in a variety of forums, including talk shows, soaps and documentaries, as well being taken up by campaigning organizations such as the trades unions, ethnic minority, LGBT (lesbian, gay, bisexual and transsexual) and various women's groups. As a result, there have been what many would regard as highly successful moves to institute organizational mission statements, policy guidelines and other quasi-official utterances designed to limit not only sexual harassment in the workplace but also nuisance sex more widely. By focusing upon what we have called nuisance sex, we are not referring solely to sexual harassment in the workplace but also to that sex which occurs in public spaces such as streets and leisure arenas. Nuisance sex thus covers an array of sexual behaviours and activities which are by no means homogeneous, and which include some sex which may be deemed by many to be 'non-consensual'. Under the umbrella of nuisance sex then, we include the regulation and control of sexual activities such as 'obscene' telephone calls, indecent exposure, stalking and voyeurism. All of these reflect wider understandings that there is a 'problem' with regard to sex in public places, and that 'problem' is largely the extent to which it has met with any agreement or approval on the part of those involved, including bystanders. But herein lies the difficulty of defining the 'problem', for nuisance sex is often about dealing with what some may regard as no more than everyday sexual banter, sexual innuendo and so on. In that sense, the informal regulations surrounding nuisance sex range over that sex which may be deemed threatening and highly upsetting for the persons on the receiving end, to that sex which creates no more than momentary discomfort and might even be seen as 'playful' or 'innocent fun'. This is also partly reflected in the way that some nuisance sex has also come to be regarded as part of the 'rough and tumble' of standard entry into public spaces, so that it is often assumed that some 'consensual' sex is conducted in the spirit of nothing more nor less than 'high jinks', adventure-seeking and experimentation, and should therefore be treated as such. For example, 'outdoors' sex involving adults (including sex in cars or other means of transport, parks, lay-bys, fields and so on) is indicative of the kinds of sexual behaviours that the public might be expected to tolerate or ignore. In some cases, however, sexual behaviour, if taking place in offices or other workplace settings, runs counter to that which has been deemed publicly 'acceptable'. There are very fine lines to be drawn here, but what is clear from all this is that the many indeterminate, contested definitions and interpretations that surround what we have termed nuisance sex, make it especially difficult to regulate and control in any straightforward way.

This does not preclude us from making a number of general observations with regard to the regulation of nuisance sex. Whilst much of the argument in earlier chapters discusses the official discourses which shape the illegality of sexual *offending*, in this and subsequent chapters, we maintain that there is often no widespread, agreed consensus on the 'wrongs' that have been committed, nor on the issue of who should have the power and authority to adjudicate and/or rule on behalf of those who have been 'wronged'. Informal, extra-statutory regulations often build upon and extend the coverage offered by formal regulations. In the case of 'obscene' telephone calls, for example, informal guidelines to customers/service users are issued by various companies within the private sector, whilst the Telecommunications Act (1984) lays down the law. Both speak to similar constituencies, but with different emphases, so that the status of the guidance given appears 'official', but is authored in different ways by different bodies. Furthermore, informal regulations of nuisance sex do not tend to evaluate how consensual sex 'really' is or was, and included within our discussions are regulations pertaining to nuisance sex which are couched in terms which speak of 'victims' who are deemed not to have consented, as well as 'victims' who have colluded and/or do not 'know' their own limits (of sexual acceptability and so on). For the purposes of our argument, we maintain that what is as crucial as the concern with protecting 'victims' are concerns about securing the reputation of employing organizations, leisure providers and so on, with regard to promoting 'good' public relations, and thereby generating 'healthy' business. In this case and like the formal regulations surrounding commercial sex discussed in the last chapter, we argue that there are commercial imperatives at work here as well as moral ones. Indeed, crucial to the regulation and control of nuisance sex is often the constitution of a 'respectable' reputation on the part of businesses/ organizations in both the public and private sectors. In this there is a syntactical and symbolic shift in the meaning of terms of reference surrounding nuisance sex inasmuch as regulations are often as much about public reputation as public protection. Indeed, the creation and maintenance of a 'good' reputation involves situating organizations (in both public and private sectors) on the 'side' of propriety and to some extent, asexuality. Many organizations who author and institute sexual harassment polices are thus in the business of positioning themselves as powerful upholders of the public good. They achieve this by, for example: ... *fully support(ing)* the rights and opportunities of all people to be treated with dignity and respect' and by making: '*every effort* to provide a working environment free of harassment and intimidation' (EDF Energy Group 2000: 9).

Such organizational guidelines also make it clear that they apply to everyone, for it is held that anyone (irrespective of age, gender or sexuality) is prone, or even likely, to fall victim to nuisance sex. This is because it is often assumed that sex is driven by inescapable 'natural', 'normal' desires, albeit ones that have been 'wrongly' publicly expressed, as opposed to being 'wrong' in and of themselves. In short, that nuisance sex (and especially sexual harassment) is often otherwise standard sexual 'attraction' and/or sexual 'invitations' that have gone awry in some way, or are taking place in 'inappropriate' settings. This would include sex, particularly heterosex, occurring in 'open' venues (such as beaches, parks, swimming pools and so on). Sets of assumptions concerning the 'naturalness' of much that is deemed to be 'in-appropriate' about sex also make appeal to gender differences, and this operates in particularly interesting ways in many of the policy guidelines surrounding nuisance sex. For example, it is often held that much 'non-consensual' sex between adults in organizational settings would not have occurred had it not been for the genders of those involved, such that a person is 'targeted' because of (most often) her gender (Hearn and Parkin 2001). Moreover, it is widely assumed that the exposure of genitalia, or masturbating to orgasm in public, is a sexual offence that is only committed by men. However, it is important to note that neither formal nor informal regulations reflect inequalities of gender in any straightforward way. Indeed, it is increasingly the case that all regulations pertaining to 'inappropriate' sex between adults in public settings like streets and so on, particularly those dealing with stalking, voyeurism and indecent exposure, are 'sold' as applying to everyone, irrespective of gender. For instance, guidance provided in the recent consultation document *Protecting the Public* made clear the government's intention to:

> ... introduce a *new gender-neutral* offence of indecent exposure relating to the exposure of both male *and female* genitalia in circumstances where the accused intended to cause or where it was reasonably likely that their behaviour would cause alarm and distress.
>
> (Home Office 2002: 32 emphasis added).

In this way then, both the 'perpetrators' (and 'victims') of nuisance sex are treated as having little to distinguish them, in terms of their gender. This is an important point which will be returned to later in the chapter.

In as much as they appear to apply to everyone then, many informal regulations regarding nuisance sex are presented as fairly non-problematic, straightforward and common-sense 'rules of engagement' for public expressions of adult sex. However, this belies a number of underlying complexities and contradictions. Firstly, because of the lack of agreement over the 'problem' which needs regulating, it has become something of a commonplace that pinpointing what constitutes nuisance sex generally, and sexual harassment in particular, is an institutional and conceptual minefield. Definitional wrangles abound and many of the policy guidelines we examine in this chapter reflect and wrestle with this ambiguity and uncertainty. Despite their appearing to apply to everyone, it is often not clear who is speaking to whom, about what, precisely. Having said that, it is also important to note that there is also much duplication of terms/definitions across a range of policies emanating from different organizations, both in the private, public and voluntary sectors. In other words, many informal policies appear simply to 'borrow' from one another in a fairly standard, uncritical way. Secondly and maybe because there is a lack of agreement over definitions of sexual harassment, it would seem that many policies aim to include as much as possible under the widest possible umbrella and, as will be seen in later sections of this chapter, often consist of little more than long lists of what counts as 'unacceptable' sexual behaviours. In this respect, they appear on the face of it to be comprehensive and clear, supported by means of lengthy illustrations of the kinds of sexual conduct which is 'off limits'. However, quite why some sex is described and prohibited, and other sex is not, remains unclear. Thirdly, the various political agendas surrounding sexual harassment have long been seen by some commentators as having been set and hijacked by 'political correctness'. As a result, many of the policies that address issues of nuisance sex have an air of 'bureaucratic-speak' about them, and are indeed regarded as 'lip service' pronouncements made on behalf of human resources departments and the like, designed to suggest that there are definitive rulings in this area to which all 'good' employers and employees alike should adhere. Accordingly, many of the informal regulations in this area are revealing as much for what they do not speak about, as for what they highlight as 'wrong'.

But the problems of specifying what is being dealt with in regard to nuisance sex goes further than this, for these informal policy guidelines move our analysis into new terrain. The symbolic landscapes which we have charted so far in this book have revealed the various contours of regulation which lie within the remit of the formal law, inasmuch as it has been the task of the law to precisely delineate what is illegal about certain kinds of sex. But we are now moving into terrain which is outside the law, insofar as nuisance sex is not always (and may not very often be) illegal, but is still subject to regulation and control. In other words, much nuisance sex is regarded by *institutions/bodies other than the state* as requiring control. Indeed, such institutions often go beyond the law as such in terms of what is to be 'outlawed'. This can be seen in the MIND (National Association for Mental Health) (1999) Guidance Document, *Dealing with Complaints of Harassment and Bullying*, which states:

> Harassment and bullying in the workplace contravenes Mind's Equal Opportunities statement. Mind recognises that it has a *legal responsibility* to ensure that no employee is subjected to such treatment at work. The intention of this policy is *to prevent all forms of offensive and unfair behaviour, whether or not such behaviour is lawful*
> (MIND 1999, emphases added)

In other words and insofar as organizations such as MIND are to decide on what is 'outlawed', it is clear that the informal regulation of nuisance sex is not only about setting out 'rules of engagement' but also about widening the net of regulation. Indeed, in this and subsequent chapters, we argue that this extended terrain is largely about shaping and proclaiming the 'wrongness' of that sex which is not viewed as so dangerous or harmful as to require the intervention of formal law, but is nonetheless deemed to be 'not right' in some way. In that sense, we are now in fraught and contested territory for the 'wrongness' of much 'consensual' adult sex can never be specified in any easy formulation.

What is clearly crucial, however, in terms of the regulation of nuisance sex, is the issue of where to draw lines between that sex which is deemed 'wrongful' and that which is not. It is sometimes thought unnecessary, even heavy-handed, for any institution/body to attempt to codify and control what could be regarded as 'private' affairs involving 'consenting' adults. The 'wrongness' of nuisance sex, then, has to be very carefully couched if it is to be made meaningful at all. Hence the various interpretations, definitions and illustrations found in the informal regulations surrounding sex, whilst often having widespread resonance in terms of common-sense understandings, are nonetheless often highly contentious in terms of how, specifically, sex is to be understood, codified and controlled, if at all. Indeed, this reluctance to interfere in 'private' sexual encounters between 'consenting' adults, even when these spill over into public settings like workplaces and so on, is apparent in much informal regulation. It is reflected, for example, in widespread suggestions that sexual harassment in the workplace should be dealt with by and on behalf of the organization. Hence, it is not thought to be a legitimate matter for state concern. This tendency towards the personalizing or privatizing of nuisance sex is partly because such exchanges usually, but not always, involve 'competent' adults who are considered to be responsible for and capable of negotiating and managing sex, particularly when it adheres closely to the conventions of the 'normal' and 'natural'. This means that to some extent and at odds with the official discourses which underpin the legal rulings discussed in previous chapters, there is in the case of nuisance sex an added and complicating dimension – namely, that the nature of the illicit sexual relations that seemingly 'consenting' adults enter into in public, will always and inevitably be contingent upon the distinctions drawn between 'private' and 'public' spheres of responsibility. In many cases, it is simply not deemed a matter of state concern whether or not, for example, insensitive sexual jokes and pranks, lewd comments about someone's appearance or speculations about their 'private' life occur in public places (indeed, much does), for this is often regarded as no more than the 'spilling over' of the 'natural' and 'normal' from the 'appropriate' to the 'inappropriate', from the 'private' into the 'public'. In the case of sexual nuisance then, what underlies the framing of informal regulations are anxieties not only over what, where and how illicit adult sex is conducted in public settings, but also over who has the power and authority to 'draw the line'. So despite much more vocal and vociferous campaigning around issues such as sexual harassment in the workplace, the regulation of nuisance sex remains a contested moral and political enterprise. Indeed, in terms of the new sexual enterprise or moral authoritarian project that we seek to explicate in this book, the search is on for ever more 'respectable' institutions/bodies to act as spokespeople or arbitrators in terms of framing 'legitimate' guidance regarding sex and sexual conduct. The issue of sexual harassment in particular illustrates these wider concerns with who has the (moral authoritarian) 'right' to regulate adult sex in public places, since sexual harassment has fallen under the remit of both statutory and extra-statutory controls.

Regulating sexual harassment – a case in point

It may appear that placing the issue of sexual harassment in a chapter entitled nuisance sex (as opposed to dealing with it in the chapter on harmful sex) is in itself contentious, given that many have seen sexual harassment as a widespread and pervasive form of sexual offending from which victims should expect and receive legal redress (MacKinnon 1978, Lawrie and Jenkins 2000). It is also important to acknowledge that whilst sexual harassment is notoriously difficult to define, there have been several attempts in law to address this particular 'problem'. Indeed, there have been and still are many attempts to categorize sexual harassment in law; for example, as in the case of what has been called *quid pro quo* (something-for-something) sexual harassment, in which a threat is made or benefit offered in order to obtain sex. Sexual harassment under certain conditions is also currently illegal in the UK because it is considered to be a form of sex discrimination and is thus prohibited under the 1975 Sex Discrimination Act (as amended) and EC regulation (December 1991) as it applies to UK law. In addition, sexual harassment has been defined as illegal under the 1978 Employment Protection Consolidation Act. Later on, the 1994 Criminal Justice and Public Order Act made *intentional* harassment a criminal offence. This Act did not define intentional harassment specifically but stated that a person commits an offence:

> ... if, with the intent to cause a person harassment, harm or distress, she/he: (a) uses threatening, abusive or insulting language or behaviour, or disorderly behaviour, or (b) displays any writing,

sign or other visible representation which is threatening, abusive or insulting, thereby causing another person harassment, alarm or distress.

(Criminal Justice and Public Order Act 1994, S.154)

Later still, the 1997 Protection from Harassment Act made sexual harassment both a criminal offence and the subject of civil proceedings. The principle aim of this Act was to deal with stalking, but it also covered other types of harassment including making malicious telephone calls, and/or sending 'offensive' electronic communications, letters or articles. Again, there is no specific definition of sexual harassment in the Act, but it does contain the following note: 'reference to harassing the person includes alarming the person or causing the person distress'. Importantly, the Act focuses upon *the effect* of the conduct on the 'victim', and not upon whether or not the 'perpetrator' intended to cause offence. Nonetheless, the Act does state: 'A person must not pursue a course of conduct which amounts to harassment of another person, and which *he/ she knows or ought to know amounts to harassment of another person*' (Criminal Justice and Public Order Act 1994). It is further required by law that a 'course of conduct' must involve conduct (including speech) on at least two occasions. In law then, particular conditions must be met before charges of sexual harassment can be brought.

Once sexual harassment became viewed as a particular kind of sex 'offence' concerned with employment relations, this then circumscribed the way it was and still is dealt with in law. In particular, this view has shaped decisions about whether sexual harassment is legislated for primarily under tort law or discrimination law. Tort law concerns personal injuries, harms done by one person to another, and thus sexual harassment is constituted in this way as behaviour offensive to the integrity or sensibility *of an individual*. As alluded to earlier, this constitutes the 'problem' as being one of personal/private affront to an individual 'victim'. Discrimination law, on the other hand, acts to support equality of opportunity and is thus sensitive to structural and group-based power dynamics. These distinctions between individuals and collectivities are reflected in the ways in which informal policies and guidelines are drawn up by companies and businesses in attempts to regulate sexual harassment in the workplace, so that anti-harassment and bullying policies, for example, often seek to provide both redress for individuals and reflect and secure wider organizational goals. However, there are difficulties here, for the individual is often highlighted whilst the organizational missions/goals remain buried or hidden. This means that the definitions of sexual harassment contained in many policies are usually framed in terms of it being that sex which is uninvited, unwanted and unwelcome to *individuals*. To some extent, this absolves others from any responsibility for defining sexual harassment because it is 'only' a matter for the person who has been subjected to it. Indeed, many policies of this kind make it clear that the onus has been and still is very much upon the individual to recognize and name sexual harassment. But at the same time, buried within these policies is another, different discursive construction of the 'problem' of sexual harassment. Namely, that sexual harassment is a *collective* 'problem' in terms of threatening particular constructions of good, desirable and even ideal working environments and/or workplace climates. Such desirable settings are places where, it is held: 'the dignity of individuals is (to be) respected' (Newport City Council 2002) and by extension, sexual harassment is not to be tolerated. In this way, the framing of sexual harassment as both an individual and collective 'problem' pivots around the requirement that rights and responsibilities are defined in terms of *all individuals* (including customers, clients and service-users as well as employers and staff) who, it is held, have contributions to make towards realizing organizational goals. In one respect then, sexual harassment is deemed to be that sex which *individuals* on the receiving end variously experience and name as discomforting, demeaning, degrading, and/or insulting. In addition, it is also defined as that which has the effect of undermining *collective* attempts to create, *by and for all who occupy them,* working environments which are free of sexual threat and intimidation. This collapsing of the individual/collective/organizational can be seen, for example, in Scottish and Southern Energy plc (2000) *Policy Against Harassment At Work,* in which is stated their aim:

> … to promote an environment where *all staff* conduct themselves in a manner consistent with the proper and professional performance of their duties and *the maintenance of good working relationships. The company* will not tolerate … unacceptable behaviour which is *personally offensive, socially unacceptable and fails to respect the rights of others.*
>
> (Scottish and Southern Energy plc 2000, emphases added)

In such attempts to regulate the 'problem' of sexual harassment then, it is clear that more is at stake than individuals' experiences of 'unwanted' or 'unwelcome' sexual behaviour, for there are collective, organizational and political interests at stake here too. But in this, the informal regulations surrounding sexual harassment (and nuisance sex generally) tend to elide and obscure notions of 'victims', 'perpetrators' and 'protectors'. As a result of the personalizing of victims as individuals who have been affronted, threatened or intimidated in some way, sexual harassment is deemed to be a 'wrong' or 'injury' from which individual employees should be protected by all others, especially and including their employers. At the same time, 'perpetrators' can be just about anyone within the organizational setting (including customers, clients and service-users). Meanwhile, many policies also couch issues of the 'wrongness' of sexual harassment in terms of it being a threat to the collective goals of the organization. In this respect, the specificity of who is victim and who is perpetrator tends to get lost. Finally, all this, whilst ostensibly appearing to clarify the 'problem', tends to simultaneously obscure the sex that is being talked about. This is a point that will be elaborated upon in more detail in the next section.

Constructing the 'problem' of nuisance sex

Within this framing of sexual harassment in particular, but nuisance sex generally, as both a 'problem' for individuals *and* a 'problem' for all, there are further issues at stake. What this permits is in effect a dual construction of the 'problem'. It allows, on the one hand, policy statements which can appear clear and unambiguous about who are 'victims' (and 'perpetrators'), whilst on the other hand, there is much muddle and confusion with regard to exactly what 'harms' have been done to whom (by whom). Clarity is achieved because many such policies go to some lengths to define, illustrate and litter with examples, sexual behaviour which is 'unacceptable' and 'inappropriate' in public settings. This is an important point, for in the case of other informal regulations of sexual conduct, such as the professional association codes of ethics discussed in Chapter 6, we argue that there is a widespread lack of precision in defining the exact nature of the illicit sex that is subject to scrutiny. In professional association codes of ethics, sex is not generally referred to as 'sex' at all, whereas in the case of most informal policies on sexual harassment, it would appear on the surface that a great deal of attention is given to defining and illustrating precisely what the 'problem' consists of. For example, Newport City Council (2002) *Policy on Dealing With Bullying and Harassment At Work* contains in the Appendix a lengthy list of examples of sexual (mis)conduct which, as stated in the policy, is 'clearly unacceptable'. The list includes:

> ... unwanted verbal or physical advances; sexually explicit derogatory statements causing offence to an individual; sexually

explicit discriminatory remarks which cause the individual to feel threatened, humiliated, patronised or harassed; unwanted, intrusive or persistent questioning about a person's marital status or sexual interest; intentional sexual behaviour which interferes with the employee's job performance, undermines job security or creates a threatening/intimidating work environment; suggestions that sexual favours may further someone's career on willingness or refusal to sexual favours; duplication and publication of written or photographic material likely to cause offence.

(Newport City Council 2002: 5 – 6 Appendix)

The same list goes on to state:

Sexual harassment can also extend to other forms of behaviour which may offend, such as ridicule, lewd, suggestive, embarrassing remarks or jokes, unwelcome comments about dress or appearance, speculation about an individual's private life and sexual activities, deliberate abuse, the display of what may reasonably be regarded as offensive, suggestive or pornographic pictures, unwanted and unnecessary physical contact, demands for sexual favours or physical assaults upon employees and less tangible forms of behaviour such as staring or leering.

(Newport City Council 2002: 6 – 7 Appendix)

What is offered by these lengthy examples appears on the surface to be a comprehensive if not exhaustive list of sexual behaviours and activities which seem to suggest we all 'know' what sexual harassment is, and can recognize it whenever and wherever it occurs.

But despite the comprehensive guidance offered in such policies, none of the descriptors of sexual behaviours offered are – in terms of their being *experienced* as discomforting, demeaning, degrading, insulting and so on – definitive. For much of the guidance in this area also makes it clear that any 'offence' depends first and foremost upon the *'victims' experiencing such behaviour as offensive.* So despite their seeming clarity, most policies throw the onus of definition back onto the individual, and furthermore, the individual 'victim' (rather than the 'perpetrator' or anyone else for that matter). This leads to the discursive constitution of an 'impossibly knowing victim', for such victims must rely solely upon their own subjective experience, with little recourse to any shared 'signposts' as to what is demeaning, degrading, insulting and so on. In short, it is up to 'victims' alone to 'know' that sexual harassment has taken place. This creates near-intractable difficulties for such 'impossibly knowing victims' inasmuch as many policy-makers, let alone the general public, know that what may be experienced as discomforting, demeaning, degrading and so on by some on the receiving end, may be acceptable and even pleasurable to others. Being physically 'helped' through a doorway or up stairs, or being sexually commented upon in terms of clothes and appearance, are both examples of 'sexual harassment' that may not always be experienced by everyone on the receiving end as 'unwelcome' and 'uninvited'. Hence, and despite the seeming clarity and comprehensiveness of the informal regulations in this area, 'victims' are positioned as those for whom it is impossible to 'really' know whether or not they have been sexually harassed, for they can only make appeal to their own experience and that is constituted as always and already subjective, rather than being shared collectively. What this means in effect is that much 'sexual harassment' often falls short of being defined by many recipients as 'sexual harassment', and indeed, it opens the doors for many supposed 'victims' to collude with their 'perpetrators', insofar as they may experience such behaviour as not only non-intrusive but also sexually 'wanted' and 'welcome'. This creates the further possibility of discursively constituting 'victims' as those who fail to 'know' or understand their own limits of sexual acceptability, or whose limits do not 'fit' those of others within an organization. As West Country Ambulance Services NHS Trust, *Harassment and Bullying in the Workplace Policy*, states: 'The Trust recognises that harassment and/or bullying are *subjective concepts which require sensitive handling*' (West Country Ambulance Services NHS Trust 2003: Section 2.16, emphasis added). But the same guidelines then go on to state: 'All employees should be aware that behaviour which they may find personally acceptable may not be considered as such by others' (West Country Ambulance Services NHS Trust 2003: Section 2.16, emphasis added). The important point here is that such admissions open up the discursive space in which it is then incumbent upon policy-makers, politicians, campaigning groups and so on, to construct notions of 'knowing victims', against which individuals who are potentially subject to nuisance sex can variously define themselves and their experiences. Hence the long lists meant to 'educate' and 'inform' potential victims. But ultimately, individuals cannot 'really' know if they have really been 'victims', for that is always a matter of subjective interpretation. Moreover, they cannot really be trusted to adhere to others' interpretations of the 'wrongs' being visited upon them and so they are also 'impossibly knowing victims'. Hence, what has become central in this particular area of sex regulation and control are specific notions of 'victims' and 'victimhood' emanating from those who have the power to define what (and who) constitutes the 'problem'. At first sight therefore, it can be argued that whilst informal policy guidelines appear to be clear and comprehensive with regard to what constitutes nuisance sex (and especially sexual harassment), nonetheless such guidance, we argue, rests upon securing notions of elusive and collusive 'victims', for whom no objective measures can ever exist. It is to the detailed constitution of these 'victims' (and 'perpetrators' and 'protectors') that the chapter now turns.

Elusive and collusive 'victims'

In what follows, we explore the discursive construction of 'victims' (and victimhood) in more detail and, following on from previous chapters, show how the emergence of a totalizing discourse of 'victimhood' reaches new heights with the extensive development of informal policy regulations pertaining to sexual harassment in particular, and nuisance sex generally. As hinted above, we argue that what is crucial in terms of the regulation of nuisance sex are particular and paradoxical notions of 'victims'. To begin with, we argue that what is at stake in many regulations surrounding nuisance sex is the notion of a 'wronged' or 'injured party' who can be used to elicit and call upon the support of 'reasonable others', because they (the 'injured party') can never 'truly' know the extent of their own victimhood. That is something only 'a reasonable person' can know. For example, as West Midlands Fire Service *Harassment and Bullying Policy* makes clear:

> In general terms it (harassment) can be described as unwanted and unwelcome comments, looks, actions, materials, suggestions or physical contact which a person finds objectionable, intimidating, upsetting, embarrassing, humiliating or offensive *and which a reasonable person would find unacceptable* ...
> (West Midlands Fire Service 2003: Section 3.1, emphasis added)

In other words and within this particular construction, it is not simply the case that a 'victim' subjectively experiences particular sexual behaviours as 'unwelcome' and 'unwanted', but that 'reasonable persons' also feels the same way. In this manner, what arises is a carefully-nuanced, paradoxical construction of those who are on the receiving end of sexually-harassing behaviours as both impossibly-knowing *and* rational. They are impossibly-knowing inasmuch as they do not have recourse to anything more than their own subjective experience upon which to rely in terms of deciding whether they have been affronted, assailed and insulted and, by being championed as and by 'a reasonable person', they are also configured as typical, sensible and above all, rational. Such 'victims', albeit paradoxical, are those upon whose behalf and in whose interests informal regulations are then held to operate. Moreover, it is crucial that the concerns expressed by such paradoxical 'victims' are made paramount and central. For, as the North Wales Police Force *Draft Policy on Fair Management Practice* states: 'The intention of the perpetrator is largely irrelevant – what is important are *the perceptions and feelings of the injured person*' (North Wales Police Force 2004: 9, emphasis added).

But whilst informal regulations are often couched in terms which are designed primarily to reflect victims' concerns, in leaving it up to the 'injured party'/'a reasonable person' to pronounce upon what the 'wrongness' of sexual nuisance is, there is little to distinguish or identify what it is that makes a difference to different 'victims'. In this respect, all 'victims' are held to be alike. As mentioned earlier, many policy guidelines suggest (often explicitly so) that *anybody* can be a 'victim', irrespective of gender, sexuality, age, occupational status or any other social or political characteristics. As Newport City Council (2002) *Policy on Dealing with Bullying and Harassment at Work* makes clear, there is no one to whom sexual harassment cannot happen, for the policy clearly states: 'Most people who are sexually harassed are women, but it is important to remember that it can happen to men too'. In this way, 'victims' are de-gendered, and moreover, robbed of most other social markers – *anybody* (even those who offer 'protection' to 'victims') can be subjected to sexual harassment. This has particular ramifications for the discursive space in which 'victimhood' is constituted because it also means that any references to the social specificity of nuisance sex in terms of its perpetration (and the 'perpetrators' thereof) is similarly denied. Unlike formal sex regulation, which for most of the twentieth century rested upon symbolic landscapes peopled by identifiable 'sex offenders' (the 'rapist', the 'paedophile' and so on), informal regulations operate with very little need to name or identify 'perpetrators'. Even the very notion of a 'sexual harasser' has little purchase upon the symbolic landscape which underpins these regulatory frameworks. 'Perpetrators' are always shadowy and barely discernable figures then, and even discursive constitutions of 'known/knowable perpetrators', for example so-called 'flashers' and 'stalkers', are constructed in terms of being temporary figures, there one moment and gone the next. Indeed, it could be argued that this is not accidental for as Northamptonshire Fire and Rescue Service *Fairness At Work Policy* makes clear:

> It is the *impact of the behaviour on the victim* which is the key in deciding whether or not a complaint of harassment or bullying should be investigated, *not the intention of the perpetrator.*
>
> (Northamptonshire Fire and Rescue Service 2001: Section 12.7.2, emphases added)

In this way and unlike 'victims' then, 'perpetrators' are discursively reduced to figures whose individual experiences, intentions and motivations are not deemed worthy of any consideration, and in some cases, can be constituted not as 'malicious' and 'malign', but as 'innocent' and 'naïve'. As the Newport City Council *Policy on Dealing with Harassment and Bullying at Work* states: 'It is recognised that problems can arise, *often quite unintentionally,* in any situation where large numbers of people of different sex, interests and cultures work together' (Newport City Council 2002, emphasis added). In this way, informal policy guidelines highlight the possibility that certain environments (such as workplaces) may arouse the sexual desires and interests of 'perpetrators', especially on occasions when and where any 'harm' done was unintended. But in the long run, this means that just about anybody can become a 'perpetrator' of nuisance sex for anybody can simply get it 'wrong'. Indeed, it is often held that nuisance sex has occurred only because people 'make mistakes' and/or 'misread' body language and other 'sexual' signals. Furthermore, what all this suggests is that the further sex regulation moves away from the dangerous, serious sexual offences covered by the law, the less explicitly articulated gendered power relations are. In this way then, we are all equally culpable (and equally 'at risk'). But in effect, 'victims' and 'perpetrators' become increasingly de-contextualized; we have all become 'people who work together', 'run into each other in the streets', 'happen to follow each other home' and so on.

What this means and unlike the feminist campaigning debates on sexual harassment which name the 'problem' of sexual harassment in particular, as a problem of *men* harassing *women*, there is very little or no emphasis in any of the informal regulations surrounding nuisance sex that we have examined, upon those social and symbolic identifications that are useful in making explicit the power relations which operate around sex. For example, because so many informal policy guidelines make little if any reference to whether or not 'sexual harassment' is directed or targeted in different ways at different groups of people, it is deemed to be experienced in the same way by anyone, anytime and anywhere, in virtually any organizational or public setting. This means that nuisance sex has become constituted as an ever-present, commonplace and routine danger. Indeed, it has been held to be a 'dripping tap' which can all too easily become a 'flood' if left unguarded, whilst at the same time it is unclear from where the 'flood' may emanate, nor what it may contain. Indeed and in this way, nuisance sex is that sex which appears from and gets everywhere. It can even destabilize and disturb 'environments' as well as people. For behind all the individual 'victims' and 'perpetrators' lie employing organizations who may, policies make clear, themselves be seriously affected, if not victimized, by sexual harassment. Take, for instance, the following examples:

> It is important to understand that harassment can have a devastating effect on an individual … *It can also have a damaging effect on the working environment as a whole as others may misinterpret harassment for favouritism or as an acceptable standard of behaviour.*
> (Marks and Spencer 2002, emphasis added)

> All forms of harassment and bullying can lower morale, undermine job security, interfere with job performance, cause loss of work time due to sick leave *and/or create a threatening, intimidators [sic] or humiliating work environment.*'
> (Lancashire Constabulary 2003: Appendix A, emphasis added)

Indeed, many policy guidelines are clear that the interests of individual 'victims' and the business, company and/or organization for which employees work are more or less coterminous, inasmuch as *everyone* can be harmed and damaged. As MIND (National Association for Mental Health) (1999) *Guidance Document for Dealing with Complaints of Harassment and Bullying* states:

> Both bullying and harassment … can have a serious effect on an employee's health, self-esteem and job performance. *They lead to demotivated and demoralised staff who are undermined and fearful of making decisions or using their initiative.*
> (MIND October 1999: Section 1.1.3, emphasis added)

'Victims' are not simply *individual* staff then, but the companies and businesses who employ them.

What has emerged in this area then, is a wealth of informal regulations which tend not to admit any possibility that sexual 'offences' will depend upon the hierarchical contexts in which they take place (for example, senior managers harassing more junior staff; heterosexual men harassing 'available' women and so on). Most informal regulations fail to make any reference to abuses of power, status and position of this kind. Instead, policies tend to be marked by both clarity and confusion. This is not accidental for it is deemed necessary that informal policies appear to guarantee the protection and safety of those on the receiving end of sex that is 'unwanted' and 'unwelcome', but at the same time they tend to leave definitions wide open. This permits the subjective interpretations of 'victims' (backed up by being those of a 'reasonable person') to be put at the centre of the frame, whilst at the same time fairly exhaustive lists of the kinds of sexual behaviours deemed to be 'harassing' act to circumscribe the sex that is deemed to be 'unacceptable' and/or 'inappropriate'. These paradoxical constructions are possible because the regulatory frameworks rely on both de-contextualized *and* over-determined notions of what and whom needs protection, such that 'victims' are impossibly knowing, reasonable and rational, and at the same time, anyone and everyone. Not surprisingly, this gives such policies a contradictory status, for the institutions who draft and adopt these guidelines appear to be doing something very concrete whilst at the same time, they are freed from the necessity of providing anything very specific upon which to hook the sexual 'offence' that may or may not have taken place. That determination is left to the discretion of individuals, and although this is not of direct concern to us for the purposes of our arguments in this book, it has been cited as a major factor in why so few cases of sexual harassment are ever successfully taken forward under formal disciplinary and grievance procedures, let alone ever brought to the attention of the criminal justice system.

Widening the net

We also argue in this chapter that the regulatory frameworks which have as their object of scrutiny that which is deemed nuisance sex, have expanded extensively over recent years. In particular and with regard to the shift in understandings of nuisance sex, there has in the last ten years or more been a veritable outpouring of attention directed towards the regulation of nuisance sex (Aggarwal 1992, Infield and Platford 2000). In many cases and particularly before the advent of second wave feminism, it was frequently suggested that nuisance sex was viewed as no more than a breach of sexual etiquette, including innocuous flirting, wolf-whistling, light 'brushing' and so on that had somehow been 'mis-interpreted'. As such, it was seen as no more than mildly objectionable, and certainly not in need of any informal (let alone formal) regulation and control. More recently, and particularly with the rise of feminist critiques and campaigns, a rather different view of nuisance sex has emerged which positions it (at worst) as a social 'evil' that is part and parcel of the torrent of violent sexual assault that men inflict upon women (Neville 2000). Indeed, some have argued that there has been a major sea change in terms of understanding and addressing nuisance sex generally and sexual harassment in particular, which can be heralded as no less than a triumph for feminism (Patai 1998). But it is important to acknowledge that nuisance sex is still both something and nothing; and seen in this way, what has become key is the ways in which organizations (and wider communities) are prepared to countenance 'unacceptable' sexual behaviours between arguably 'consenting' adults. Hence campaigners have maintained that even those who are not directly affected by nuisance sex are complicit in allowing or sanctioning its occurrence. As already discussed, it is often thought to be the responsibility of all those in public settings to uphold the 'social good', to engage, respond and deal with such sexual 'wrongdoing'. To this extent, nuisance sex has increasingly been constituted as the concern of everyone, particularly all of those within employing organizations, workplaces and so on. As the North Wales Police *Draft Policy on Fair Management Practice* makes clear: 'All staff have the right to be treated fairly and with dignity and respect at work *and it is the responsibility of everyone in the workplace to make this happen*' (North Wales Police 2004: 5, emphasis added). In this sense there has been a widening of the net within which nuisance sex is codified and controlled, such that it is now held that it is the responsibility of everyone to be constantly vigilant and 'on guard'. As the Royal Berkshire Ambulance NHS Trust *Harassment and Bullying at Work Policy* states:

> All staff have a responsibility to behave in an appropriate manner at work. Every member of staff also has a duty to deal responsibly with any instances of bullying or harassment that they are aware of. *It is not acceptable to turn a 'blind eye'.*
>
> (Royal Berkshire Ambulance NHS Trust
> November 2000: Section 4.2.3, emphasis added)

How has this increasingly widespread regulation and surveillance of 'nuisance' sex taken effect? First of all, it is important to note that over the last 30 years or so, there have been many campaigns which have sought to get various forms of sexual 'wrong doing' (not least sexual harassment) classified as serious sexual offences. These moves to elevate the status of nuisance sex, and sexual harassment in particular, have been aimed at getting not only private and public sector organizations to take nuisance sex more seriously than hitherto, but also to get the state to act to curb such 'offences'. Political moves have come in the wake of feminist campaigns, but there have also been moves from other quarters. Organizations such as local authorities, private businesses (large and small) and voluntary sector agencies now routinely regulate their customer/service user environment by means of prohibiting what they deem to be sexual activities and behaviours which are not conducive to public decency, propriety and order. This means that all manner of sexual 'intentions' have now come to be viewed as 'suspect' because they are somehow 'inappropriate' in terms of their public occurrence. For example, in the words of one small private business offering facilities such as jacuzzi, sauna, steam room, hot tub and floatation tanks, their stated aim is: 'to achieve a safe and tranquil environment conducive to deep relaxation'. To this effect, notices are displayed on the walls of the reception area stating that:

> It has come to our attention that there are a small number of people who use the Relaxation Centre in an inappropriate way. We would like to use this opportunity to clarify a fundamental: *If you have a sexual agenda in visiting the Relaxation Centre this is not the place for you.* It is wholly inappropriate to come here with an attitude that threatens to destroy all that the Relaxation Centre strives to create. Sexual behaviour inhibits other people's relaxation, as does being followed or stared at. We are treating this issue absolutely seriously and would like it to be known that the existence of some of the days we currently offer are under threat. We request that anyone who is made to feel uncomfortable in any way let us know immediately so that appropriate action may be taken.
>
> (Bristol Relaxation Centre 2003, emphasis added)

Furthermore, the assumption here is that much of the (supposedly) disturbing, disquieting sex that takes place in public settings is always and already an affront to 'decent' people and should be dealt with accordingly. It is also clear that there are increasing numbers of institutions/bodies who now position themselves as the voices of caring concern, the benign guardians of public morality. Witness, for example, what was said by Home Office Minister Charles Clarke, in announcing proposed new legislation to deal with:

> the nuisance associated with prostitutes' cards (in public telephone boxes) ... *Prostitutes' cards are explicit and offensive, can be seen by*

children, create a bad impression for overseas visitors and can cover up
important information such as adverts for the Samaritans and Childline.
(Clarke, Home Office Minister 2001,
Home Office Press Notice 150/99, emphasis added)

With this, it is clear the regulation of nuisance sex has increasingly become invested with moral authority. All sex in public places, it is held, offends decency, propriety and order. This assumption allows powerful bodies (including private business organizations) to be seen as legitimate upholders of moral standards. As such, there has not only been a net widening of regulation and control inasmuch as regulations have 'layered up' upon themselves (with authoring institutions/bodies all 'speaking' with one voice) but they have also extended their coverage into all manner of non-public spaces, most notably into the 'privacy' of the home.

One way in which this net widening operates can be seen in the case of the regulation and control of 'obscene' and 'nuisance' telephone calls. The regulatory frameworks leave the public in no doubt that such telephone calls are serious infringements which will not be tolerated by those who are there to protect them from such (often ill-specified) sexual 'threats'. Building and extending upon Section 43 of the Tele-communications Act (1984), various police authorities and telecommunications companies have issued guidance to the public in terms of distinguishing 'malicious' from 'nuisance' calls. The tone and tenor of such 'official' guidance is, it can be argued, soothingly reassuring but at the same time morally paternalistic. Witness, for example, that offered by Telewest Broadband (2003), which advises its customers:

> In most cases you will be in no doubt that you have received a distressing phone call. If you wish to report the call you need to try and distinguish between the two types of problem phone call, as only one type is a serious criminal offence. Nuisance calls can range from an excessive amount of 'wrong numbers' to persistent unsolicited calls.
>
> (Telewest Broadband 2003)

The guidance then goes on to outline 'malicious' calls as follows: 'If you receive a call containing any of the following, then it's a malicious call: obscene suggestions, personal threats, abusive language' (Telewest Broadband 2003). In all these cases, no mention is made of sex in terms of it being 'sex' as such, but customers are left in no doubt that they are 'protected' by service providers who are guarding and upholding their 'best interests'. Even and especially in the privacy of their own homes then, customers are told that there is an array of sexual 'offences' that can be perpetrated upon them any time they pick up a telephone receiver or log on to a personal computer. Furthermore, although these sexual 'offences' are never clearly identified as sexual, they are constituted as an ever-present danger that can occur to anyone, any time of the day or night. Indeed, we want to argue that with the extensive widening of the net around sexual 'wrong doing' that has now occurred, there is not much sex at all which is not seen as being in need of regulation.

Furthermore, we maintain that the more 'consensual' adult sex that comes to be proclaimed as illicit, the greater the possibilities for subjecting more and more sexual behaviours, activities and practices to formal regulation. In other words, rather than informal policy guidelines acting to rein in 'unacceptable' sex between adults which has fallen short of being made illegal as such, we argue that the informal regulation of sex produces more and more sex for potential inclusion within formal legal frameworks. In this respect, we give some consideration in the closing section of this chapter to the 'new' offences delineated in the Sexual Offences Act (2003) of sexual behaviour in a public place. As the consultation document *Protecting the Public* made clear, this offence:

> … will send out a strong signal of our intention to protect people from being *unwilling witnesses* to overtly sexual behaviour that most people consider should take place in private.
>
> (Home Office 2002: 32, emphasis added)

Again, it is not sex itself that is the issue here, but rather (as argued above) the extent to which such activities are deemed troubling, upsetting and distressing to others ('the public', 'innocent' by-standers and so on). Later in the same document, this is made more explicit:

> … it is not our intention to interfere in everyday behaviour in public that does not cause offence to the vast majority of people such as kissing and cuddling. It is also not our intention to criminal-ise sexual activity that takes place outdoors but in an isolated place where one would reasonably expect not to be observed.
>
> (Home Office 2002: 32).

As such, sex regulation is reduced to little more than the upholding of public decency.

Upholding public decency

Given the arguments above, it should come as no surprise that there have been moves to extend formal controls into hitherto unregulated 'sexual' realms. For example, 'outdoor' public settings where people may engage in consensual, adult sex are now more closely regulated, public lavatories being a case in point (Sexual Offences Act 2003: Section 66). The indecent exposure of genitalia, knowing or intending: 'that someone will see them and be caused alarm or distress' (Sexual Offences Act 2003: Section 67) is also now illegal, albeit circumscribed by particular intentions on the part of legislators. Witness, for example, the proclamation made in the consultation document *Protecting the Public* which states:

> This is designed to catch those whose behaviour is specifically intended to shock another person and would not be used to criminalise, for example, *naturists in regulated environments or streakers at sporting events.*
>
> (Home Office 2002: 32, emphasis added)

Whilst falling short of assuming that in and of themselves naked bodies, when displayed in public places and amongst strangers, are necessarily sexually offensive or a threat to public decency, such regulations nonetheless draw upon long-standing assumptions that collapse nudity into sex. Such assumptions have a long history of being informally applied in piecemeal and *ad hoc* ways. For example, tanning studios, saunas, beauty and massage parlours are all 'public' settings in which bodies are often naked or semi-clad, and they have also been deemed 'suspicious', and thus subject to piecemeal, informal regulation. Public swimming pools, for example, have been known to display notices to the effect that 'no kissing or heavy petting' is allowed. It is also notable that there have been formal regulatory moves to rein in (sexual) 'voyeurism', even where nothing more than the unclothing of another's body is the object of curiosity on the part of the 'voyeur'. This has the effect, as will be unpacked in more detail in the following chapter, of instilling any unclothing of the body, whenever and wherever that is overseen by another person, with some measure of disreputability. For example, the surveillance of people undressing in changing rooms or sunbathing areas is now a criminal offence, subject to there being 'sexual gratifica-tion' on the part of the voyeur. Nonetheless, this is still a messy and muddled area, and one on which, we would argue, the issue of where to draw the line has reached particularly tangled and contorted proportions. For example, the interpretation of voyeurism, as outlined in Sections 68 and 69 of the Sexual Offences Act (2003), includes operating equipment in order to record (without consent of the person(s) involved) 'private acts', where such 'private acts' mean: '(a) the person's genitals, buttocks or breasts are exposed or covered only with underwear, or (b) the person is using a lavatory' (Sexual Offences Act 2003: Section 69). All this raises issues of what precisely are the sexual 'wrongdoings' that are being perpetrated here, and it is very often only by recourse to 'expert' voices which carry moral authority that the regulation of such illicit sex can be made meaningful. It is also clear from all this, that we are now moving from the terrain of 'risk' and 'risk factors' into the terrain of ethics and morals, not just with regard to what is 'wrong' with sex but what is 'wrongful' full stop. In order to further explicate our analysis of the moral authoritarian project that is at work here, we now turn our attention to illicit sex which has been subject to regulation by particular institutions/bodies who lay claim to being 'moral guardians' *par excellence*, namely professional associations.

Chapter 6

Professional sex: ethics, trust and moral guardianship

Doctor denies prostitute advice

A pioneering psychotherapist has denied instructing a male patient to sleep with prostitutes as part of his treatment. Dr Stuart Lieberman allegedly told the 34-year old – who had a 'kaleidoscope of mental problems', that he should have sex with both male and female prostitutes. But Dr Leibermen, giving evidence to a disciplinary hearing on Thursday, denied that he had 'pushed him' into using prostitutes, merely mentioned it as 'an afterthought'. Other possibilities for meeting people he claimed to have mentioned included cycling clubs, church groups and dating agencies. 'I was providing him with information, not telling him what to do,' he told the General Medical Council (GMC) hearing. The GMC was told that the patient, referred to as 'Mr A' looked on Dr Leiberman as a 'god-like figure', and endeavoured to follow his instructions. However, after contacting female prostitutes on two occasions, but being unable to have sex with them, and following a disastrous encounter with a gay friend, he made an unsuccessful attempt to kill himself. Miss Joanna Glynn, barrister for the General Medical Council, alleged that the advice was given to Mr A in front of his parents at the Prudence Skinner Family Therapy Clinic in Tooting, South London, in July 1992. Earlier Mr A's mental condition, which included worries about his sexuality and obsessive compulsive disorder, had led him to being treated as an inpatient in hospital. Miss Glynn said that he saw the therapy sessions with Dr Lieberman as 'his best chance' to put his life in order. Dr Lieberman, the GMC had earlier been told, had advised Mr A at their sixth therapy session to 'lose his virginity' before the following session, a month later.

135

'Caution advised'
But Dr Lieberman himself denied this, saying he cautioned Mr A against
rushing into having sex. 'I even went to the lengths of not fixing a date for the
next session, as I normally did, because I didn't want him to rush into anything'.
Mr A had earlier told the GMC that he had been desperate to solve his mental
problems, so he followed the advice of the doctor. 'My parents were against the
idea but who was I to believe – an expert with medical knowledge or my parents
without medical knowledge?' Dr Lieberman, who qualified in Nova Scotia,
denies failing to keep adequate records of his therapy sessions, failing to keep
himself adequately acquainted with his medical records or history, and advising
him to lose his virginity by sleeping with prostitutes. The hearing continues.

(BBC News Health, 13th April 2000)

Introduction

In order to further develop our arguments with regard to the regulation
and control of 'consensual' adult sex, this chapter examines the informal
guidelines surrounding what we have called professional sex. The focus
here is upon what has been deemed illicit sex involving adults, and
which takes place within the context of professional caring, helping or
other occupationally based relationships. We need to make clear that the
focus is not on illicit sexual conduct involving colleagues or co-workers,
but on that involving professionals and the adults whom they heal, treat,
educate, serve or otherwise minister to. Sex in such contexts is not illegal
as such (because it involves adults over 16 who are deemed to be capable
of consent) but it is widely regarded as illicit, and may carry with it
penalties such as (at most) being subject to official complaints and, if
claims are upheld, being struck off professional registers. Hence it is fair
to say that sexual exchanges and encounters involving professionals and
their patients, clients, students or service-users is conventionally
regarded as harmful, disreputable and unacceptable. It is held by
professional institutions/bodies themselves, that such sex calls into
question the motives and desires of the two (or more) adults involved
and raises issues of professional power, authority and responsibility. In
some cases and dependent upon the extent to which consent has been
given, professional sex may be a matter for legal proceedings, but most
of the time it is no more than an infringement of professional association
guidelines and as such, there is no criminal offence. Nonetheless, it is
clear that there is widespread acceptance of the idea that there is a
'problem' with sex in professional relationships, and this is reflected in
the informal regulations issued by professional associations, most of

whom have devised codes of ethics to which their members are expected to adhere. In this chapter, we will take an overview of the quasi-official discourse that operates in this area and examine what it is that lies behind the moves to codify and control that which falls within the scope of 'consensual' adult sex in professional contexts.

Before doing so, however, it is necessary to engage in a more general discussion about the notion of professionalism. By unpacking both traditional and contemporary notions of professionalism, it is possible to understand how and why even 'normal' and 'natural' manifestations of sex (including consensual heterosex between adults), when conducted in professional contexts, has come to be constituted as illicit, suspect and even dangerous. Traditionally, notions of professionalism have deployed structural and organizational indicators as markers of professional status and standing. Powerful professions such as law and medicine have had a monopoly over the control of recruitment, training and credentializing; control over entry numbers into the profession and some degree of financial control. Professions have also been described as *self-regulating* occupations in that professional associations have monitored education and training requirements, accredited institutional provision of training, awarded and renewed professional licenses, controlled aspects of professional practice and disciplined recalcitrant members (Evetts 2002). But professionalism is never established once and for all in any monolithic way and contemporary notions of what it is to be professional also seek to capture the dynamic processes of professionalization. It has been suggested that the strategies adopted by aspiring professions constitute 'professionalization projects' and that such projects involve, amongst other things, the constant *performance* of professional legitimacy (Fournier 1999, 2000, Deverell and Sharma 2000). In short, professions are based on *being seen to be professional*, as well as *simply being professional*. It is in this way that codes of ethics for the professions have been devised and revised in order to act as legitimating strategies for professionalization (Stone 2002).

The various professional institutions/bodies that are the subject of this chapter have also been positioned as 'authority figures' dispensing medical, psychological, educational, welfare and/or spiritual knowledge and expertise for the benefit of others. Such professional bodies have even been referred to as 'anointed' guiding lights and professional codes of ethics as 'secular expressions of sacred covenants' (Peterson 1992: 25). At the heart of any professional relationship then, is the notion that certain expectations can be met within professional relationships; for example, it can be argued that there is an expectation of deference to seniority on the part of the recipient or service-user, who thereby relinquishes a degree of control to the professional concerned. Professionals are also expected to place recipients' needs before their own, to monitor their self-interests and to exercise self-restraint (Dryden 1985). Furthermore, dependency and gratitude on the part of recipients or service-users is traditionally seen as inherent in the relationships they have with professionals. Crucially, any taint of any sex at all threatens such notions of what it is to be in professional relationships of this kind. In this chapter then, we seek to explicate the ways in which professionalism is constituted as a site in which virtually all sex is construed as 'off-limits'. Part of this construction rests in the notion of professional performativity. It is argued that professional relationships are deemed to be trust-based relationships, and sex in and of itself threatens to breach that trust. Not only is sex between professionals and the groups whom they seek to heal, protect or serve seen as 'wrong' then, inasmuch as it is widely viewed as compromising recipients' welfare, but sex is also seen to subvert the ethos of altruistic care and commitment that is associated with being, and being seen to be, professional. Hence any suggestion of sex between professionals and their patient, client or service-user groups threatens to bring professions into disrepute, weaken their power and ultimately erode their legitimacy. In short, professional sex is highly destabilizing in terms of professional performativity. But more is at stake than illicit sex merely posing a threat to notions of professionalism, for the maintenance of a particular discursive construction of 'professionals' has ramifications, we argue, for the moral authoritarian project that we seek to unpack and explicate in this book. This is a point that will be returned to later in this chapter.

But first to clarify the extent and content of the professional sex with which we are dealing here. It follows from what has been argued above that virtually all and any professional sex has come to be constituted as a serious 'problem', particularly for those working in people-orientated, health and welfare fields. Professionals involved in the frequent and routine provision of one-to-one and/or hands-on care and support, such as that offered in medical and allied health occupations, complementary health care and 'talking' therapies like psychotherapy and counselling, are obviously deemed to require active and close monitoring. But recreational, youth work and sporting activities such as those that take place in fitness coaching or personal training settings, are also open to imputations of professional boundary violations inasmuch as close, trust-based relationships are usually developed in these settings, and so consideration is given in this chapter to the regulatory guidelines that operate in these areas. Similarly, professional guidelines in lecturing and social work are also included. Following on from this, the regulations pertaining to the clergy are examined in order to highlight not only the position of professions which are particularly sensitive to accusations that their 'leading lights' are engaged in illicit sex with their congregations, but also because the regulations that exist within religious organizations speak volumes about the moral and ethical concerns underpinning the regulation and control of professional sex. For much of this chapter then, we are dealing with informal organizational guidelines which carry no statutory weight, but in the final section of our discussion and following on from similar considerations in Chapter 5 on Nuisance Sex, we wish to draw attention to the recent inclusion in the Sexual Offences Act (2003) of new legislation designed to regulate 'trust-based relationships' between adults, since these recent developments in the formal regulation and control of illicit sex illustrate our wider arguments regarding the moral authoritarian project that is at work here.

As already outlined, we want to emphasize that many but not all of the professional association codes of ethics examined in this chapter cover professionals engaged in close if not direct bodily contact with recipients or service-users. This is in part the basis for selecting particular codifications for exploration; namely, that such regulations pertain to professions in which there is anything from a suspicion to a real danger, historical or otherwise, that illicit sex may be taking place. One of the key arguments of this chapter, and developing that which was briefly outlined in the previous chapter, is our contention that professional sex is a particularly difficult and fraught 'problem' precisely because of its close proximity to 'natural' and 'normal' sex. After all, professionals and recipients or service-users are adult men and women who have consented to be in often intimate relationships with one another. Hence if not guarded against, many professionals are thought to be all too easily at risk of forming relationships with recipients and service-users which may not only become overly close and exclusive, but which may also imitate 'natural' and 'normal' partner, conjugal or even parent-child relations. But there are other, related difficulties here too, for the possibilities for professional sex do not simply arise because of shared, sexual attractions between individuals. In practice, many professional relationships in people-orientated fields such as health care, take place in settings which mimic private and domestic spaces, with recipients or service-users lying on beds, couches and in chairs. At the very least, examinations or treatment sessions are usually conducted in 'private' surgeries, clinics, offices or other 'intimate' spaces such as bedrooms. In short, many professional relationships, particularly in health and other care work, are often and literally, carried on 'behind closed doors'. In and of itself this marks such relations as 'intimate'. As such then, imputations of sex necessarily go with the wider terrain, for many professional relationships involve a degree of intimacy or hands-on touch, as for example between doctors/nurses and their patients, or bodywork therapists and their clients, that would be deemed sexual if practised or delivered in other contexts (Oerton and Phoenix 2001). It is thus important to acknowledge that the removal of clothes, the lying down on couches or beds, the touching of various parts of the body (including the genitals) and in some cases, close-up 'internal' examinations, routinely feature in many of these occupational contexts. Moreover, in many contexts where professional care, help and support is offered, it is often experienced by recipients as deeply expressive, spontaneous and even 'loving'. In other contexts, such close and 'loving' contact between adults would be construed as a sexual invitation, or might even constitute sex itself (Lawler 1991). As a result, many people-orientated professional relationships have been marked by assumptions that they are at constant risk of becoming overly sexual. Indeed, anxieties about the trustworthiness of certain doctors, therapists and other allied health professionals, and the abilities of professional associations to deal with 'offending' members, are indicative of a wider public concern about the 'dangers' thought to be associated with professional sex (Pilgrim 2002).

Before entering any further into such dense terrain, it is necessary to clarify the limits to what is being discussed here. In those professions of interest, our concern is with quasi-official codifications or regulations. The quasi-official discourse generally takes the form of what have been variously termed codes of ethics, codes of practice, ethical guidelines, ethical principles, rules of order and so forth, as laid down by the relevant professional associations. This chapter focuses largely, but not exclusively, upon ethical guidelines in people-orientated professions, especially those involving direct, hands-on contact. The aim of this chapter is to discuss the various ways in which the informal guidelines governing sex in professional settings are codified, and ultimately, to uncover and chart the symbolic landscape which underpins such regulations and helps explain why they take the forms they do. To do this and in common with what has come before, we want to make clear that in selecting the particular guidelines that have been included here, no claims are made for a representative sample. In summary then, this chapter deals with various typical (and some atypical) codes of ethics across a non-standardized sample of people-orientated professional associations. In order to explicate what the underlying concerns around professional sex might be, it then goes on to discuss the symbolic landscapes that underlie those regulatory frameworks. To begin with, however, we turn to the 'problem' of professional sex insofar as it is sex that is not 'sex'.

Professional codes of ethics: sex is not 'sex'

This section is concerned with the sex, or related conduct, that professional codes of ethics proscribe. To begin with, it is important to note that few professional regulations explicitly state that sex *per se* is prohibited, since the imputed sex and/or sexual behaviours hinted at tend not to be referred to as 'sex' at all. In other words, most (but not all) professional association codes of ethics fail to make any explicit mention of specific sexual activities and behaviours being 'off-limits'. Even in those guidelines where prohibitions against 'sexual behaviour' as such is mentioned, it is usually unclear whether this refers to genital exposure and contact, kissing and stroking, touching and hugging, sexual humour and suggestive remarks, sexual overtures or other expressions of sexual attraction. However, this does not mean that illicit sexual activity between 'consenting' adults is not of serious concern to professional associations. Many guidelines make extensive reference to professionals upholding the 'best interests', 'rights' and 'dignity' of recipients or service-users in ways which may or may not be read as indicators that it is sex that is being proscribed. Fairly typical of this is the fifth ethical precept contained in the Education Counselling Service of the British Council *Good Practice Guides*, which states:

> Members shall act at all times in the *best interests* of students or prospective students and shall offer advice and counselling and provide information in a manner consistent with this principle.
> (Education Counselling Service of the British Council 2000,
> emphasis added).

Similarly, the Chartered Society of Physiotherapy *Rules of Professional Conduct on Relationships with Patients* states: 'Chartered physiotherapists shall respect and uphold the *rights, dignity and individual sensibility* of every patient' (Chartered Society of Physiotherapy 2003: Rule 2, emphasis added). One of the assumptions that is often made here, however, is that these are 'taken-for-granted', coded references to sexual 'misconduct'.

Nonetheless and with regard to regulating sex between professionals and their recipients or service-users, guidance such as that outlined above is ambiguous in that it could refer to almost anything from a prescription against stealing, to avoidance of damage to health or property, to the protection of anonymity and confidentiality. Indeed, it is still the case that such regulations are taken to mean as much, and as a result suggestions that sex is prohibited tends to remain buried and hidden. However, it is important to note that when worded in terms of 'best interests', 'good practice' and so on, such guidelines make it clear that professionals are expected to take responsibility for being beyond reproach in all manner of (albeit largely unspecified) ways. Vague references are often made to maintaining 'appropriate boundaries' and so on. For example, and in much the same vein as the guidance referred to above, the General Dental Council's *Standards of Dental Practice* exhorts dentists to:

> ... *demonstrate respect* for your patients and your profession by *maintaining appropriate boundaries* in the relationships you have with patients. *Do not abuse those relationships for your gain or gratification.*
> (General Dental Council 2003: Section 2, emphases added)

The key point here is that exactly what constitutes 'appropriate boundaries', 'abuse' and so on is generally left unspecified. Thus many professional codes of ethics suggest that sex is prohibited only insofar as it constitutes that which lies outside 'good practice'. However, what constitutes 'malpractice' or 'misconduct' hardly ever gets specified in any clear or direct way. This point warrants further elaboration, and to do so we now turn to those contexts where the 'risks' of sex which is not 'sex' takes particular forms, and has particular meaning.

Health care contexts: regulating intimacy and touch

What appears to be at work in such professional codes of ethics is an assumption that references to 'malpractice', 'misconduct', 'impropriety' and the like will in and by themselves suffice. This can be seen in the way that buried in many professional association guidelines for health care professionals (including medical and allied health professions, as well as complementary and alternative practitioners) are vague warnings about 'boundary violations'. 'Boundary violations' can be understood as being about *bodily-based* boundaries. But these stipulations are couched not in terms of sexual behaviours and activities *per se*, but in terms of breaches of 'intimacy'. In the case of most of the health care professions discussed in this chapter, this is usually construed as the avoidance of 'indecent' bodily exposure and contact. It is well understood and a commonplace of

health care, that during examination and treatment sessions, patients
and clients often get undressed (some may get fully undressed). In such
situations, professionals are advised to protect and promote the client's
'modesty'. Typical of such exhortations is, for example, the International
Therapy Examinations Council (ITEC) *Code of Practice* (2002), which
states:

> ITEC professionals shall at all times act in a professional, ethical
> and honourable manner towards their clients and members of the
> public. *Client modesty shall be maintained at all times.*
>
> (International Therapy Examinations Council
> (ITEC) 2002, emphasis added)

All manner of 'props' including screens, drapes, robes, towels and
blankets are thus deployed by health care professionals engaged in direct
bodily contact with patients and clients. In theory, the use of such devices
acts not only to provide the patient/client with a warm, comfortable
treatment environment but also acts to delimit 'inappropriate' bodily
contact and/or sexual 'misconduct' on the part of health care professionals. References to 'modesty' then, appear to afford some measure
of protection against stolen glances, accidental brushing against bare
skin and so on, all of which can be read as markers of bodily contact
which is overly-sexual. However, much of the time stipulations to
maintain client 'modesty' also appear rather coy.

Hence in the case of some health care professional associations, more
clear-cut guidance is offered. For example, the British Register of
Complementary Practitioners *Code of Ethics and Practice for Members*
clearly states:

> Practitioners must appreciate the patient's need for privacy and
> modesty and *allow them to have another person of their choice present if
> they so wish.*
>
> (British Register of Complementary Practitioners 2001:
> Section 5.5, emphasis added)

What is being suggested here is effectively a form of chaperoning and
indeed, several professional associations do make clear reference in their
codes of ethics to the need for a 'chaperon' to be present in what might be
regarded as potentially compromising sexual situations. Such situations
appear to be synonymous with the removal of the patient/client's
clothing, and particularly their underwear. Chaperoning is an interesting
issue for the purposes of constituting the 'risks' of professional sex. On

the one hand, some professional codes of ethics in the field of health care stipulate that not only the patient/client but also their family and friends are 'off-limits' sexually. For example, the General Council for Chiropractors *Code of Practice* states:

> Chiropractors shall not use their professional position as a means of pursuing an improper personal relationship with a patient or *with a close relative or personal companion of a patient.*
>
> (General Council for Chiropractors 1999:
> Section 2.6.1, emphasis added)

Yet at the same time, health care professional associations also advise their members that having another person present (such as a close relative or personal companion of the patient/client) is necessary in order to guard against the 'dangers' deemed to inhere in hands-on examinations or treatments. This can be seen in the case of the British Register of Complementary Practitioners *Code of Ethics and Practice for Members,* which states that complementary practitioners must not: 'conduct a genital examination of a patient without a chaperon being present unless written consent has been given' (British Register of Complementary Practitioners 2001: Section 5.8.3). Similarly, the General Medical Council provides guidelines for doctors conducting genital examinations which state that before conducting any intimate examination, doctors should:

- Explain to the patient why an examination is necessary and give the patient an opportunity to ask questions.

- Explain what the examination will involve, in a way the patient can understand, so that the patient has a clear idea of what to expect, including any potential pain or discomfort.

- Obtain the patient's permission before the examination and be prepared to discontinue the examination if the patient asks you to. You should record that permission has been obtained.

- Keep discussion relevant and avoid unnecessary personal comments.

- Offer a chaperon or invite the patient (in advance if possible) to have a relative or friend present. If the patient does not want a chaperon, you should record that the offer was made and declined. If a chaperon is present, you should record that fact and make a note of the chaperon's identity. If for justifiable practical reasons you cannot offer a chaperon, you should explain that to the patient and, if possible, offer to delay the examination to a later date. You should record the discussion and its outcome.

- Give the patient privacy to undress and dress and use drapes to maintain the patient's dignity. Do not assist the patient in removing clothing unless you have clarified with them that your assistance is required.

What is at stake here is not simply that medical professionals (in this case doctors) are held to be at risk of violating bodily-based 'boundaries', for if these guidelines are taken at face value, it is clear that they are deemed to be in almost ever-present danger of this. The matter is more complex than this, for it is explicit in these guidelines that any hands-on examination of particular areas of the body (most obviously, the genitals), involving two – and only two – people of any age, gender or sexuality, is deemed inherently risky. This is why it is considered necessary to stipulate that such examinations must be conducted in the presence of a chaperon who somehow guards against the likelihood of anything untoward happening. In effect, a chaperon acts as a 'third party', becoming a 'safety valve' in an otherwise potentially litigious situation which, it is widely assumed, involves both illicit, and possibly illegal, sexual behaviour on the part of the professional concerned. In this way, adult patients/clients are viewed as relatively passive and power-less inasmuch as they require chaperoning in order to be kept, or to feel, sexually 'safe'. Health care professionals, by extension, are viewed as unwilling or unable to maintain 'appropriate boundaries' if left on their own with a semi-clad or naked patient/client. Amongst other things, this serves to elide professional sex with 'natural' and 'normal' sex since such situations, akin to those which arise between consenting sexual partners, come to be regarded as unquestionably tempting to almost any and every health care professional, and must therefore be strenuously guarded against by means of ensuring the presence of a third person.

But there is a further 'problem' with regard to professional sex, for whilst it is implicitly accepted that even (and perhaps especially) 'natural' and 'normal' professionals might be tempted to commit sexual 'offences' whilst engaging in 'intimate' bodily contact with patients/clients, nonetheless patients/clients are not seen as entirely passive and powerless either. In many cases, it is assumed that health care professionals are wide open to unwarranted accusations of 'unprofessional' behaviour. Thus the chaperon becomes constituted, in effect, as a potential witness as well as a 'safety valve'. This serves a multiplicity of ends, but the important point to stress here is that in contexts where chaperoning is required by professional regulations, it is assumed that health care professionals are (potentially at least) untrustworthy and possibly even abusive. In other words, this opens up the space in which the very people in whom trust is placed all too easily become sexual 'perpetrators'. But these are 'offenders' who need 'protection' for they themselves are highly vulnerable inasmuch as recipients/service-users are often positioned as malicious, irrational and volatile, subject to making unwarranted accusations of professional 'malpractice' or 'misconduct' to suit their own ends. Whether or not this is actually the case is not of concern here; what is important is that all of this reflects underlying sets of assumptions about the uncontrollability of sex generally, and about the risks and dangers deemed to inhere in even that supposedly most 'safe' sexual encounter, that between a 'caring' professional and adult recipient or service-user. In this case, it is possible to argue that the constitution of caring, benign 'perpetrators' and all too easily seduced 'victims' moves our analysis into new terrain, for professionals are paradoxically positioned as potential 'perpetrators' in whom trust, responsibility and security can never be completely placed (nor completely eroded). In addition, what this does is magnify widespread fears that sex is always ready to 'break out' even (and perhaps especially) in the most ostensibly 'caring' of contexts, where adults are involved and when consent to examination and/or treatment has already been given. In other words and although never directly admitted as such, virtually any and all sex can now be constituted as a 'problem' because the 'dangers' of sex are that it lies just beneath, and sometimes even mirrors, the thin surface of supposed respectability, safety and propriety thought to attach to those 'upholders' of public decency and the 'social good', namely professionals.

Non-health care contexts: regulating dual relationships

Nor does the matter end there. This chapter also argues that something more is at stake than a need to regulate and control professionals working in health care contexts, since it is clear that not all the professional associations which operate guidelines in this area do so in order to regulate the 'dangers' involved in hands-on or intimate care of patients/clients. Some professional associations covering those working in people-orientated professions which involve little or no hands-on touch, or where there is no obvious need for recipients or service-users to be semi-clad or naked, nonetheless explicitly stipulate what is 'off-limits' sexually. Perhaps not surprisingly, 'talking' therapies (such as counselling and psychotherapy) offer guidelines which are relatively clear about what is or is not acceptable practice with regard to sex. For example, the British Association of Counselling and Psychotherapy, *Ethical Framework for Good Practice* states unequivocally that: 'Sexual relations with clients are prohibited. *Sexual relations include intercourse, and any other type of sexual activity or sexualised behaviour*' (British Association of Counselling and Psychotherapy 2003: Section 18, emphasis added). Similarly, the British Association for Sexual and Relationship Therapy stipulates that professional practitioners:

> ... must not abuse the client/therapist relationship financially, *sexually*, emotionally or in any other way. Where the use of sexually explicit material is considered to be appropriate within the overall context of therapy, then the matter must be discussed with the client and the nature of the material and the reasons for its use explained so that the client can give informed consent as to its use.
> (British Association for Sexual and Relationship Therapy 2003: Sections 3.1, 3.5 and 3.6, emphasis added)

In the case of 'talking' therapies of this kind then, the potential 'dangers' are much more explicitly acknowledged and hence something more is at stake here than a concern with sex as it inheres in health-care professions where hands-on touch and bodily exposure is required.

We argue that what is crucial in the case of 'talking therapies' is the nature of the professional care and support offered. It is often claimed that in the case of the in-depth work of counsellors and psychotherapists, the clients' energetic and/or emotional 'boundaries' are precarious and permeable and must not therefore be unduly 'violated'. In all this then, a particular construction of 'victims' and 'victimhood' is made manifest, for what operates herein is a notion of consenting, adult 'victims' whose bodily (and 'extra-bodily') 'boundaries' are considered to be so weak and fluid that they can all too easily be 'penetrated'. This notion of 'victims' characterized by the excessive permeability of their energetic and/or emotional 'boundaries' can also be seen in some of the complementary and alternative therapies. For example, professional associations governing modalities such as Reiki explicitly state that no sexual contact is permissible. Yet Reiki has little or no hands-on or 'talk' element, clothes are not removed during treatment sessions and Reiki practitioners work in a 'hands-off' position in what is known as the 'subtle' or 'astral' body of the client. Nonetheless, the UK Reiki Federation *Codes of Ethics and Standards of Practice for Reiki* (2003) states:

> Reiki Practitioners must not exploit their clients financially, sexually, emotionally or in any other way. The Practitioner *will not undertake any form of sexual activity* with a client in their care or with a student in their tutelage or supervision
>
> (UK Reiki Federation 2003, emphasis added)

In this way then, there is an extension of the discursive constitution of 'victims' such that 'victims' of professional sex are adults for whom no resistance or withdrawal of consent is relevant or possible. This is because upon entering into relationships with professionals, the 'boundaries' of such 'victims' are deemed to be so fluid as to render them immaterial. In short, these are 'victims' for whom 'boundaries' are already effaced.

So it is neither 'intimacy' nor hands-on bodily contact *per se*, nor the extent to which 'modesty' is compromised by states of undress, that is at the heart of this symbolic constitution of the 'wrongfulness' of professional sex. Although all of these are not insignificant, what is crucial in terms of what is being regulated here are not shadowy, unknowable 'perpetrators' who prey upon weak, powerless 'victims'. Indeed, what we have here are often otherwise responsible and trustworthy *professionals,* who somehow violate 'boundaries' that are already constituted as fluid and elastic. Indeed, such 'perpetrators' can all too easily be considered blameless, for it is assumed that they have somehow unwittingly overstepped lines which are so finely drawn as to be almost indiscernible. This in effect shifts the ground upon which professional associations devise the 'rules of engagement' concerning illicit sex. For what becomes the object of regulation is very often not sexual activities, behaviours or conduct, but 'improper' relationships. But even here, the regulation of sex in terms of an 'improper relationship' (even and especially when it is consensual) is ambiguous. Indeed, many professional associations warn against 'improper relationships', but do not make it clear what this means. Take for example the General Council for Chiropractors *Code of Practice*, which stipulates that: 'Chiropractors shall not use their professional position as a means of pursuing an *improper personal relationship* with a patient' (General Council for Chiropractors 1999: Section 2.6.1, emphasis added). Despite the vague and coy references, however, it can be argued that what matters most is not the delineation of which activities and behaviours might constitute sex, but *who it (sex) is done with, when, where and under what conditions.* Illustrative of this is, for example, the Register of Exercise Professionals (2003) *Code of Ethical Practice*, which stipulates that: 'fitness professionals will avoid sexual intimacy with clients *while instructing, or immediately after a training session'* (Register of Exercise Professionals 2003: Principle 2, emphasis added). So the 'problem' is not that the sex that takes place (if it does) is 'wrong', but that it takes place between the 'wrong' people, at the 'wrong' times and in the 'wrong' places. However, rationales for why informal regulations draw lines (as above) between illicit sex during or immediately after training sessions (but not hours, days or weeks later), remain unspoken and unspecified.

In Chapter 4, arguments were put forward regarding the constitution of 'victims' and 'victimhood' of sexual harassment. In the case of those regulations, it was argued that 'victims' are paradoxically constituted as both impossibly knowing *and* reasonable. It was also argued that equal opportunities, anti-harassment and bullying policies of the kind put in place to regulate 'uninvited', 'unwelcome' and 'unwanted' sex between employees, colleagues and so on, make little reference to disparities of power and status. Not so in the case of professional codes of ethics, for here there are clear indications that the illicit sex taking place between professionals and their recipients or service-users may well be invited, welcome and wanted. Indeed, it may even be initiated by 'victims'. Hence such consensual, adult sex can only be pronounced as 'wrongful' because of the *disparities of power and status between the adults involved*. This then takes us to the nub of the 'problem' which policy guidelines on nuisance sex rarely if ever make manifest; namely, that what is 'wrong' about sex between 'consenting' adults is that it can breach the 'trust' which is somehow thought to belong in adult–adult sexual relationships. Indeed, professional associations' codes of ethics often do not need to provide lengthy illustrations of what constitutes 'wrongful' sex, for this sex is 'wrong' simply because it is between the 'wrong' people. In short, professional associations establish the 'inappropriateness' of the sexual relationships they regulate in terms which make it clear that even if consensual, 'normal' and 'natural', these are still the 'wrong' people to be having sex. However, this opens up a further dimension, for such discursive constructions of 'wrongful' relationships allow for *any* relationship between professionals and recipients or service-users to be constituted as 'wrong', including romantic and 'courtship' relationships. As such, sex does not have to take place. Witness, for example, the Association of University Teachers (2003), where professional guidelines make clear that:

> To embark upon a sexual/*romantic relationship* with a student will always involve serious risks and may involve serious difficulties rooted in the unequal power, and hence choice, of the parties concerned.
> (Association of University Teachers 2003: 1, emphasis added)

At this point we want to emphasize that all this opens wide the floodgates, for no longer is the 'problem' of professional sex considered to lie only in settings where 'modesty' and 'intimacy' are compromised or 'boundaries' are violated. Instead, understandings of professional sex as 'wrong' because it is that which takes place in relationships marked by unequal power and status, means that endless possibilities are opened up for the inclusion of all and any sex in these informal regulatory frameworks. For it is clear that 'wrongful' sex, when collapsed into constructions of the 'wrong' people, means that that which requires regulation is 'sex' that occurs anywhere, anyhow or at any time that anyone comes into contact with a professional within (and often beyond) professional contexts. Hence, in this hugely extended construction of 'wrongful' sex, what needs to be controlled includes those 'consensual' sexual relationships which overlap with 'professional life' in all manner of ways. This is the 'problem' of what is known in many professional circles as 'dual relationships' (Borys and Pope 1989; Pope 1991) or 'overlapping relationships' (Saks Berman 1985). What this means in effect is that wherever professionalism is, no one and nowhere is entirely sexually 'safe', since 'wrongful' sex may be perpetrated even when a professional relationship is over. Indeed, such sex may even be subsumed under some other legitimate relationship such as casual and/ or long-term partnership or even a legal, monogamous marriage *and still be 'wrong'*.

At this point, it can be argued that several professional codes of ethics have huge difficulties in wrestling with this 'problem' of dual relationships. This is because such 'rules of engagement' are dealing with the requirement of identifying and delimiting 'wrongful' sex in terms of the *who*, rather than the *what*, of sexual encounters between consenting adults. Professional guidance thus lists the categories of people with whom the professional must not come into 'sexual' contact. Witness for example, the British Association of Social Work *Code of Ethics*, in which members are warned:

> ... not to engage in any form of intimate or sexual conduct with *current service users, students, supervisees, research participants, or with others directly involved in a professional relationship which involves an unequal distribution of power or authority in the social worker's favour.*
> (British Association of Social Work 2003:
> Section 3.4.2.g, emphasis added)

Moreover, it is not simply current or on-going relationships with any of these people that are subject to regulation. For in the case of some of the professional associations already mentioned, consensual sex involving adults who were *former* patients, clients and service-users is also deemed to be 'wrong'. For example, the UK Council for Psychotherapy *Codes of Ethics* states:

> Engaging in sexual activity with a *past client or student* is normally inadvisable, is only to be taken after a time appropriate to the length and nature of the relationship and with the knowledge of the practitioner's supervisor.
>
> (UK Council for Psychotherapy 1999, emphasis added)

Similarly, the British Association of Social Work (2003) *Code of Ethics* advises members:

> … not to enter into an intimate or sexual relationship with a *former* service user without careful consideration of any potential for exploitation, taking advice as appropriate.
>
> (British Association of Social Work 2003:
> Section 3.4.2.h, emphasis added)

In effect, such quasi-official discourse acts to control *all* professional relationships even when they are, for all intents and purposes, no longer professional relationships. What this means in effect is that any sex with anyone professionals have come into contact with in the past, even (and perhaps especially) when sex mirrors otherwise 'normal', 'natural' and legal relationships, is open to being constructed as 'wrongful'. Indeed, several professional associations specifically forbid dual relationships, and advise members, once sexual and professional relationships overlap, to 'terminate' the professional relationship with the recipient or service-user. For example, the UK Reiki Foundation *Codes of Ethics and Standards for Practice* unequivocally requires that a registered practitioner: 'formally ends the therapeutic or educational relationship *before* starting a sexual relationship' (UK Reiki Foundation 2002, emphasis added).

Hence if professionals are to be (and be seen as) responsible and respectable, safe and trustworthy, it would appear that no sex with anyone they heal, treat, educate, serve or otherwise minister is ever permissible. However, there are further complications here, for some professional association guidelines also admit the possibility that professional sex may actually 'benefit' (rather than 'damage') recipients or service-users inasmuch as the latter may be granted 'special favours' as a direct result of such relations. In other words, we argue here that what this allows for is the possibility of 'victims' who are not 'victims' at all, but are – paradoxically – 'beneficiaries'. For example, the College of Occupational Therapists (2000) *Code of Ethics and Professional Conduct for Occupational Therapists* explicitly states:

> The College considers it unethical for occupational therapists to indulge in relationships which may impair their professional judgement and objectivity and/or give rise to the *advantageous/ disadvantageous* treatment of the client.
>
> (College of Occupational Therapists 2000:
> Section 4.2, emphasis added)

In other words, whilst the unequal power and status of professionals as against their patients and clients confers 'wrongness' upon any sex involving the parties concerned, at the same time, it is possible to reconstitute 'perpetrators' of professional sex as positively benign (rather than malign and so forth) precisely because they are able to offer their 'victims' favourable treatment. This opens up a further possibility, since (as hinted at above) it allows for the inclusion of all and any sexual relationships, including legal and marital relationships, which are entered into by 'benign benefactors' and 'favoured beneficiaries'. In the case of professional sex then, it can be argued that such sexual/ professional relationships are simultaneously constituted as both 'right' and 'wrong'. Indeed, all this rests upon novel and highly paradoxical discursive constructions of 'perpetrators' and 'victims' since these are deemed to be 'inadvisable' but otherwise legitimate relationships, in which notions of who 'benefits' and who is 'at risk' have become especially contorted and confused. Hence it is that professional sex can be constituted as desirable and rewarding for both parties, whilst at the same time it gives rise to suspicions and concerns about the 'wrongness' of such sex because these are still the 'wrong' adults to be having sex.

Such contortions and confusions in the regulation of professional sex become particularly pronounced in cases where a consensual and legal sexual relationship between two adults exists prior to any professional relationship. Such relationships are constituted as both problematic and risky as well as 'normal' and 'natural'. This is because they tend to confound the boundaries between, on the one hand, the 'private' and familial and on the other, the 'public' and professional. The ethics of such relationships are frequently contested, with many professionals claiming that the 'wrongness' of sex in such contexts is not a matter for organizational regulation because it is not 'harmful' or 'exploitative'. Indeed, the difficulty of specifying the 'wrongness' of some dual relationships is reflected in many professional associations' codes of ethics. For example, the British Psychological Society (2000) operates with a policy statement which admits that:

Some dual relationships may not be harmful although the risks of damage to the normally impartial professional role of the more senior partner, or to the personal or social status of the more junior partner, are high.

(British Psychological Society 2000: 39, emphasis added)

Hence, whilst some professional associations do admit that consensual, adult sexual relationships which pre-date and/or run parallel with professional relationships pose particular problems in terms of what is 'right' or 'wrong', nonetheless precisely what the 'high risks' are is only specified in vague terms, for example, of 'impaired judgement'. However, that some professional associations admit any difficulties at all in this respect is an interesting turn inasmuch as sex within legally and socially recognized relationships such as marriage is not traditionally viewed as a 'problem' at all. Indeed monogamous couple sex is usually regarded as just about as 'safe' and legitimate as any sex can possibly be, and any notion that within such relationships there may be 'perpetrators' and 'victims' is hard (although not impossible) for the symbolic landscapes which underpin sex regulation to sustain in any meaningful way.

The analysis undertaken so far has highlighted the point that drawing the line around that which is beneficial or harmful, benign or exploitative, in terms of sex involving consenting adults, is a highly problematic undertaking. It is particularly difficult for professional associations to regulate and control sex between professionals and recipients or service-users where the latter are also partners, spouses or family members of the professional concerned, since it is clearly difficult for such a moral authoritarian project as the one we explicate here to establish how 'inequalities of power and status' can still operate within and/or overlap with 'natural' and 'normal' sexual relations involving consenting adults, such that these relationships are to the detriment of 'victims' (and the benefit of 'perpetrators'). For what is required in order for the regulations to make sense is that heterosexual couple relationships, generally held up to be the epitome of 'rightful' sexual relations, become reconfigured as 'suspect' and 'wrong'. In effect, sex within the context of such relationships has to be proscribed as 'unethical'. Such governance of illicit sex in these particular contexts, however, is made possible because it is the very 'perpetrators' (professionals themselves) who occupy a unique and often unquestioned platform from which to pronounce upon ethics and morality. Indeed, we argue that regarding sex, 'professional experts' are often constituted as moral guardians *par excellence*.

Religious professionals: regulating sex from the moral high ground

From here, we take our analysis forward by examining particular settings in which the regulation of professional sex takes on special moral meaning, namely in the churches and associated organizations. It is possible to argue that what all the professional guidelines discussed so far have in common is an overwhelming concern with *ethics*. Professional ethics rest upon the need for those in positions of power within official institutions (like medicine, law and the Church) to be seen to be in 'right' relation with those they heal, educate, represent, minister to or otherwise care for. It is interesting to note that the vast majority of 'professionals' who make up the various religious denominations in the UK do not tend to belong to professional associations as such and the churches (or other bodies) for whom they work do not tend to have codes of ethics of the kind already discussed. In that sense, they are 'above the law'. However, this is not to say that there are no quasi-official guidelines within these organizations, and whilst they do not currently have the power of professional associations to discipline members (clergy being answerable in the final instance to God and their conscience), they are moving in that direction. A flavour of all this can be gleaned from the Presbyterian Church of Wales, for example, which operates with a *Book of Order and Rules* which under 'Rules of Church Discipline' states:

> *It is not practicable to draw up a list of transgressions and specify the appropriate discipline for each one.* This must be left to the conscience and judgement of the church and it must administer judgement in accordance with the nature of the transgression, taking into consideration on the one hand the age, experience, history and circumstances of the transgressor, and on the other the discipline which would be appropriate.
> (Presbyterian Church of Wales 2003, emphasis added)

However, informal policy guidance such as this could be used to argue that the professionalism of religious ministers is deemed to be unassailable. Certain professions then are always and already positioned as those who can 'do no wrong'. If, however, we turn to bodies like the Scouting Association, a different picture emerges and, although Scouting was originally a movement with organized religious connections, Scout leaders are clearly seen as potential 'perpetrators' of sexual 'wrong-doing'. This may be because Scouting, albeit a respectable and reputable 'profession', has been deemed a 'problematic' arena in terms of the elisions between adult–adult and adult–child sexual relationships.

It is interesting to note that the Scouting Association (2003) offers explicit guidance with reference to sexual relations between leaders and members in the same Scouting group. Their guidelines state:

> Such a relationship is unacceptable even when the young person is over the age of consent or emotionally mature. A Leader has re-sponsibility and authority over the young people in his or her Group or Section, and therefore has a power over Members of their Section or Group which is open to manipulation in a sexual relationship.
>
> (Scouting Association 2003)

However, these guidelines include an additional proviso concerning 'genuine' sexual relationships. In this respect, the regulations go on to state that:

> ... this should not be interpreted to mean that no genuine relationship can start between two people within a relationship of trust. But given the inequality at the heart of a relationship of trust, the relationship of trust should be ended before any sexual relationship develops.
>
> (Scouting Association 2003)

On the face of it, such guidance speaks of moral prescriptions against sex in trust-based relationships but ultimately, a deft sleight of hand is at work here inasmuch as it is deemed that 'relationships of trust' can be 'genuine relationships' where it is accepted that consensual sex can legitimately enter the frame. At the same time such relationships are also deemed to be 'unacceptable' because they involve 'power' which is open to 'manipulation'. At this point then, it is clear that professional guidelines which attempt to draw the line between what is 'right' and 'wrong' with regard to professional sex, run into the near-impossibility of so doing. This is because in such symbolic constructions, *trust* must be collapsed into *power inequalities* and this is a difficult formation to achieve. Not surprisingly, even what we have referred to as 'moral guardians' (namely, professional experts occupying the moral high ground) may find themselves caught in bizarre constructions of what is 'right' and 'wrong' about trust-based sex. For example, in the case of consensual sexual relationships between two youth members of the Scouting Association which are defined, according to the guidance given, as *'unlawful'* (presumably because one party is under the age of 16), the guidelines state:

> … Leaders … should give guidance in the best interests of each of the young people. This will depend upon the emotional maturity of each of the young people, and their relationship with their parent(s)/guardians. Leaders should explain the legal position, and the consequences, to them, but *should be warned that a determinedly legalistic approach is unlikely to be helpful.*
>
> (Scouting Association 2003, emphasis added)

In short, even where *illegal* sex is taking place, the professionals concerned are advised to act more as moral guardians rather than heavy-handed police. These quasi-official codifications then, ultimately position professionals as above the formal law even.

Such guidelines also carry symbolic weight inasmuch as they provide informal guidance based, on the face of it, upon ethical and moral principles. Ultimately, however, such regulations are highly contra-dictory. We argue that this is because at heart they are based upon sets of assumptions concerned not with the 'protection' of 'victims' (although they may appear to be all about that), but with the conferring of moral authority upon professional institutions/bodies. In other words, we argue that the informal regulation of adult sex in professional, trust-based relationships is not primarily about safeguarding 'victims' as such, but is more about constituting professionals as moral guardians. Herein lies the crux of the matter, for the regulations concerning professional sex, as laid down by professional associations, do not make sense unless they are understood as being not solely or even primarily about protecting recipients or service users *but about promoting the status and standing of professionals as a self-regulating body.* Why and how such developments have become vital to the moral authoritarian project we unpack in this book, will become clear in the next section.

Constituting professionals as moral guardians

We need to make clear what is being argued here, for the constitution of professional sex is key to our overall analysis of sex regulation and control in contemporary UK society. Firstly, this chapter has argued that many people-orientated professional associations do not offer clear, unequivocal guidelines on 'sex' *per se*. Sex in such codifications is not usually referred to as 'sex' and is typically spoken of in terms of 'mal-practice', 'misconduct' or other 'transgressions'. The absence of many precise references to 'sex' speaks volumes for, amongst other things, it allows professionals to separate themselves from those who are non-professional or unprofessional, including those in sex-related sectors of the economy, including those working in the prostitution and pornography 'industries'. This means that, with few if any exceptions (such as sex therapists), professionals do not ever speak of or undertake 'sex' as part of their legitimate work or business. This has extremely wide-ranging ramifications in terms of placing sex outside the remit of what professionals do. For to be professional, it is not deemed per-missible to undertake any sexual contact with recipients or service-users at all, even when it is fully consensual. Secondly, it has been argued that the underlying concern with 'professionalism' in many professional regulations is to do with delimiting 'wrongful' sex from the pro-fessional's point of view. In health care and other therapeutic settings, for example, being seen to be professional is often constituted in terms of creating safe 'space'. Without this professional 'safety', patients/clients are thought to be at risk of becoming confused over the boundaries between treatment, intimacy and sex, and hence it is always deemed to be the responsibility of the professional to be clear about and maintain 'appropriate boundaries' around the potential elisions between treat-ment, intimacy and sex (Clarkson 1995, Gonsiorek 1995, Shardlow 1995). Indeed, it is almost never deemed to be the patient/client's responsi-bility to hold 'appropriate' boundaries, and with this, they are constituted as utterly powerless in relationship to professional 'experts'. Thirdly, it has been argued that there is a need for professionals to appear altruistic, motivated not by self-interest but by the 'best interests' of those they serve. In situations where professionals become sexually involved with a current (or even former) student, patient or client, they are deemed to be compromising their professional status and standing and bringing their profession into disrepute. Many professionals believe that it is important that the public have confidence in them and imputations that any sex is taking place are thought to shake that con-fidence and deter people from approaching, and remaining in the care of, professionals. Clearly, this is a threat to professionalism that must be carefully monitored. Fourthly, professional codes of ethics reflect underlying concerns about impartiality; if professionals engage in sex with those with whom they have professional relationships, then it is thought that certain 'favours' may be bestowed or 'rewards' offered.

Whilst this may appear to be problematic because all professionals are meant to be fair, even-handed and impartial, many professional association guidelines also permit (indeed, sanction) the notion that professionals can be benign (as well as malign) in terms of their sexual relationships with those they serve. Such contorted discursive constructions of 'wrongful' sex (for example, as 'beneficial' rather than 'damaging' to recipients or service-users) uphold notions of professionals as caring and altruistic, working for the welfare of others and not for the good of themselves. However, they also permit what we argue is a very dangerous discursive construction, namely the possibility of the 'professional-perpetrator', the 'benign benefactor', upholding the 'social good' and supporting the very moral authoritarian project we explicate in this book.

So whilst it is not surprising that embedded in many professional associations' codes of ethics are notions of professional responsibility and accountability, we argue that here (as elsewhere) there are novel extensions to the terrain upon which the discursive constitution of illicit sexual conduct is being mapped out. From what has been argued above, it would appear that on the face of it, no professional is ever permitted to have *any sex* with *anyone* with whom they have (or have had) a professional relationship. In that respect we are dealing here with what Rutter (1995) has called 'sex in the forbidden zone', a term he uses to describe: '*any sexual contact* that occurred within professional *relationships of trust*' (Rutter 1995: 11, emphases added). Notwithstanding all this, many professionals are simultaneously constituted as 'subject to temptation', particularly when the sex in question, albeit illicit, closely mirrors 'normal' or 'natural' sex. As Lakin (1988) puts it with regard to psychotherapy:

> ... intimacy and client neediness can also tempt the therapist to respond – to express caring and affection – in ways that are appropriate ... *to ordinary, loving relationships.*
>
> (Lakin 1988: 65, emphasis added)

In effect, professional relationships can all too easily be reconfigured as 'loving' relationships. This permits highly anomalous discursive constructions of 'perpetrators' who are caring authority figures ('benign benefactors') and since 'perpetrators' may be configured as 'benign benefactors', 'victims' too are effectively 'victimless' because they are robbed of any possibility of their own 'victimhood', becoming instead 'beneficiaries' of professional 'favours' and so on. Finally, we also want to draw attention to the manner in which most professional association guidelines do not allow for any differentiation between professionals who are deemed sexually predatory and professionals who, it is supposed, unwittingly and inappropriately wander across ill-defined 'boundaries'. As such then, professionals circumvent any suggestions that they may be 'sexual offenders' by positioning themselves as largely operating for the 'good of all'.

Because there is a widespread consensus that at face value, the professional regulation and control of illicit sex has less to do with protecting professional interests and more to do with promoting the well-being of recipients or service-users, professionals (and their regulatory associations) therefore escape scrutiny and censure. Their motives and intentions appear always and already honourable and blameless. For as has been shown, most professional associations maintain that the regulations surrounding 'sex in the forbidden zone' (Rutter 1995) exist because whenever and wherever there is sexual 'misconduct' or 'malpractice', there are serious consequences, first and foremost, *for those on the receiving end of professional help and support.* Indeed, frequent mention is made by professionals themselves of the ambivalence, confusion and guilt experienced by those who are 'victims' of professional 'misconduct' or 'malpractice'. As such, professionals are constituted first and foremost as the people who do the protecting. And by positioning themselves as protectors who do not themselves need protection, as trustworthy rather than as abusers of trust, the moral authoritarian project around 'sex' that, we maintain, has taken a particular 'turn' in the period in which New Labour has held office, is safely buttressed and sustained. Such a project elevates professionals, including professional politicians, to the standing of powerful, unassailable protectors of morality, benign purveyors of justice and the 'greater good' and ultimately, trustworthy 'public servants'. This serves to create further discursive closure not only around the notion of illicit sex, but more particularly around the notion of who has the power and authority to pronounce upon that sex which is to be constituted as illicit and illegal.

Conclusions

In the final analysis then, it is clear from what has been argued above that professional association guidelines reflect ethical and moral concerns which are held to be about the 'social good' (Koehn 1994). Indeed, professionalism is axiomatically seen as being about acting ethically and morally beyond reproach (Sim 1997, Tadd 1998, Dowrick and Frith 1999,

Banks 2001). Moreover, many of the ethical and moral precepts contained in professional association codes of conduct have been well-rehearsed in the literature on professional ethics (Gabriel and Davies 2000). What this means is that because professionals are deemed always to uphold this wider 'social good', any sexual conduct at all presents 'problems' in terms of exposing professionals to charges of being potential 'perpetrators'. Indeed, underlying concerns with the 'dangers' of professional sex are made most manifest in relationships where consenting adults enter into sexual/professional relationships with one another, for it is here that 'professionals-as-perpetrators' stand at risk of being unveiled. As a result, many of the professional codes of ethics we have examined in this chapter operate to obscure who is perpetrating what 'wrongs' upon whom. For whilst appearing to be about protecting 'victims' against inequalities of power, the underlying concerns in all this are much more about infringing *'norms' of unequal power*. As Jehu (1994) glibly reveals in relation to sex between psychotherapists and counsellors and their clients: 'For therapists to *misuse* this unequal power for their own sexual gratification is unfair and unethical' (Jehu 1994: 9, emphasis added). What this means is that it is not the exercise of unequal power and authority in itself that is 'wrong', for that would be to destabilize the edifice upon which professionalism is built. In effect, what professional codes of ethics do is maintain that it is only when such power and authority is 'misused' that it is 'wrong'. As a result, it is interesting to note, New Labour has recently moved to curb the power of those 'professionals' who are thought to be most in danger of 'abusing' positions of trust. In the consultation document, *Protecting the Public*, for example, an extension to the construction of 'victims' of sex enacted in trust-based relationships was proposed, so that the legislation covered: *'children aged 18 or under* in educational establishments and various residential settings such as prisons' (Home Office 2002: 26). The document went on to make clear the government's intention to:

> … expand the scope of this offence to include *personal advisers* and *those who care for, advise, supervise or train young people in the community on a one-to-one basis in pursuance of a court order made in the criminal justice system.*
>
> (Home Office 2002: 27, emphases added)

At this point, some of the fine cracks or fissures in the edifice of professionalism are exposed, for it could not be made more clear that those in whom public trust has been placed to *care for* 'offenders', are nothing more than (potential) 'sex offenders' themselves.

This is not to suggest, however, that the regulation of professional sex does not ultimately serve the wider purpose of legitimating the unequal power and authority of those who 'rule' on all matters of sexual conduct. As Allison (1997) states:

> In a professional role, the professional *makes an ethical covenant with society* to exercise self-restraint, to give and not take from the parishioner/patient/client/student, and to monitor self-interests.
> (Allison 1997: 2, emphasis added)

It is in the guise of ethical, honest and trustworthy moral guardian or 'public servant' that the 'professional-perpetrator' of illicit sex can most readily afford to stand fully revealed for who they are – no longer a hidden, shadowy figure but a bright and shining 'guiding light'. Furthermore, the power of such discursive constructions of 'professional-perpetrators' as 'protectors' (rather than 'abusers') should not be under-estimated, for what all this illustrates is the enormous weight and standing that professionals carry in contemporary society. This is a crucial point as it permits the erasure, re-writing and 'silencing' of other constructions around the 'problems' and 'dangers' of illegal and illicit sex. For we argue that not only have professionals positioned themselves as moral guardians *par excellence* but that it is increasingly the case that only professions can occupy this space. Despite their attempts, no other social institutions/bodies have the moral authority associated with professions like law, medicine, education and counselling, social work and the like. When all else fails, these are the 'good people'. And given the ways in which the moral authority that was traditionally thought to rest in institutions like the 'family' has now come to be seen as eroded, professionals have now assumed rights and responsibilities which permit them to act as powerful, benign and trustworthy purveyors of the 'social good' in most matters concerning the conduct of sexual activities, behaviours and relationships. So just at that historical moment when the family has been emptied of its protective guardianship of vulnerable members (children and young people), in its stead have come powerful bodies deemed to be not only trustworthy 'public servants' but also caring and loving 'parents-in-loco'. Just how secure a moral project this is, and where the outermost limits to it lie, will be explored in the next chapter.

Chapter 7

Transgressive and digital sex: margins, edges and limitless victims

German 'cannibal' charged with murder

A German man who confessed to killing and eating a man he met through a website for cannibals has been charged with murder, prosecutors have said. The 41-year old suspect, identified as Armin M, is alleged to have killed the 43-year old victim in March 2001 in the town of Rotenburg in central Germany, after meeting him through the site. He then carved up and froze portions of the man's flesh, later eating some of it, prosecutors allege. The crime was apparently carried out with the victim's full consent, however state prosecutor Hans-Manfred Jung told French news agency AFP that the victim's supposed 'death wish' did not change the fact that the killer had wanted to commit murder. The suspect's arrest in December last year caused a sensation in Germany, as the country's tabloids competed to report the most grisly details of the case.

'Sexual enjoyment'
The suspect and victim met in early 2001, after Armin M is said to have posted a personal ad on several websites and in chatrooms asking for 'young, well-built men aged 18 to 30 to slaughter', the German daily newspaper Bild reported at the time of his arrest. The victim was a 43-year old Berlin computer technician who had sold his car, written a will and taken the day off work to sort out what he called a 'personal' matter. He then went to Armin M's home, where the pair reportedly agreed to cut off his penis. The victim was then allegedly stabbed to death – still apparently with his approval – and cut into pieces. The whole incident was filmed on videotape, and prosecutors say that the whole crime was committed for the purpose of sexual enjoyment.

(BBC News World Edition 17 July 2003)

Introduction

In this chapter we continue to explore the concerns that have underpinned much of the previous two chapters dealing with quasi-official discourses of sex. Our focus in what follows is upon the regulation of sex which is for the most part regarded as adult, 'consensual' and, to some extent, freely chosen. Much regulation of 'consensual' sex between adults which is deemed 'wrongful' has, as we have seen, tended to fall under the remit of extra-statutory bodies such as public sector organizations, private business and professional associations, and is thus not illegal as such. Indeed, informal sex regulations appear to deal with what might be deemed less serious 'wrongdoings'. This chapter, however, takes a slightly different approach in that it focuses upon adult sex which is deemed to be at the unruly margins of possibility, either because it is constituted as bizarre, 'unnatural', 'abnormal' and so on, or because it is considered to be unreal, and in some cases so imaginary and fantastic as to be nigh on unthinkable, and by extension, 'un-doable'. In other words, we turn our attention in this chapter to the regulation and control of those sexual activities and behaviours which might be considered to be at the borders or edges of the permissible, desirable or conceivable. To that extent, we are entering uncharted terrain inasmuch as what we have here is sex over which both official and quasi-official discourses range, and around which it has been difficult to enact very much in the way of regulation, whether formal or informal. This is because it is held that any sex at and beyond the outermost limits tends to be implausible and impossible. For example, the regulation of sex with non-human species such as animals (what is popularly known as bestiality or cross-species sex); and sex with the comatose, unconscious or dead (popularly known as necrophilia), constitute some of the 'edgy' or marginal sexual behaviours which we consider here. Such sex might be regarded as so completely 'off-limits' as to require little regulatory intervention, for it can be regarded as but a rare occurrence and thus hardly worthy of the attention of any of the regulatory institutions/bodies we discuss. In that sense, it might not be seen as 'wrongful' inasmuch as it has, until recently, escaped any public or regulatory attention. What has been designated by media commentators as 'vampire sex' (consensual sex involving blood-letting and ingestion of bodily fluids) is a case in point for, to our knowledge, whilst it may not be as unusual as some of the sex we focus upon in this chapter, it has not (as yet) been officially codified in any of the formal or informal regulations we examine.

Nonetheless, although and perhaps because much transgressive – or what the Spanner Trust (2003) term non-conventional – sex might indeed be rare and unusual, there has been a tendency, historically at least, to regulate and control it in somewhat fragmentary, *ad hoc* and inconsistent ways. This means that whilst some transgressive sex has been criminalized, much of it has escaped any formal censure at all, or has been dealt with under psychiatric or mental health legislation. This means that, unlike the sex discussed in the previous two chapters, there are on the face of it, no obvious official or quasi-official regulatory institutions/bodies under whose authority the marginal and 'edgy' sex discussed in this chapter, falls. For example, the RSPCA does not operate 'rules of engagement' for the sexual abuse of animals in the same way that it does cruelty to animals. This may be because such sex is always and already at the outer limits of possibility, undisciplined and to some extent, un-disciplinable. But whilst it may only surface in *ad hoc* regulations, nonetheless, we argue that the interesting, recent and for the purposes of our arguments, important regulatory moves that have taken place in the last decade or so, act to further illustrate the analysis we have developed regarding the underlying sets of assumptions which currently shape the regulation and control of all illegal and illicit sex in the UK. In particular, we argue that both official and quasi-official codifications dealing with transgressive sex raise acute and difficult issues regarding the discursive constitution of 'victims' and 'perpetrators'.

In addition to transgressive sex, we also take as the object of inquiry in this chapter what we have termed digital sex involving explicit verbal, pictorial and/or photographic representations of sex between 'unknowable persons' who, on the face of it, appear to be adult. By virtue of being situated at the 'outer limits', it often appears that on-line sex involves strangers who never meet in 'real life' or engage in any 'real' sex at all (although clearly some do). It is not the 'casual' nature of such sex, however, that is of primary concern to regulatory bodies, but its unknowability. It is argued that because of the anonymity afforded by on-line exchanges, the conventional demarcations between adult–adult, adult–child and child–child sexual encounters (based upon their respective chronological ages) breaks down completely, and it is this that is seen as a 'problem'. Digital sex offers possibilities for 'perpetrators' to become particularly shadowy, slippery and elusive, for it is held that they can all too easily become almost completely indeterminate in terms of conventional markers such as gender, and more worryingly for those who seek to regulate and control illegal sex, age. So whilst we take as the subject of this chapter the regulation of sex involving adults, it is increasingly the case in the digital age that there are no means of knowing whether those involved are really 'adults' at all since they can pass on-line as 'children'. This seems to be at the heart of some of the difficulties of the regulation and control of digital sex. Indeed, concerns are frequently expressed that 'perpetrators' can all too easily pass as other than they are, in attempts to appear attractive to potential 'victims'. As in the previous chapter on professional sex, trust (or lack thereof) appears to be a central motif in the symbolic landscape of 'victims' and 'perpetrators' of digital sex. 'Perpetrators' using digital means of communication can (and do) constitute themselves as trustworthy, caring, potential friends, lovers and/or partners and so forth, when they may 'in reality' be none of these. We are arguing that in effect then, the authors of digital sexual exchanges are the ultimate unknown and unknowable 'perpetrators'. And as in the case of the transgressive sex outlined above, this raises acute and difficult issues regarding the discursive constitution of 'victims' and 'perpetrators', particularly in contexts where humans can no longer be seen to 'really' exist at all.

It is important to note that in terms of the quasi-official discourses surrounding digital sex, what is being regulated is not 'real' sex between 'real' people. However, it is widely held that there is something 'wrong' about on-line sexual encounters/exchanges because, via the internet, 'adults' can enter worlds in which anything is possible, sexually speaking. In many ways then, digital sex offers the ultimate sexual experience, with numerous 'partners' in endless 'permutations'. How is such sex to be regulated (if at all)? The possession and sale of sexually explicit materials is not criminalized as such in the UK at the present time but, as with other commercialized sexual activities, the distribution and consumption of sexually explicit material in digital formats occupies an ambiguous legal position. In both academic and political forums, and not least driven by right-wing crusades and feminist anti-pornographers, there have been well-rehearsed debates about what constitutes 'unacceptable', 'exploitative' and 'objectifying' sexual representations, on the internet and elsewhere (Akdeniz 1999; Akdeniz et al 2000). Taking on board these concerns, some of the informal regulatory frameworks pertaining to digital sex have to date been industry-led but even so, there are difficulties keeping pace with fast-emerging developments regarding 'virtual' sexual possibilities. For example, the Internet Watch Foundation, the UK on-line 'porn watchdog' set up in 1996 to govern the internet and which is largely funded by internet service providers, has only just begun to start looking at the potential 'misuse' (for sexual purposes) of 3G mobile phone technology in which callers can have sight of each other as they talk. Hence we argue that much of the regulation in the area of what we have termed digital sex is as yet embryonic and for the most part, reactive and cautionary.

So ultimately, the central issue we focus upon in this chapter is that of addressing, through an examination of both official and quasi-official discourses, the permissible (and permissive) limits to which any sex, in any form, can be allowed to go. To that extent, the underlying symbolic landscape which we identify and expose herein is premised upon the desirability of constructing and controlling the who, how, where, when and what that marks the 'edges' of sexual possibility. We argue that the regulatory frameworks in the case of both transgressive and digital sex, such as they are, variously construct notions of 'perpetrators' and 'victims' as going beyond the boundaries of the 'human'. We explore how such markers fit with the constructions of 'victims' and 'perpetrators' discussed in previous chapters and in particular, focus upon the discursive distinctions drawn between 'natural' and 'unnatural', 'normal' and 'abnormal', acceptable and unacceptable sex.

Moreover, buried within the regulatory frameworks we discuss is another underlying assumption, namely that in order to wrest power away from the unruly (and seductive) margins of sexual possibility, there is a need to maintain some kind of 'stable centre' in relation to what might be deemed 'normal' and 'natural' sex. Adult, consensual heterosex is still held to be the central motif for the normal and natural, and its discursive maintenance requires that it is cleansed of any 'queer' possibilities. As already argued, one of the assumptions that operates in terms of positioning adult, consensual heterosex as acceptable and legal, normal and ideal, lies in identifying (and outlawing) that sex which is unacceptable and illegal, abnormal and less than ideal. What we are focusing upon here then, might appear at face value to be all those regulations which have as their aim the marking out not only of what (and who) can be regarded as sexually degenerate, depraved and obscene, but also what (and who) can be inscribed as so 'truly' shocking and scandalous as to be beyond the bounds of any 'normal' or 'natural' sexual conduct. In line with our earlier arguments, we want to suggest that what is at stake is a highly political enterprise designed to subject all 'edgy' sexual possibilities to contemporary concerns around 'protection'. In the case of the 'edgy' or marginal sex discussed in this chapter then, the main concern underlying the regulations is how far sex can extend (or rather, be permitted to extend) before it is no longer containable, and before it does harm to those 'adults' whom the regulatory frameworks seek to protect *from themselves*. This is particularly problematic in instances involving sex in which there are no identifiably human 'victims' (or even 'perpetrators') as such.

But before we address the issue of the 'problem' posed by transgressive and digital sex, it is first necessary to examine the ways in which notions of sexual degeneracy and obscenity have been constituted in laws dating back through much of the last 50 or so years, for it is through the regulation of the 'obscene' that normality can most effectively be constituted. It is also possible to see, through tracking such regulatory frameworks, the particular difficulties that inhere in constructing 'victims' and 'perpetrators' where there are, on the face of it, no such persons.

Regulating the obscene

It is possible to argue that regarding sex deemed to be at the 'outer edges' in terms of degeneracy, depravity, obscenity and so on, contemporary society has reached its current impasse because of earlier openings of the 'floodgates'. Indeed, it is suggested that there has already been a dangerous loss of control in terms of drawing very clear lines around the 'threats' posed by sexual degeneracy. New Labour has of late begun targeting the 'permissive' 1960s as the source of all social ills with regard to supposedly licentious sex, with Blair's ethos being made most manifest in his well-publicised attack in July 2004 upon the 1960s as the decade which brought about the erosion of respect, responsibility and discipline. In this regard, it is important to consider the backdrop of formal laws concerning obscenity in the UK which were passed in the late 1950s, and against which more recent moves to regulate and control transgressive and digital sex can be contextualized. We made reference in Chapter 4, in relation to commercialized sexual activities, to the Wolfenden Committee Report (Home Office 1957), where it was pointed out that:

> ... certain forms of sexual behaviour are regarded by many as sinful, morally wrong, or objectionable for reasons of conscience, or of religious or cultural tradition; and such actions may be reprobated on these grounds. But the criminal law does not cover all such actions at the present time: for instance, adultery and fornication are not offences for which a person can be punished by the criminal law.
>
> (Home Office 1957: 10)

We maintain that such admissions make clear the state's reluctance, as far back as the 1950s, to curtail what were deemed to be matters of private sexual morality. As such then, and increasingly over much of the last century, the state sought to distance itself from interfering in what were held to be the *'private* wrongdoings' of consenting adults, since these were regarded as no more than matters of individual conscience. But if and when private immorality strayed into the public realm, it was considered an altogether different affair, although even then, the state occasionally attempted to stand back in the name of individual freedom of expression and so on. This can be illustrated with reference to the debates that took place during the twentieth century around the granting of various 'freedoms' to those who produced and consumed what were variously considered to be erotic/pornographic materials. Although such debates have a 'long tail' dating back to the eighteenth century, it is worth noting for the purposes of our arguments, that it was the 1950s, not the 1960s, that was the key decade with regard to the liberalization of formal controls of 'obscene' materials in the UK. By the end of the decade, the Obscene Publications Act 1959 (followed by the 1964 Amendment to the Act) was passed. Both these Acts wrestled with two overlapping issues. Firstly, how far issues of 'private' sexual morality were an appropriate object of legal control; and secondly, how far the state should go in attempting to regulate for what were held to be the corrupting, corrosive effects of 'obscene' materials should they fall into the hands of those held to be impressionable and vulnerable. What resulted was a reassertion of the liberal principle of not suppressing any individual sexual conduct or activity unless or until it could be demonstrated that harm, injury or offence was caused. In effect, this meant that formal regulation hinged on the necessity of producing 'victims' (and denouncing 'perpetrators'). The difficulties of so doing were made manifest in contexts where no clear 'victims' (or 'perpetrators') could be identified, largely because whatever sex took place involved, on the face of it, fully consenting adults whose choice was to produce and consume erotica/pornography in the comfort and safety of the 'private' realm. This increasingly came to be regarded as a matter of legitimate (and even 'safe') individual freedom of expression, individual sexual proclivity, taste and so on.

It is important to note that in such a 'victimless' landscape, aspiring 'professionals' (writers, artists, photographers, film-makers) were able to position themselves as the 'victims' of draconian censorship. Indeed, calls for reform to the laws on obscenity in much of the twentieth century were made on the grounds of more clearly distinguishing 'true' obscenity from works of art or literature, particularly when the latter could be legitimately classed as 'high' cultural products or artefacts. Indeed, the Obscene Publications Act (1959) starts with the declaration that it was drafted in order to 'provide for the protection of literature'. To achieve this, the Act makes explicit the notion that an article is to be deemed 'obscene' if its effects, when taken as a whole, tend to deprave or corrupt the adult persons who are likely to read, see or hear the material contained within. Hence the 'problem' with 'obscene' materials was reconstituted in official discourse as being about the effects of *public* visibility of *private* depravity. Analysis of the contents of the Williams Report of the Committee on Obscenity and Film Censorship (1979) (hereafter Williams Report) provides further illustration of how and why mid to late twentieth century statutes regulating 'obscenity' took the shape they did. It can be argued that underlying all the regulations in this area are assumptions about what is 'natural' and 'normal' sex (and by extension, what is not). More importantly for our purposes here, the formal controls that were put in place to deal with what was deemed to be 'obscenity', involved complicated and contradictory constructions of public and private moralities. Indeed, we argue that one of the central issues surrounding the regulatory framing of all 'edgy' sex is the extent to and ways in which privately expressed sexual proclivities and preferences are to be allowed public freedom of expression. The symbolic separation of private moralities from the public realm, however, is one that can never be entirely sustained. Nonetheless, the inheritance from all these earlier regulations has been a legacy whereby the 'problem' of depravity is primarily constituted as one of its public presence – namely, of its having corrosive and corrupting effects on 'ordinary' and 'decent' citizens, particularly those who are impressionable and vulnerable by virtue of their particular sensitivities and sensibilities. But as for the 'private' consumption of explicit sexual materials, in the words of the Williams Report (1979), that was, and still is, regarded as 'a matter for private taste'.

We argue that at its centre, the 'problem' of 'obscene' sex has been constituted as a liberal one of ensuring that the otherwise legitimate but 'depraved' sexual preferences and proclivities of some (albeit immoral, unnatural and abnormal) adults do not overly contaminate the sexual tastes of those (moral, normal, natural) adults who make different choices. In short, this has been held to be simply and solely a 'problem' of where to draw the line in terms of what is permissible with regard to conventional/non-conventional sex involving consenting adults. Indeed, for much of the past five decades, what this has led to, as in the case of the formal regulations surrounding the sale of sex through prostitution-related activities, is not 'rules of engagement' which target 'obscene' sex itself, but controls to deal with the commercial and trading activities surrounding 'obscene' sex. In short, it is the public visibility of sex which offends ordinary citizens and/or is deemed an insult to public decency, and as such the result has been a vast regulatory infrastructure

to them. By definition, these were *individual* rather than collective and as such, much transgressive sex was considered to be asocial inasmuch as regulations only operated to protect 'normal' citizenry from the worst excesses of those who made 'depraved' sexual choices. This is not what is assumed to be the case in more recent official and quasi-official discourses, where the 'risks' associated with and posed by transgressive and digital sex are considered to be more fully social. But these newly collectivized 'dangers' are held to be simultaneously hyper-real and unreal. Furthermore, in such constructions, notions of 'consent' (and 'adulthood') are robbed of any meaningful contextual underpinning, such that anybody (including non-human, sub-human and post-human 'victims') can be unknowingly targeted in all manner of unspecified ways. Such discursive re-workings have rested upon a symbolic extension of precisely who (or what) are the 'victims' of such sex, and who (or what) are the 'perpetrators'. This has been made possible because of shifts in the conditions of possibility for sex, such that it is widely assumed in both official and quasi-official discourses that there has been a widespread 'seepage' or 'leakage' of sexual degeneracy from the 'margins' to the 'centre', so that everyone (including the comatose, animals and the dead) is now in need of 'protection' from a host of hyper-inflated, unknown and unknowable 'perpetrators'. To that extent, every body (conscious or unconscious, alive or dead, whether belonging to human or non-human species) is now considered to be a 'victim' inasmuch as they may fall prey to transgressive, fantastic and unruly sexual appetites and desires. Hence it has now, according to recent government proclamations (Home Office 2002), become necessary to outlaw very specific sexual practices, such as sexual activities with the dead and with animals, which were until very recently untouched by law.

As already explained and in addition to our focus upon the formal regulation of sex which is regarded as almost completely 'off limits' (such as sex with the dead or with animals), our other concern in this chapter is with the regulation (or attempted regulation) of digital sex, particularly that which takes place in virtual 'cyber sex' forums such as the internet, interactive sex games, instant picture messaging and so on. Digital sex has a history of largely ineffective regulation, since it involves that which is simulated and imaginary; it is not actually happening between embodied 'real' persons in 'real' spatial and temporal locations. Sex is often given meaning because it is assumed to be a material, bounded experience that takes place *in situ*. Sex is also assumed to take place primarily between embodied persons, not re-formulated 'figures' who have been reduced to computerized bytes and pixels. But, as was touched upon in the previous chapter on professional sex where the permeability of energetic and emotional 'boundaries' was discussed in the context of rendering clients/patients particularly 'vulnerable' to off-body sexual 'violations', much official and quasi-official discourse now constitutes any and every illicit and/or illegal sexual encounter as involving a breaking of undefined 'borders', an immersion into realms which do not only or solely involve bodily-based sexual experiences, and may in some respects not be 'embodied' (or even 'sexual') at all. In this way, both official and quasi-official discourses constitute 'sex' as an utterly inclusive category for it now includes that which is only ever possible through being non-material, disembodied and to an extent, fantastic. Indeed, that it is 'purely' or 'only' fantasy has long been held as the attraction of much 'obscene' erotic, pornographic material. Some of the transgressive, bizarre and digital sex we discuss here is also fantasy – for in a sense it can never be 'real' – and this poses particular problems for its regulation and control. But there are further aspects to the 'problem' of digital sex. We have argued that with the growth of more sophisticated communications technology, no longer can sex be said to be constituted by the conventional 'limits' that marked out much of what, for most of the nineteenth and twentieth centuries, sex was. Until recently, the regulatory frameworks which operated in relation to what was variously deemed to be pornography, erotica or even 'art' were largely applied to 'live figures' (albeit representational) in mediums such as books, magazines, photographs, films and videos. But even within those media, the production, distribution and consumption of sexually explicit images (as opposed to the written word) increasingly became the central focus of regulatory attention. However, it is only in recent years that new digital and electronic media, such as the internet, world wide web and mobile phones offering 'new' services such as 3G technology, have come to pose particular 'problems' for the regulation of sex involving 'persons-who-are-not-persons'. Indeed, much of the symbolic landscape underpinning contemporary 'utterances' about illegal and illicit sex is now peopled by those who are held to be 'dangerous' precisely because they constantly and continuously transmogrify into uncontained (and uncontainable) formations. This 'problem' of not knowing who anybody is any more is made explicit in quasi-official discourses surrounding sexual abuse. Witness, for example, proclamations issued by Stop It Now! UK and Ireland (2004), an organization which proclaims itself to be an 'innovative project' built on partnerships between: 'leading children's charities working with government and child protection agencies'. As Stop It Now! UK and Ireland (2004) starkly warns: 'You cannot pick out an abuser in a crowd'. In other words, it is impossible to now know – even if anyone ever did – who (or what) is a 'perpetrator' and who (or what) is not. In such a hyper-real symbolic landscape then, everyone ('perpetrators' and 'victims') looks unlike anyone else and yet utterly like everyone else. And with that, the near-impossibility of drawing any lines between 'victims' and 'perpetrators' becomes apparent, for we are all part of the world-wide, micro-chip 'crowd'.

Our concern in this chapter is not only with the increasingly sophisticated technological innovations in the arena of digital sex, some of which have rendered formal regulation of sexual 'obscenity' virtually impossible. Although it is often argued that there is a growing 'voice' calling for something to be done about the vast outpourings of 'sex on the net', we maintain that the regulations in this area are *ad hoc*, localized and/or still in their infancy. Prevailing quasi-official discourse surrounding 'sex on the net' has largely been centred on the 'problem' of the ease of access to digital on-line sex, such that at the touch of a button, millions of adults (and children) can log on to 'virtual' sex sites and can swap potentially contentious 'sexual materials' in a wide range of different formats. The 'portals' through which we view (and are viewed by) one another have become increasingly expanded and un-boundaried, and there is little in the way of law or policy to regulate this. Indeed, it could be argued that bedrooms (and beds) have now become globally shared spaces which respect fewer and fewer geographical, temporal or bodily limitations. Furthermore, within much of the official and quasi-official discourse surrounding digital sex, 'perpetrators' (and 'victims') are constituted as occupying an exclusive, unreachable enclave whereby they become not only highly anonymous, but also privileged, technically-competent and enabled members of a global 'crowd', who to an extent adhere to no rules at all. As a result, the regulations we examine here move the issues well beyond those identified in earlier debates around censorship and control of 'obscenity', based as they were upon private morality and public decency. What is at stake with regard to the 'outermost limits' of sex regulation and control is the issue of who has the power and authority to police such ostensibly 'open' and 'free' sex, particularly in terms of where sovereign powers begin and end in relation to international electronic 'spaces'.

This does not mean that nothing at all has happened in the way of regulation and control. There are currently a whole set of internet providers who are attempting informally to police the net, largely by positioning themselves as global 'moral guardians'. For example, in the absence of any rigorous way of confirming on-line identities, Microsoft announced in September 2003 the closure of thousands of UK-based chatrooms in an attempt to curb what was referred to as 'misuse'. Informal guidelines relating to the use of computing facilities are also issued by many 'respectable' institutions, including private and public sector organizations and most UK universities. In the case of the latter, the guidelines are designed to deal with the 'problem' posed by staff and students accessing what is referred to as 'unacceptable material'. For example, the University of Strathclyde states in its *Codes of Practice* that it:

> ... will not permit the use of its computer facilities and resources for the access to or transmission of information which is considered by the University to be unacceptable; illegal; in breach of University policies such as those on Equal Opportunities and Harassment; wasteful of resources; or not commensurate with the provision of facilities for legitimate educational purposes.
>
> (University of Strathclyde 2003: Section 5.2)

It defines as 'unacceptable':

> ... material which, in the opinion of the University, is offensive, abusive, defamatory, discriminatory, obscene or otherwise illegal which brings or may bring the University into disrepute.
>
> (University of Strathclyde 2003: Section 4)

We would suggest that akin to the points made in the previous chapter regarding those professionals who position themselves as upstanding 'moral guardians', many 'respectable' institutions/bodies providing networked information services similarly seek to announce that 'sex is not here', not on 'our' channels and so on. This permits such institutions to assert their own status and standing as 'moral guardians', upholding the 'collective social good' and so on. However, and again like the professional associations discussed in the previous chapter, there is very little in the way of precise identification of what such sexual 'wrongdoing' actually involves, particularly when it is adult and consensual, let alone when it is for 'legitimate educational purposes'.

To an extent then, it is clear that the various attempts to regulate sex which is free-floating and detached from the human body, and which operates in the borders not only between humans and humans but also between human and machine, moves our analysis into ever expanding terrain. The movement beyond identifiably live, human 'victims' in the case of much transgressive and digital sex is crucial, for in the case of the sex discussed here, it is clearly difficult to specify what the 'dangers' are that can be said to have been done to and by non-persons and/or non-existent persons. In the next section, we unpack in more detail the symbolic landscapes underpinning the regulations that pertain to such sex, to include what might, on the face of it, appear to be totally victimless 'victims'. This involves laying bare how, by whom and in whose specific interests, 'victims' who are not 'really' victims at all are to be constituted, and thereby championed, by those who lay claim to the power and authority with which to institute the 'rules of engagement' regarding sex at the margins of possibility. In effect, we maintain that the positing of particular sorts of victimless 'victims' is necessary in order for the regulation of marginal and 'edgy' sex to make sense as a moral authoritarian project. This point will be more fully elaborated in the next section.

Victimless sexual victims

At this point, we want to argue that the distinction made thus far between official and quasi-official discourses has begun to break down, inasmuch as we are now discussing regulatory frameworks which emanate from all manner of institutions/bodies, including that contained within government papers, consultation documents and in particular, the Sexual Offences Act (2003), as well as informal codes of conduct drawn up by extra-statutory institutions/bodies such as Microsoft. It also needs to be acknowledged that for any analysis of the regulations surrounding 'edgy' and marginal sex to be undertaken, it is necessary to unpack the symbolic landscape which constitutes 'victims' (and 'perpetrators') as lying on the cusp of imagined possibilities. This means examining 'victims' who, like the 'perpetrators' discussed previously, are themselves constituted as shadowy, unknowable figures. Transgressive and digital sex clearly raises difficult issues about the extent of 'choice' and 'consent' between adults involved in sexual encounters and exchanges. As alluded to earlier, the sex with which we deal here is to some extent 'victimless' in that there is no uncontaminated notion of a blameless, vulnerable, passive or coerced 'victim' to be found (indeed, there *never* is such a 'pure victim'). One of the key points here, and like the elisions hinted at in the previous chapter on professional sex, is that 'victims' may not 'really' be victimized at all and may at the self-same time be 'perpetrators'. Because what is being regulated and controlled includes 'freely chosen' sex, the symbolic landscapes which map out 'victimhood' must allow for the possibility that 'victims' have willingly chosen and consented to be 'victims'. Let us be very clear, we are not here referring to sex involving those who are deemed to have been 'tricked', 'coerced' or otherwise 'forced' into sex, for that is the subject of a slightly different analysis, and one that forms the central focus for our discussion of criminalized sexual offending in the first half of the book. Indeed, we cannot stress strongly enough that what is the focus of concern in this – and the previous two chapters – is 'consensual' sex involving adults. Here the problem is that of unknown possibilities, and the extent to which freely chosen, adult sex can be permitted to extend. Hence what we have termed victimless 'victims' are those who have been constituted by official and quasi-official discourses in two non-mutually exclusive ways: (a) as troubled and troublesome 'perpetrator-victims' who are a danger to themselves and (b) as non-human or post-human 'victims'. It is with these two discursive constructions that the remaining sections of this chapter deal. There is also a third possibility: that of the non-existent 'victim', namely the victim who has never existed outside the realm of the imaginary and for all intents and purposes has never been nor never will be 'real'. The discursive contortions of victimless 'victims' are in some ways, very real. To some extent, victimless 'victims' are symbolically marked out as those who share in common with children and vulnerable adults (those with learning disabilities and so on), some of the self-same characteristics as 'pure victims': namely they can be held to be blameless, weak, passive and in need of protection for their own safety and so on. But they also differ from such 'victims' inasmuch as they are constituted as highly culpable, collusive and in need of protection from themselves, and particularly from their own 'shadow sides'.

To further expand upon such symbolic constructions of victimless 'victims', we argue that even though it is apparent that there are no obvious 'victims' in many instances of transgressive or digital sex, much of the sex which takes place at the outer margins of possibility is deemed to require regulation and control because it is considered harmful and injurious to the parties involved, who must be protected for their own safety. This can occur despite such 'victims' being fully consenting adults, because as in the case of consensual bondage/discipline, sado-masochism or prohibited sexual relations between blood relatives, for example, issues are raised concerning whether, and under what conditions, adults can freely 'choose' to endanger themselves. In other words, the underlying concern here appears to be with protecting adults who, on the face of it, freely consent to their own 'victimhood'. To wit, in cases where bodily wounding takes place in the course of sexual activity, then consent and choice become highly compromised issues in which the state has shown itself more than willing to adjudicate. For example, the law as it stands at present does not allow a person to consent to what would be serious or lasting injury to their own body (Offences Against the Person Act 1998). However, the status and extent of injury regarded as permissible in many sadomasochistic sexual practices is often unclear, especially as the courts have decided criminal culpability differently for different persons, even where the activities undertaken and injuries caused were similar. In many cases, however, what is upheld is a construction of a 'pure victim' whose body (and bodily integrity) can all too easily be hurt. See, for example, the infamous Spanner case in Brown and others (1992) 94 Cr. App R 302 CA [1994] 1 Ac 212 HL, in which it was decided by the House of Lords that a person could not consent to any injury that was more than 'transient and trifling'. In this respect, 'victims' who consent to their own bodily injuries are deemed to be 'pure victims' inasmuch as they are easily damaged, violated and so on. To an extent, such 'victims' are also infantilized and robbed of their bodily self-determination, for they are deemed little more than a baby-like 'surface' upon which harm can be inflicted, albeit by themselves. By opening up the discursive space in which sexual harms inflicted by and upon 'victims-perpetrators' can be regulated in much the same way as the harms done (and any protections offered) to 'pure victims', the distinction between shadowy 'victims' and shadowy 'perpetrators' is maintained, if only insecurely. This is crucial, for without 'victims' and 'perpetrators', the edifices of the regulatory frameworks surrounding sex (and the symbolic landscapes which underpin them) would be little more than grains of sand which collapse into meaningless 'nothings'. In effect then, there must always be 'victims' and 'perpetrators', even if they are the self-same person and no matter how insubstantial or immaterial they are, for these discursive constructions to make sense. Furthermore and as in the case of consenting adult 'victim-perpetrators' involved in sexual activities with blood relatives (those related by both kinship and legal ties), it is abundantly clear that consenting adults are always deemed to need protection from their 'shadow' selves. For even in the very 'safest' circles of their immediate family and kinship networks, 'dangers' are held to abound. With regard to inter-familial sexual relations, for example, *Protecting the Public* clearly states:

> *Despite involving consensual adults* it is generally believed that all such behaviour is wrong and should be covered by the criminal law. Furthermore, there is evidence to suggest that some adult familial relationships are the result of long-term grooming by an older family member *and the criminal law needs to protect adults from abuse in such circumstances.*
>
> (Home Office 2002: 26, emphases added)

Witness in this construction, the invocation of another variant of the victimless 'victim', namely the groomed/abused *adult* who simultaneously colludes in, and thereby perpetrates, his or her own 'victimization'. Herein lies a further twist, for inter-familial sexual relations, like the sadomasochistic sex discussed above, also threaten to collapse and conflate 'victim' and 'perpetrator' into insubstantial 'nothings', but the symbolic landscapes that map out such constructions manage to circumvent such possibilities by virtue of constituting a novel version of the shadowy 'victim-perpetrator', namely the abusive/abused *adult* who is preyed upon but also colludes in sex with close family members. So whilst allowing for the possibility that such a 'victim', whilst being groomed and abused by an older relative, is at the self-same time a 'perpetrator', the differences between the two constructions ('victim' and 'perpetrator') are (thinly) maintained. For as the Sexual Offences Act (2003) makes clear, the 'victim' who has *consented to sex with an adult relative* is also a 'perpetrator'. Section 65 (1) of the Sexual Offences Act (2003) states:

A person aged 16 or over (A) commits an offence if:
(a) another person (B) penetrates A's vagina or anus with a part of B's body or anything else, or penetrates A's mouth with B's penis,
(b) A consents to the penetration,
(c) the penetration is sexual,
(d) B is aged 18 or over, and
(e) A is related to B in a way mentioned in subsection (2) and,
(f) A knows or could be expected to know that he is related to B in that way.

Sub-section (2) identifies the ways that A may be related to B as: 'parent, grandparent, child, grandchild, brother, sister, half-brother or half-sister'. In cases of consensual, adult, sadomasochistic *and* inter-familial sexual relations then, it is clear that what is at stake is the 'protection' of 'victims' from their shadowy 'perpetrator' selves. In certain circumstances, and as already highlighted in the previous chapter, even sex involving freely consenting adults can be deemed 'wrong', both because the sex itself is 'harmful' and because it is between the 'wrong' people.

Despite using contemporary examples as above, we also argue that notions of 'victim-perpetrators' who collude in or freely choose their own 'victimhood' have a long and stark history in official discourse of sex. For example, much sexual 'perversion' has been publicly identified (and often diagnosed by 'professional experts') in terms of psychosexual deviancy. There are long-established traditions in both law and medicine for considering certain sexual activities and behaviours as indicative of serous psychiatric 'disorders' such as for example, erotomania, necrophilic and necrosadistic vampirism. In these cases, 'perpetrators' are often identified and treated as 'victims' because of the 'disturbed' nature of their 'abnormal' sexual desires (Persaud 2003). So in the extended discursive construction of sexual 'victim-perpetrators', we would also want to point to long-standing constructions of consenting adults whose sexual behaviours have been considered 'mad' as well as 'bad'. It is also worth noting that not all 'deviant' adult, consensual sex is outlawed – for example, vigorous, harmful and injurious forms of autoeroticism and/or the use of 'foreign objects', 'sex aids' and 'sex toys' to achieve sexual enjoyment, is not illegal, or even particularly illicit in contemporary UK society. 'Deviant' sex, therefore, is always historically and socially specific and context-dependent. To wit, in the eighteenth century, much regulatory concern was with reining in masturbation, which was thought at the time to lead to all manner of individual and social 'ills'. Today, there is very little if any concern at all about sex with oneself, and certainly (unless undertaken in public) no formal or informal regulatory controls pertaining to such once 'harmful' forms of sex. But whatever the 'object' of sex regulation and control, it must always at some level involve the notion of 'harms' inflicted upon 'victims' by 'perpetrators', for without this, such regulations cannot be made meaningful at all. Indeed, this supports our earlier argument that underpinning all sex regulation in the UK is the overwhelming will not to govern sex *per se*, but to govern sexual *relationships between various constituencies and categories of people*. Furthermore, where and when this is individualized (such that no others are involved) or psychiatricized (such that the 'wrongs' are reinscribed as 'illnesses'), then again the discursive contours are always re-drawn in ways which encompass what is 'inside' rather than what is 'beyond'. For to go beyond the 'edges' of the sexually possible is to threaten the very notion of sex regulation and control itself.

However, we do argue that included in the extended discursive construction of victimless 'victims' are those who have no meaningful capacity to consent by virtue of their status as 'non-persons'. Until the passing of the Sexual Offences Act (2003), there were no laws against sex with the deceased. Indeed, there were no laws against any sort of interference with human bodily remains, as corpses have no legal status (Howarth, forthcoming). However, this is not to argue that this issue had not come to the attention of regulatory authorities. The Home Office explicitly commented that until the Sexual Offences Act 2003 there was nothing illegal about sex with corpses or cadavers. *Protecting the Public* clearly states:

> There is currently no law that covers sexual interference with human remains. Although there is no indication that such activity is anything but extremely rare, we believe that this behaviour is so deviant as to warrant the intervention of the criminal law and are proposing a new offence of sexual interference with human remains, which will carry a maximum penalty of 2 years' imprisonment. Where a defendant is suspected of killing their victim, the first priority will clearly be to charge murder or manslaughter. Where there is evidence of sexual penetration of the body after death, *it is important that the sexual deviance of the offending behaviour is properly recognised* by a separate indictment of sexual interference with human remains. This will ensure that a defendant who is found guilty on both charges is sentenced accordingly and is treated and monitored as a sex offender both in prison and after release. The offence could also apply to cases in which the offender has no contact with the victim prior to death but sexually abused their corpse.
>
> (Home Office 2002: 33, emphasis added)

In the event then, recent legislation has now made it a *sexual* offence to engage in penetration of a 'corpse'. Section 71 (1) of the Sexual Offences Act (2003) states:

> A person commits an offence if:
> (a) he intentionally performs an act of penetration with a part of his body or anything else,
> (b) what is penetrated is a part of the body of the dead person,
> (c) he knows that, or is reckless as to whether that is what is penetrated and
> (d) the penetration is sexual.
>
> (SOA 2003: Section 71(1))

However, we want to argue that sex with non-living or deceased 'victims' begins to throw into confusion any secure notion of who (or what) a 'victim' 'really' is (or might be).

In this finely extended discursive construction of those requiring the full protection of the law, the dead (presumably at any stage after death?) have now come to be deemed as 'victims', and 'victims' furthermore who have no meaningful capacity whatsoever to consent. Indeed, there is now no 'living' body (with the exception arguably of the unborn and 'inanimate' plant material) which stands outside this extended discursive construction of 'victims'. But what has taken place here is a shift away from the medico-legal identification and treatment of 'deviant', psychiatric sexual proclivities and 'perversions', to an understanding that all supposedly 'bizarre' sexual desires and fantasies, when perpetrated with and upon others (be they adults, relatives, animals and/or the deceased) need now to become objects of control by regulatory institutions/bodies, particularly if every body is to be kept sexually 'safe'. In other words, no longer is the concern primarily with the identification of bizarre and unusual 'disorders' from which 'perpetrator-victims' are thought to suffer, but with the necessity of controlling those deemed, in many cases, to be nothing more nor less than 'beyond' being human, whilst at the same time they are all too human. Hence regulatory moves in the case of much transgressive sex are now increasingly underpinned by an understanding of particular sexual desires, even when practised in adult, consensual relationships (such as sadomasochism) or where consent cannot enter into the frame in any meaningful way (because 'victims' are non-humans or deceased), as literally 'monstrous', because no 'real' humans engage in them, although clearly someone (and possibly) everyone does, at least in their sexual imaginings. What this does, however, is open up the discursive space in which any and all sex has the potential to slide inexorably into the outermost excesses of depravity, because all humans can become 'monsters', and indeed cannot escape from so becoming. Hence there is no body (and no sex) that can ever lie outside or beyond such discursive constructions, for once the unruly margins begin to collapse onto the 'centre' in this way, then no one (and nothing) is ever sexually safe or secure. In other words, there is no place/space beyond the reaches of the regulatory frameworks where 'perpetrators' (and 'victims') can lurk or hide. In short, everyone is now both dangerous and in danger.

However, we do not want to dismiss the liberal or libertarian traditions which maintain that the state should only exercise power in regulating the sexual choices of 'consenting' adults where there is definable and proven 'harm' to others. We have argued in this section that one of the central 'problems' of transgressive and digital sex is that it only affects those adults who on the face of it, willingly consent, or where there are victimless 'victims' such as when there are no other, conscious, living persons involved (besides the 'perpetrator'). In true liberal fashion, what the symbolic landscape of sex regulation does is present much of the 'harm' being perpetrated as 'harm' to the social fabric, particularly as and when 'too much' sexual freedom or permissiveness prevails at the 'edges'. Such a discursive construction has a strong purchase upon New Labour rhetoric, as we explained earlier. Hence we argue that one of the underlying assumptions at work here is the re-invocation of the 'threats' to society posed by permissiveness. As explained, this has become a cornerstone of much political campaigning rhetoric concerning 'unruly' and 'outlandish' sex. From the 'stable centre', too much permissiveness is made to signal degeneracy, confusion and uncertainty; a disregard for authority; and ultimately, the collapse of traditional morality. Indeed, it could be argued that some of the 'dangers' of 'edgy' and marginal sex are the fears, anxieties and uncertainties that accompany unbridled choice, particularly where and when such choices that are hitherto configured unthinkable then become all too publicly visible and possible. However, from the margins, so-called permissiveness is desirable; it signals the relaxation of supposedly 'outmoded' norms and values; a humanizing modernism and pluralistic democratizing of sexual pleasure and sexual desire. So what is at stake in the new sexual enterprise of moral authoritarianism which we outline in this book includes, amongst other things, dealing with the shifting tensions between conservative orthodoxy on the one hand, and liberalism or libertarianism on the other. Buried herein too are feminist concerns with the gender power dynamics of 'edgy' and 'marginal' sex, such that it is held that the discursive construction of sex 'fiends', 'monsters', 'beasts' and so on are not gender neutral, and in most cases are nearly always informed by hegemonic masculinity. To wit, sex 'monsters' and 'beasts', including those to be now charged under the Sexual Offences Act (2003) with the new offence of 'sexual grooming', are almost invariably constituted in feminist critiques of on-line sexual abuse and so on as highly rapacious and calculating adult men. Hence characteristic of the sets of assumptions which lie behind much of the move to regulate and control transgressive and digital sex, where codified at all, are all kinds of conflicting and paradoxical anxieties about where to draw the line between consent, choice and the freedom of individuals on the one hand and the 'dangers' and 'threats' to the collective social fabric on the other. And once again, within this are buried issues of who has the power to control sex at the 'outer limits', and who – in the final analysis – are the 'real perpetrators'.

Sliding into the 'murky' depths

There are other issues at stake here besides those of re-working dis-cursive constructions of 'victims' and 'perpetrators'. As the distinctions, borders and boundaries between the two become increasingly hard to draw or decipher, it becomes more and more imperative to do so. We have argued that the regulation of hitherto bizarre, outlandish and to an extent unthinkable sex appears on the surface to be fuelled by concerns that 'deviant' sex is only ever a minority interest to which the majority are unlikely to be drawn. But, as was acknowledged even in the 1950s, this is not just a concern with rare or unusual forms of sex which have no purchase on the imaginings (or practices) of 'decent' citizens. It has long been recognized by academic, political and social commentators, media pundits and policy-makers alike that 'edges' are attractive and addictive, and must thus be strenuously guarded against. Indeed, there is a long history of viewing 'outrageous' and ostensibly 'sick' forms of sex as having a corrosive and corrupting effect on the public imagination, precisely because prohibited sex is held to be so 'alluring'. Witness, for example, the fascination with 'nasty' sex stories which appeared to grip many readers and viewers alike during 1995, when the Fred and Rosemary West story, dating back over two decades, broke into the public domain. Often underlying the concerns around such sexual 'dramas' are fears that the public appetite for more and more titillating and sensational forms of sex will lead to over-exposure and desensitization, and thus a growing desire for more and more 'nasty' sex. At first sight this may appear to be the old fear of the 'slippery slope' in a (not so very) new guise; the concern being that the more exciting/ shocking the 'edgy' and marginal sex which comes to light, the more sexual 'kicks' will be sought, and the greater the need for regulation and control on these 'outer edges'. But the 'freedom to choose' around and apropos 'nasty' sex, even where consenting adults are involved, is always contingent upon the contexts in which such 'choices' are expressed. And as with the underlying concerns in relation to recreational drug use, it is held that choosing to engage in 'softer' or less serious forms of sexual transgression will inevitably lead to 'harder' or more serious sexual violations which will impact significantly upon public morality. What this means is that attempts at regulation and control can be made to appear as if they are generated by widespread, common-sense demands that 'something should be done', even if this runs counter to individual freedoms. What this means is that all sex regulation can be made to appear as if it is undertaken solely and primarily in the interest of allaying widespread public fears of *everyone's* 'slide into degeneracy'. Protection from 'sex offenders' then is ultimately constructed as being about protection from the individual's own murky, disreputable self.

This supposed slippage into the 'murky' depths of sexual self-immolation can be seen to work in a particularly pervasive way with regard, to take just one example, to the supposedly 'rare' and 'unusual' sexual proclivity commonly known as bestiality. Whilst there may be widespread societal indifference to the wearing of animal skins (furs, leathers) and little or no formal prohibitions against such, there is more societal disquiet about animal lovers routinely taking their pets to bed, caressing, cuddling, kissing and tickling them and certainly much greater societal unease around adults (or children) engaging in 'foreplay' with their pets or other domestic animals. Until recently, however, such sex was not subject to any formal regulation. The government rectified this lack of protection offered to 'victims' (in this case non-human species) from human 'perpetrators' who on the surface appear to be sub-human – although simultaneously they can be anyone and everyone who comes into contact with a pet or other domestic animal – in the Sexual Offences Act 2003. In *Protecting the Public*, the potential 'perpetrators' of such offences are marked out as nigh on 'sub-human', but nonetheless as in need of regulatory attention. To wit:

> Sexual activity with animals *is generally recognised to be profoundly disturbed behaviour.* A new offence of bestiality will criminalise those who sexually penetrate animals or allow an animal to penetrate them.
>
> (Home Office 2002: 33, emphasis added)

In the case of such 'extreme' sexual offending, it appears on the surface that there is little discursive connection between sexually abused animal 'victims' and sexually abused child 'victims'. But we would argue that the discursive constitution of sexually abused 'animal-victims' who share much in common with sexually abused children, serves the moral authoritarian project that we unpack in this book. It could be argued that, even immediately and before the passing of this recent legislation, little public attention was given to the sexual 'abuse' of animals, yet they (like children) can all too easily become a *cause célèbre*, to be championed by a whole litany of 'moral guardians', not least 'animal *lovers*'. Indeed, it could be suggested that in the case of some domestic animals, particularly pet dogs, their tameness, availability, amenability (and 'silence') is somehow suggestive of their 'consent', namely that they can be seen as willing 'participants' in sexual activities. Hence the Sexual Offences Act (2003) makes provision for a slightly different construction of a complicit even actively desiring 'non-human victim' (the animal 'victim'), compared with (the impossibility of) the willing or active 'post-human victim' (the dead 'victim'). For, whilst there is no suggestion that the 'perpetrator' in the case of sexual offences against a 'corpse' might be charged with having allowed a dead person to penetrate them, this is not so in the case of sex with an animal, where the law permits such a construction. Section 70 (Intercourse with an animal) (2) states that:

A person (A) commits an offence if:
(a) A intentionally causes, or allows, A's vagina or anus to be penetrated,
(b) the penetration is by the penis of a living animal, and
(c) A knows that, or is reckless as to whether, that is what A is being penetrated by.

(Sexual Offences Act 2003: s71(2))

In short, what is being posited here is the possibility of a non-human 'victim-perpetrator' (an animal who has sex with a human) and is complicit in the 'degradation' of both. So in the final analysis, 'perpetrators' both need 'protection' from their own selves and from the 'collusion' in their crimes by those non-human 'victims' (animals) they seek to abuse. In this way, 'victims' who are deemed totally incapable of any meaningful adult consent (by virtue of being non-human), can nonetheless become constituted as 'willing participants' in illegal forms of sex. And at this point, just who (or what) requires 'protection' from what (and whom) becomes particularly difficult to keep track of.

This creates and reflects the conditions of (im)possibility around sex, whereby sex becomes nothing more nor less than an empty 'centre', vacuum or vortex into which virtually anything (and anybody) can be sucked. We argue that this is the 'real' danger to which the regulation and control of 'edgy' and marginal sex is directed, since there is in the final analysis, no line which can be drawn (or certainly ever be made to 'stick') between the 'normal'/'abnormal', 'natural'/'unnatural', 'acceptable'/'unacceptable'. Hence, even though some bizarre, outlandish and unusual forms of sex may be considered to pose little in the way of 'real' danger, nonetheless they loom large in publicly-voiced concerns regarding what it is that is 'wrong' and 'dangerous' about unregulated and freely-expressed sex. Although it would appear that some sexual 'degradations' (particularly when they take place in the privacy of one's home and are or appear to be consensual) are indeed very difficult to regulate and control, there is now increasing public acceptance of the idea that all sex should be routinely and systematically monitored, if only to prevent the possibility that it may suddenly and somehow turn out to be 'monstrous'. Hence the 'flood' of (unregulated and unregulatable) sex that has come to be the object of scrutiny in the late modern era is not simply an expression of a sexually open, diverse and free society but is always and already posited as 'sex-which-is-highly-threatening-and-dangerous'. It cannot ever be other than this if it (sex) is to be deployed as a means of achieving power and control.

Conclusions

We argue in this chapter that the moves to regulate transgressive and digital sex to date, represent a shift of attention away from the 'far end' or 'outer limits' of 'unruly' sex and a move towards a focus on what can all too easily go 'wrong' with sex if and when it is not stringently monitored. We also argue that the trawl is on for more effective ways and means of controlling any sex that crops up in virtually any guise at all. As a result, attempts to regulate and control all manifestations of sex in the current day and age have become a virtual witch-hunt. This has led to some novel 'inventions' of new sexual 'offences' which the government is all too clear about championing in the public interest. Witness, for example, some further 'new' offences contained within the Sexual Offences Act (2003) and officially known as 'preparatory offences', which do not have 'sex' as their object of scrutiny at all (since no sex is done in these cases). *Protecting the Public* (2002) makes clear the government's aims in respect of what is referred to as 'drug-assisted rape'.

> … existing law includes an offence of administering drugs in order for a man to have unlawful sexual intercourse with a woman and carries a maximum penalty of 2 years. We intend to retain this offence, amended so that it covers the administering of drugs or other substances with intent to stupefy a victim in order that they can be subject to an indecent act without their consent, and to increase the maximum penalty to 10 years' imprisonment. This offence can apply both where the substance has been administered to sexually exploit a person *even though the sexual activity does not for whatever reason take place* and where the purpose is for the victim to be subjected to sexual activity with someone other than the person who administered the drugs.
>
> (Home Office 2002: 22, emphasis added).

In this way, the hunt is on not just for more and more sex which can be subjected to regulation, but more and more 'non-sex' that can be reconfigured, regulated and controlled as 'sex'.

To conclude, in this and other chapters of the book, we have argued that the policing of 'boundaries' and 'borders' is fundamental to the regulation of all and any sex. We argue that it is at the 'edges' or 'outer limits' of sex that sex becomes both almost impossible to regulate, and yet also most in need of regulation. For it is not the 'niceties' of modesty, nudity or other effrontery that we are dealing with here, nor is it even the so-called widespread 'dripping tap' of sexual harassment, including what has become popularly known as flashing and/or streaking. This – particularly the 'offence' of sexual harassment – has not been subjected to much consideration at all in the recent moves to regulate sexual conduct in twenty-first century. Indeed, sexual harassment is remarkable if only for its complete omission in any discussion of what was or was not to be included in the Sexual Offences Act (2003). In this respect we argue that the regulation and control of 'edgy' sex is key, for clearly the control of any adult sexual activities involving close relatives, the dead, the drugged, animals, computers, machines and so forth is, if not the stuff of sexual 'fantasy' (and sexual enjoyment), is now regarded as highly alluring. Indeed, we argue that the attempts to control such 'unruly' sex at the 'outer limits' are not a matter of regulating that which lies at the so-called 'extreme' edges (in terms of its 'obscenity', 'depravity' and/or 'deviancy'), but are indicative of the way sex as an 'empty centre' or vacuum constitutes its own project. In other words, we return at this point to what was said in Chapter 1 about sex having no meaning outside its constitution. With the expansion of sex regulation into the 'outermost limits', it becomes ever more apparent that all sex is nothing more than a vortex into which more and more can be sucked in ever-increasing and widening extensions, collisions, collusions and elisions. Not surprisingly, much of the attempt at regulation and control comes full circle in that the concerns that operate at the 'hard core' centre are remarkably similar to those that operate at the 'outer edges'. At heart then, the crux of the 'problem' of all illicit and illegal sex is that it (sex) is always both 'inside' and 'outside' control. It can only become the object of regulation and control by being inscribed in particular ways which draw upon highly paradoxical (and difficult to sustain) discursive constructions of 'victims' and 'perpetrators' – and, of course, those who are their ultimate but largely hidden 'protectors'. These are points that will be returned to in the next and final chapter.

Chapter 8

Conclusion: victims, perpetrators and the new sexual enterprise

Our argument in this book began by holding out the possibility that with regard to sex, there has emerged a wealth of new official and quasi-official discourses which speak about and to the 'problem' of sex. These discourses have given rise to a whole gamut of official 'utterances' which take the form of what we have variously referred to as formal and informal regulations, regulatory frameworks, 'rules of engagement' and so on. Indeed, we argue that there has been a discursive explosion around and apropos illicit and illegal sex in recent times, drawing upon and co-creating many strands of late twentieth century feminist and liberal concerns. We have further argued that the official and quasi-official discourses that we unpack in this book are underpinned by sets of assumptions or what we have called symbolic landscapes, and by particular configurations of gendered power relations. These relations never quite get explicitly recognized and are more often transformed into non-gendered asocial relationships. Taken together these symbolic landscapes cohere in the form of regulatory frameworks which emanate from, amongst other bodies/institutions, the state, professional associations, employing organizations and so on. But in this book we point to there being something more at stake than the identification of, and solutions directed towards, the 'problem' of sex.

We maintain that the 'problem' of sex lies not so much with sex *per se*, but with *sexual relations*. What cannot be admitted is that in contemporary Britain, *all* sexual relationships occur within a broader social context of gendered inequalities and as such are, at once, 'ordinary' relationships (because they make up much of the 'ordinary' fabric of day-to-day life that much, of necessity is taken-for-granted) and 'extraordinary' (because of their potential for being abusive). This is most evidently the case with heterosexual relationships. We also maintain that in effect, this means that there are inevitable, persistent and ongoing crises of legitimacy in the official and quasi-official discourses concerning sex. These legitimation deficits have their origins in the complex lived social, economic, political and ideological 'realities' shaping most relationships between men and women, adults and children. These realities cannot be spoken, and therefore become constrained, rewritten and reinscribed into formal and informal rules of engagement, in ways which take normative and prescriptive forms. By and through an explication of such regulatory frameworks, we highlight the workings of an on-going, palimpsest project – a project which, we argue, has permitted a new moral enterprise concerned with sex regulation to take hold. Such a new moral enterprise appears to 'better' deal with sexual 'offences' of all kinds. Yet tellingly, what we have demonstrated is that this enterprise speaks of the 'wrongness' of sex without ever clearly explicating and delineating what the 'wrongs' of sex might 'really' be.

It is necessary to state clearly that it was never our intention in this book to identify the 'problem' of sex in terms of what is 'really' wrong with it, but we do argue that because of the distortion and erasure of the underlying social realities of men's sexual violence, power is thereby effectively exercised in ways which obscure those underlying 'realities'. In the present era and more specifically in the UK context, this new sexual enterprise of sex, this rewriting and erasure, constitutes what we have termed moral authoritarianism. This book has attempted to chart the workings of moral authoritarianism in relation to the formal and informal regulation of sex. Moral authoritarianism presents us with a picture of 'reality' in which it is held that there has been a 'revolution' in terms of how we think of ourselves sexually and in particular, how we inter-connect sexually with others. This 'revolution' is partially held to be a response to what are perceived to be increasingly 'risky' times regarding sex and sexual relations, especially in relation to the risks of violence, sexually transmitted diseases, abuse and so on. It is also seen as having its roots in progressive sexual movements, with their origins in the radicalism and 'liberal' permissiveness of the 1960s and 1970s. In this book, we have referred to both 'state-sponsored moral authoritarianism' as well as that which resides outside the structures of the state. We do not suggest that these are two versions of moral authoritarianism because both interlock and in part constitute each other. State-sponsored moral authoritarianism may well be backed up by the force and capacities of criminal justice interventions, but the moral authoritarianism present within professional associations, employing organizations and so on is nevertheless highly impactful in the various ways in which it positions individuals as 'victims' or 'perpetrators'.

On the face of it then, moral authoritarianism highlights particular 'problems'; for example, that much sexual violence and abuse, once hidden, is now 'out in the open' and requires societal response and intervention. Such 'problems', it is thought, are largely technical ones which require technical solutions of the kind provided by law and policy. Much of the emphasis has been upon the protection of 'victims' – and the surveillance and punishment of 'offenders' and 'perpetrators'. As a result, moral authoritarian reforms to the regulatory frameworks concerned with sexual 'misconduct' can be seen as attempts to deal with these 'problems' by drawing upon 'better' and more 'expert' under-standings, by leaving no 'gaps' uncovered and so on. But there are unacknowledged difficulties here, for the sexual 'wrongness' of which the discourses speak cannot be articulated without underlying power relations being reworked in particular ways so that ultimately, the powerful – and most especially men – are not implicated in any sexual 'wrong doings'. In short, the various sexual crimes, offences and infractions of which both the formal and informal regulations speak, do not present the 'problem' of sex in terms of there being a 'problem with men', or – to be more precise – any problem with what men do sexually, especially heterosexually. Indeed, despite what we claim have been seen as feminist successes in opening the discussions of sexual politics, the possibilities for speaking of the 'problem' of sex as being first and foremost a problem of what men do heterosexually has been and still is systematically clouded and obscured. Central to this endeavour, and its highly successful execution, are the symbolic landscapes which con-struct 'victims', 'offenders' and 'perpetrators' in specific (albeit contra-dictory) ways, thereby permitting the official 'utterances' to make sense without bearing much relationship to the realities of sexual violence.

This book has attempted to trace and lay bare the contours of such symbolic landscapes. We have argued in the six main chapters that much contemporary official and quasi-official discourse is predicated upon powerful notions of securing justice for 'victims' and meting out punishment to 'offenders' and 'perpetrators'. In many ways and on the face of it, these are neither new nor remarkable constructions, for it can be argued that the law exists solely to secure such means and ends. But what are new and remarkable are the totalizing effects of such discursive constructions, conditioned as they are by the workings of gendered power, such that particular sorts of 'victims' and particular sorts of 'perpetrators' are made manifest whilst at the same time, other possible writings/readings are silenced. In this book, we have attempted to expose the workings of such symbolic landscapes as they take shape and form in the modern era. We maintain that, firstly, such often sharply drawn landscapes involve an extension of the existing discursive terrain upon which sex regulation has in the past been mapped out. So, for instance, Foucault (1978) referred to the 'hysterization of women's bodies', 'pedagogization of children's sex', 'socialization of procreative behaviour' and 'psychiatrization of perverse pleasures' as the key sites of knowledge and power which permitted the increasing regulation of sex throughout the nineteenth and early twentieth centuries. By way of development, we have shown that current sex regulation is extended mainly through discourses of victimhood as they emanate from and within the state and other informal sites of authority. Not only does this mean that we have had to take as the object of our enquiry a wider and wider remit of laws, policies and guidelines pertaining to sexual conduct and relations, but we also are able to argue that there is now more and more sex to be analysed in terms of its being seen as requiring regulation. Secondly, we argue that at first glance, such an ever-widening regulatory framework, based as it is upon extending the symbolic landscape of 'sex', appears to stem from and thereby signal greater sexual toleration, openness, freedom and so on, and this chimes with – importantly – its apparent gender-neutrality. Yet at the same time and somewhat counter-intuitively, such regulatory frameworks appear to be much more feminist, offering greater protections from gendered and (hetero)sexual violence, abuse and so on. As we have already stated, this has been made possible and plausible through the re-inscription of particular notions regarding 'victimhood', and especially the instigation and extension of 'protective mechanisms' that are thought to be necessary for 'victims'. But we want to stress that the symbolic landscapes we deconstruct are not simple, static or straightforward. Central to these is the discursive constitution of a host of 'victims', a wide variety of 'offenders' and 'perpetrators' and, importantly, *unified* 'protectors'. The 'protectors', comprising what we have termed moral guardians (which take different forms according to whether or not the regulations are state-centred or extra-statutory) are held to be trustworthy public servants in whose hands the 'problem' of sex and sexual relations can be dealt with and secured. All this adds up to a new sexual enterprise or radical brand of moral authoritarianism which, we argue, has come to dominate sexual politics at the dawn of the twenty-first century.

Sexual 'victims'

We have argued in each of the preceding chapters that if there is anything problematic about sex *per se*, one 'problem' is that it has come to be seen as much more dangerous and risky than hitherto. However, this view of sex as troubling and troublesome cannot be mapped out without being shaped and moulded by (albeit slippery) constellations of 'victims' and 'perpetrators' of sexual 'wrong doings'. Such constructions allow the 'rules of engagement' which follow from them to 'make sense'. Various notions of 'victims' are scattered throughout both the formal and informal regulations we have unpacked in this book. All these varying constructions of 'victims' have at their heart the archetypal 'genuine victim' who is above all else weak, passive, vulnerable, blameless and in some cases, extremely traumatized. These 'genuine victims' have suffered a violation to their very integrity, their self, and their body/soul, up to and including social, spiritual and psychological 'death'. As such, it is easy to maintain, publicly, that such 'victims' must be championed and protected. Indeed, much formal and informal regulation is replete with unspoken assumptions regarding the need to protect those who have been 'genuinely' victimized. Such a symbolic landscape is further reinforced by notions of such 'victims' as those who have been unjustly treated because, it is held, 'protections' in the past were insufficient and/ or un-workable, or 'victims' were unwilling or unable to make use of the 'protections' offered. This 'lack of protection' is *not* held to be the outcome of powerful vested interests blocking victims' capacities to call upon the 'protection' of the law, or indeed even the relationship of the law with social structures and power relationships, but *rather the direct result of past ignorance and failings on the part of those offering such protection*. But 'remedies' for past 'mistakes' can always be found, from any number of quarters – including those critical of existing regulations – and hence the situation is constituted as one to which more sophisticated understandings can now be brought to bear. This holds true for the 'discovery' in recent years of what are seen as hitherto unacknowledged and neglected forms of abuse and violence, including for example, sexual grooming. However, discursive constructions of 'victims' and 'victimhood' are never fully stable because there is always some slippage and elision, particularly as many individuals cannot carry the mantle of 'victimhood' in any simple or straightforward way.

In this respect, we have highlighted in several of the book's six main chapters a whole host of other 'victims' who are not constituted as weak, passive, vulnerable and blameless. These less-than-genuine 'victims' are often but not always adults and they may (or may not) have consented to their 'victimhood'. They are highly problematic 'compromised victims' then, who occasionally are seen to be culpable for their own sexual 'victimization'. Witness for example, 16 or 17 year olds involved in prostitution who despite their actual victimization are nevertheless seen as 'offenders' when voluntarily returning to prostitution. Other 'compromised victims' are those who are seen to simultaneously sexually offend, such as sexually abusive children who are constituted as proto-adults insofar as they are engaging in sexual offending behaviours whilst not being exposed to the full force of criminal justice by virtue of being a child. Furthermore, some 'compromised victims' are held to be passing as 'victims', but ultimately are thought to be in the business of 'victimizing' their 'perpetrators', by falsely accusing them, for example, of sexual assault, sexual harassment and so on. Some 'compromised victims' are also constituted as 'beneficiaries' of sexual 'wrong doings' inasmuch as it is thought that they may profit from advantageous treatment, enjoy special 'advantages' as in the case of students who may be involved with their own university lecturers. Finally, appearing at the outer edges of this symbolic landscape are a whole host of 'victimless victims', those who are in effect 'non-victims' because they are held to be sub-human, non-human or post-human. Sexual 'victims' therefore encompass a whole host of slippery, contingent categories, many of whom, *in practice,* might never be afforded the status of 'genuine victim'.

Moreover, in some instances, it is held that victims are 'victims' only because of the personal offensiveness, the affront to decency and so on, which has been caused by the illicit/illegal sex to which they are subjected. In this case, only 'victims' themselves can determine the extent and status of their 'victimhood' since such 'offences' can never really be objectively established. This holds for those who are 'victims' of nuisance sex, sexual harassment and so on[1], who are in this case denuded of their social context, insofar as it is only their *own subjective* experience of being sexually affronted, assailed and so on that counts. Once the ultimate 'unknowingness' of sexual 'offences/offensiveness' is (or has to be) admitted into the frame, 'victims' are of necessity required to have the backing of being 'rational' in order to become legitimate 'victims'. The 'reasonable person' becomes the motif for the all-knowing, right-thinking citizen, the one who can take a 'proper moral' stance on sex and sexual conduct but can simultaneously identify 'wrong doings' (and 'wrong-doers'). But we want to argue that at this point, the contours of the symbolic landscape that we chart here are in danger of becoming particularly elusive and vague. Indeed, 'victims' who are without reference points themselves become elusive and vague, for as they become more adult and more freely consenting, they are less easily constituted as 'genuine victims'. Much, we argue, will depend upon how consent and choice is viewed. As detailed in various chapters, both informal and formal regulatory frameworks often invoke a literal notion of consent and choice. We next turn to sexual 'offenders' and 'perpetrators'.

Sexual 'offenders' and 'perpetrators'

The moral authoritarian project discussed throughout takes additional shapes and forms, the contours of which can be further and more finely traced via an examination of the paradoxical notions of 'offenders' and 'perpetrators' deployed. We maintain that on the one hand, 'offenders' and 'perpetrators' are seen as shadowy, excessive figures, often constituted as inhabitants of the most extreme reaches of 'terror' and 'threat'. They are often held to be little more than non-human 'fiends', 'beasts' and 'monsters'. But 'offenders' and 'perpetrators' are also ever-present, unknown (and sometimes unknowable) both to their 'victims' (or potential 'victims') and to themselves. In this they are constituted as all-too-human; as 'ordinary' people who make mistakes, overstep unclear boundaries and sometimes even bring about unforeseen and unfortunate consequences for their 'victims', towards whom they can profess to have caring, loving and otherwise 'good' intentions. 'Offenders' are almost always defined in relation to the formal process of criminal justice. Any fragmentation of this category occurs in the process of identifying the potential 'offender' rather than in the process of prosecution. In contrast, 'perpetrators' are defined in much less clear-cut ways. As well as being seen as 'near offenders', they may also be seen as otherwise impartial benefactors who have inadvertently 'favoured' their 'victims', albeit in a sexually 'unprofessional' or unwise manner. In this way and unlike the 'victims' discussed in the previous section, 'perpetrators' are bifurcated into two categories; those at the extremes, and those who are all too ordinary. This is also the case for 'offenders' but for different reasons: 'offenders' become all too ordinary because they are not easily identifiable by either criminal justice agencies or occasionally by 'victims' themselves (cf. child sexual abusers in the family). In remaining unrecognizable figures, 'ordinary offenders' and 'perpetrators' are thus very little different from 'natural', 'normal' people. In this regard, 'ordinary offenders' and 'perpetrators' can also be the self-same individuals whom their actual victims most trust.

The interlocking articulation of these sliding constructions of 'victims' and 'offenders'/'perpetrators' has a complex, subtle but specific effect. As noted above, there is a fraying of the notion of a 'genuine' victim in the face of the constantly fragmenting categories of victimhood such that more and more 'victims' come to be seen as culpable, blameworthy and so on. There is also a similar, but different movement in regards to 'offenders' and 'perpetrators'. As the constructs fray according to ever more finely distinguished and increasing degrees of culpability on the part of the 'wrong doers', there is a drive to subject them to harsher and harsher punishments and censures. However, the movement towards increasing punitiveness is utterly contingent on the successful identification of the 'genuine victim'. Where no 'genuine victim' is present, there is a tendency to 'let perpetrators off the hook'. To be clear: in the face of fragmenting constructions of both 'victims' and 'offenders'/'perpetrators', there is a simultaneous tendency to push actual individuals to the margins of 'normality' ('beasts', 'fiends' and 'monsters') whilst also pulling some back into the centre of 'ordinary lives' ('anyone', 'everyone'). Hence, it is never possible to *really know* who is who. In other words, the 'realities' of which the official and quasi-official discourses do not speak, lie just beneath the surface, ever ready to erupt and break out of their (sometimes thinly veiled, sometimes deeply buried) depths. Following on from this, we maintain that moral authoritarianism relies upon these discursive conflations for the securing of its project.

The politics of sexual politics

It could be argued that the sort of deconstruction of sexual victimization that we have undertaken in this book is politically short-sighted. For the efforts and hard work of many feminist campaigners and researchers around the issue of victimization have, indeed, created many beneficial interventions for actual and real victims of sexual violence and abuse. Their successes are in no small part attributable to the recognition of the lived experiences of actual victims and the ability of these campaigners and researchers to affect law and policy in line with that recognition. However, as we have demonstrated throughout this book, the incorporation within official and quasi-official discourses of these recognitions has not been without cost. In particular, the sexual enterprise that these discourses constitute is one that confronts the challenges of (largely) feminist critiques through a normative language that makes it, literally, impossible to name the 'problem' in the same way. The drive to gender-neutralize ensures that the complex social realities of many women's and children's lives are lost in the service of reforming law and policy in ways which appear to treat men and women as *the same*. Coupled with the shifting and sliding constructions of 'victims', 'offenders' and 'perpetrators', this drive to gender-neutralize forecloses the space to effect meaningful political change in the fashion envisaged by many feminists. So for instance, the recognition that women in prostitution are victimized and exploited has many benefits such as increasing the range of services offered to them at the same time as challenging straightforward notions of their offending. But, as this is translated into official discourse, those benefits disappear in the face of shifting notions of victimhood and the individualizing and responsi-bilizing strategies also put in place. Thus, the actual change such regulations may bring to women in prostitution might well be minimal.

At heart, we suggest that the sexual enterprise currently underway presents feminists, and those with a keen eye to reform of law and policy for actual sexual victims, with particular dilemmas. For it would seem that just at that historical moment when it became possible to recognize the sexual victimization of women and children, other forces came into play which have made that possibility less and less realizable. As we have continually demonstrated throughout this book, official and quasi-official discourses of sex are incapable of this full recognition. They operate by erasure of the material origins of their legitimation deficits. Instead, the political messages of feminism *vis à vis* sexual violence, abuse and infractions get translated into the *extension* of official and quasi-official discourses and a net widening of formal and informal regulatory frameworks. Simply, more and more people, relationships and behaviours come to be identified as 'problematic' and in need of intervention. In this fashion, the very strategy of reform invoked by feminists creates perverse and unintended consequences. And so, another real challenge lies ahead. sTo create the space in which it is possible to recognize the actual sexual vicitmization of women and children, it would seem that, politically, it might be best not to reify their victimhood and indeed, to displace the construction of them as little more than 'victims'. Given that so much of the construction of 'offenders' and 'perpetrators' hinges on the construction of 'victims', such a strategy might also create the space in which it is possible to envisage reforms that are located outside 'traditional' sites of moral authority – especially those associated with the state and other 'moral guardians' – and which may be in the longer run, much more liberating.

Notes

1 Interestingly, it was precisely these categories of sexual infractions that were left out of the Sexual Offences Act 2003.

Bibliography

Aggarwal, A.P. (1992) *Sexual harassment in the Workplace*, 2nd edition, Toronto: Butterworth.

Akdeniz, Y. (1999) *Sex on the Net: The Dilemma of Policing Cyberspace (Behind the Headlines)*, South Street Press.

Akdeniz, Y. *et al* (ed.) (2000) *The Internet, Law and Society*, London: Longman.

Allison, N.E. (1997) 'The Professional and Boundary Issues', www.advocateweb.org/hope/theprofessionalandboundaryissues.asp.

Aries, P. (1967) *Centuries of Childhood*, London: Penguin.

Ashenden, S. (2004) *Governing Child Sexual Abuse: Negotiating the Boundaries of Public and Private, Law and Science*, London: Routledge.

Ashworth, A. (2000) *Sentencing and Criminal Justice*, London: Butterworths.

Ashworth, A. (1995) *Principles of Criminal Law*, London: Butterworths.

Association of University Teachers (2003) 'Staff-student relations' www.aut.org.uk/index.cfm?articleid=134.

Banks, S. (2001, 2nd edition) *Ethics and Values in Social Work*, Houndsmill, Basingstoke: Palgrave.

Barnardos (1998) *Whose Daughter Next? Children Abused Through Prostitution*, Ilford: Barnardos.

Barrett, D. with Barrett, E. and Mullenger, N. (eds) (2000) *Youth Prostitution in the New Europe: The Growth in Sex Work*, London: Russell House Publishing.

Barry, K. (1979) *Female Sexual Slavery*, New York: New York University Press.

Bevacqua, M. (2000) *Rape on the Public Agenda: Feminism and the Politics of Sexual Assault*, Boston: Northeastern University Press.

Blunkett, D. (2004) 'Tough, Fair, Modern – Sex Laws For The 21st Century', Home Office Press Release, homeoffice.gov.uk/n_story.asp?item_id=930.

Borys, D.S. and Pope, K.S. (1989) 'Dual Relationships Between Therapist and Client' in *Professional Psychology: Research and Practice* 20(5), 283–93.

Bristol Relaxation Centre (2002) 'Notice to Patrons', www.relaxationcentre.com

British Association for Sexual and Relationship Therapy (2003) 'Therapist Responsibility and Competence', www.basrt.org.uk.

British Association of Counselling and Psychotherapy (September 2003) 'Ethical Framework for Good Practice', www.bacp.co.uk.

British Association of Social Work (2003) 'Code of Ethics', www.basw.co.uk.

British Psychological Society (2000) 'Code of Conduct, Ethical Principles & Guidelines', Leicester: British Psychological Society.

British Register of Complementary Practitioners (2001) 'Code of Ethics and Practice for Members', London: Institute of Complementary Medicine.

Brownmillar, S. (1975) *Against Our Will: Men, Women and Rape*, London: Secker and Warburg.

Burke, V. and Selfe, D.W. (2001) (2nd edition) *Perspectives on Sex, Crime and Society*, London: Cavendish Publishing.

Burton, F. and Carlen, P. (1979) *Official Discourse: On discourse analysis, government publications, ideology and the state*, London: Routledge & Kegan Paul.

Cahill, M.L. (2001) *The social construction of sexual harassment law: the role of the national, organizational and individual context*, Aldershot: Ashgate.

Carlen, P. (2002) 'New Discourses of Justification and Reform for Women's Imprisonment in England' in P. Carlen (ed.) *Women and Punishment*, Cullumpton, Devon: Willan Publishing.

Chambers and Millar (1986) *Prosecuting sexual assault*, Edinburgh: HMSO.

Chartered Society of Physiotherapy (2003) 'Rules of Professional Conduct with Patients', www.csp.org.uk.

Clark, C. (27 April 2001) Home Office Press Notice 150/99, www.nds.coi.gov.uk/coi

Clarkson, P. (1995) *The Therapeutic Relationship in Psychoanalysis, Counselling Psychology and Psychotherapy*, London: Whurr Publishers Ltd.

College of Occupational Therapists (2000) 'Code of Ethics and Professional Conduct for Occupational Therapists', http://cot.co.uk/

Collier, R. (1995) *Combating sexual harassment in the workplace*, Buckingham, Bristol, PA: Open University Press, Taylor and Francis.

Criminal Law Revision Committee (1985) *Seventeenth Report on Off-Street Prostitution*, London: HMSO.

Crouch, M. (2001) *Thinking About Sexual Harassment: A Guide for the Perplexed*, Oxford: Oxford University Press.

Department of Health / Home Office (2000) *Safeguarding Children Involved in Prostitution*, London: HMSO.

Deverell, K. (2001) *Sex, Work and Professionalism: Working in HIV/AIDS*, London and New York: Routledge.

Deverell, K. and Sharma, U. (2000) 'Professionalism in everyday practice: issues of trust, experience and boundaries' in N. Malin (2000) *Professionalism, Boundaries and the Workplace*, London and New York: Routledge.

Dowrick, C. and Frith, L. (1999) *General Practice and Ethics: Uncertainty and Responsibility*, London and New York: Routledge.

Driver, S. and Martell, L. (1997) 'New Labour's Communitarianisms' in *Critical Social Policy*, vol. 17, 27–46.

Dryden, W. (1985) *Therapists' Dilemmas*, London: Sage.

EDF Energy Group plc (June 2000) 'Group Policy Statement on Equal Opportunities', London: Templar House.

Education Counselling Service of the British Council (2000) 'Good Practice Guides', www.britishcouncil.org.

Edwards, S.E. (1996) *Sex and Gender and the Legal Process*, Oxford: Blackstone.

Evans, D. (1993) *Sexual Citizenship: The Material Construction of Sexuality*, London: Routledge.

Evetts, J. (2002) 'New directions in state and international professional occupations: discretionary decision-making and acquired regulation' in *Work, Employment and Society* 16(2): 341–54.

Finnegan, F. (1979) *Poverty and Prostitution: A Study of Victorian Prostitution in York*, Cambridge: Cambridge University Press.

Foucault, M. (1978) *The History of Sexuality: An Introduction*, trans. by R. Hurley, London: Penguin.

Fournier, V. (1999) 'The appeal to professionalism as a disciplinary mechanism' in *The Sociological Review* 47: 280–307.

Fournier, V. (2000) 'Boundary work and the (un)making of the professions' in N. Malin, (2000) *Professionalism, Boundaries and the Workplace*, London and New York: Routledge.

Gabriel, L. and Davies, D. (2000) 'The management of ethical dilemmas associated with dual relationships' in C. Neal, and D. Davies, (eds) (2000) *Issues in Therapy with Lesbian, Gay, Bisexual and Transgender Clients*, Buckingham: Open University Press.

General Council for Chiropractors (1999) 'Code of Practice', www.gcc-uk.org.

General Dental Council (2003) 'Standards of Dental Practice', www.gdc-uk.org/Standards_practice

General Medical Council (2003) 'Protecting Patients: Guiding Doctors', www.gmc-uk.org/Standards/intimate.htm

Giddens, A. (1992) *The Transformation Of Intimacy, Sexuality, Love And Eroticism In Modern Societies*, Cambridge: Polity.

Giddens, A. (1999) 'Runaway World', BBC Reith Lecture, http://news.bbc.co.uk/hi/english/static/events/reith_99/week4/week4.htm

Goggins, P. (2004) 'Tough, Fair, Modern – Sex Laws For The 21st Century', Home Office Press Release, www.homeoffice.gov.uk/n_story.asp?item_id=930.

Gonsiorek, J. C. (1995) *Breaches of Trust: Sexual Exploitation by Health Care Professionals and Clergy*, Thousand Oaks, CA, London, New Delhi: Sage.

Griffiths, S. (1999) 'Criminal Justice Conference: Violence Against Women', Special Conferences Unit, Macclesfield, 24–25 November, www.homeoffice.gov.uk/docs2/cjcviolence20.html.

Hall, R. (1985) *Ask Any Woman*, London: Falling Wall Press.

Harris, J. and Grace, S. (1999) *A Question of Evidence? Investigating and prosecuting rape in the 1990s*, London: HORS 196.

Hearn, J. and Parkin, W. (2001) *Gender, sexuality and violence in organizations: the unspoken forces of organizational violations*, London: Sage.

Hoigard, C. and Finstad, L. (1992) *Backstreets: Prostitution, money and love*, Cambridge: Polity.

Home Office (1957) *The Wolfenden Committee's Report on Homosexual Offences and Prostitution*, London: HMSO.

Home Office (2000) *Setting the Boundaries*, London: The Stationery Office.

Home Office (2002) *Protecting the Public*, London: The Stationery Office.

Home Office (2004a) *Paying The Price: a consultation document*, London: The Stationery Office.

Home Office, (2004b) *Protecting the Public from Sexual Crime: An Explanation of the Sexual Offences Act 2004*, London: The Home Office Communications Directorate, April 2004.

Howarth, G. (forthcoming) *Matter of Life and Death*, Cambridge: Polity.

Howarth, G. and Leaman, O. (eds) (2002) *Encyclopedia of Death and Dying*, London: Routledge.

Howe, A. (ed) (1988) *Sexed Crime in the News*, Leichhardt, NSW: Federation Press.

Infield, P. and Platford, G. (2000) *The law of harassment and stalking*, London: Butterworths.

International Therapy Examinations Council (ITEC) (2002) 'Code of Practice', www.itecworld.co.uk.

Jackson, S. (1999) *Heterosexuality in Question*, London and New York: Sage.

Jehu, D. (1994) *Patients As Victims: Sexual Abuse in Psychotherapy and Counselling*, Chichester: John Wiley and Sons.

Kappeler, S. (1988) *The Pornography of Representation*, Cambridge: Polity.

Kelly, E. and Radford, J. (1996) 'Nothing Really Happened: the Invalidation of Women's Experience of Sexual Violence' in M. Hester, L. Kelly, and J. Radford, (eds) *Women, Violence and Male Power,* Buckingham: Open University Press.

Kelly, L. (1988a) 'What's in a name? Defining Child Sexual Abuse' *Feminist Review*, No. 28, 65–73.

Kelly, L. (1988b) *Surviving Sexual Violence*, Cambridge: Polity.

Kelly, L., Regan, L. and Burton, S. (1991) *An Exploratory Study of the Prevalence of Sexual Abuse in a Sample of 16–21 Year Olds*, London: Child and Woman Abuse Study Unit, University of North London.

Kinnell, H., Bindel, J. and Lopes, A. (2000) 'Violence Against Sex Workers', press release, EUROPAP, Justice for Women and Safe in the City, 6th December.

Koehn. D. (1994) *The Ground of Professional Ethics*, London and New York: Routledge.

Lakin, M. (1988) *Ethical Issues in the Psychotherapies*, Oxford: Oxford University Press.

Lancashire Constabulary (2003) 'Equal Opportunities Policy' hutton08/legalweb/local/51065.htm

Law Commission (2000) 'Appendix C: Consent in Sex Offences: A Policy Paper' in Home Office (2000) *Setting the Boundaries*, London: The Stationery Office.

Lawler, J. (1991) *Behind the Screens: Nursing, Somology and the Problem of the Body*, Melbourne: Churchill Livingstone.

Lawrie, C. and Jenkins, K. (2000) *Women in the workplace: sexual harassment and discrimination*, St. Leonards, NSW: Prospect Media.

Lees, S. (2002) *Carnal Knowledge: Rape on Trial*, London: Women's Press.

Lees, S. and Gregory, J. (1993) *Rape and sexual assault: a study of attrition*, London: Islington Council.

Lees, S. and Gregory, J. (1996) 'Attrition in rape and sexual assault cases', *British Journal of Criminology* 36(1), 1–17.

Levitas, R. (1998) *The Inclusive Society? Poverty, Social Exclusion and New Labour*, London: Macmillan.

Lombroso, C. and Ferrero, G. (2004) *Criminal Woman, The Prostitute and the Normal Woman*, Raleigh, NC: Duke University Press (originally published in 1895).

MacKinnon, C. (1978) *Sexual harassment of working women; a case of sex discrimination*, New Haven, CT: Yale University Press.

MacKinnon, C. (1987) *Feminism Unmodified: Discourses on Life and Law*, Boston, MA: Harvard University Press.

Mahood, L. (1990) *The Magdalenes: Prostitution in the Nineteenth Century*, London: Routledge.

Marks and Spencer (October 2002) 'Equal Opportunities and You: A Guide For All Staff', M & S Print.

Matthews, R. (1986) 'Beyond Wolfenden' in J. Young and R. Matthews (eds) *Confronting Crime*, London: Routledge & Kegan Paul.

Matthews, R. (1993) *Kerb-Crawling, Prostitution and Multi-Agency Policing*, Police Research Group, Crime Prevention Unit Series, Paper 43.

Melrose, M., Barrett, D. and Brodie, I. (1999) *One Way Street? Retrospectives on Childhood Prostitution*, London: The Children's Society.

McKeganay, N. and Barnard, M. (1996) *Sex Work on the Streets: Prostitutes and Their Clients*, Buckingham: Open University Press.

MIND (National Association for Mental Health) (October 1999) 'Guidance Document for Dealing with Complaints of Harassment and Bullying', www.mind.org.uk

Neville, K. (2000) *Internal Affairs: the abuse of power, sexual harassment and hypocrisy in the workplace*, New York, London: McGraw-Hill.

Newport City Council (April 2002) 'Dealing With Bullying and Harassment At Work' Policy, Newport: Human Resources Department, Newport City Council.

North Wales Police Force (April 2004) 'Draft Policy on Fair Management Practice', Colwyn Bay: Human Resources Department, North Wales Police.

Northamptonshire Fire and Rescue Service (July 2001) 'Equality and Fairness At Work' Policy, www.northamptonshire.gov.uk.

O'Neill, M. (1999) *Feminism and Prostitution*, London: Routledge.

Oerton, S. and Phoenix, J. (2001) 'Sex/Bodywork: Discourses and Practices' in *Sexualities: Studies in Culture and Society* 4(4), 387–412.

Painter, K. (1991) *Wife Rape, Marriage and the Law*, Manchester: University of Manchester, Department of Social Policy and Social Work.

Patai, D. (1998) *Heterophobia: sexual harassment and the future of feminism*, Oxford: Rowman and Littlefield Publishers.

Persaud, R. (2003) *From the Edge of the Couch: bizarre psychiatric cases and what they teach us about ourselves*, London: Bantam Press.

Peterson, M. (1992) *At Personal Risk; Boundary Violations in Professional–Client Relationships*, New York, London: W.W. Norton and Company.

Phoenix, J. (2001) *Making Sense of Prostitution*, Basingstoke: Palgrave.

Phoenix, J. (2002a) 'In the Name of Protection: Young People In Prostitution', *Critical Social Policy* 22(2), 353–75.

Phoenix, J. (2002b) 'Youth Prostitution Policy Reform: new discourse, same old story' in P. Carlen, (ed.) *Women and Punishment* Cullumpton, Devon: Willan Publishing.

Phoenix, J. (2003) 'Youth Prostitution Policy: Summary Findings', Bath: University of Bath.

Pilgrim, D. (2002) 'The Emergence of Clinical Psychology as a Profession' in J. Allsop and M. Saks (eds) (2002) *Regulating the Health Professions*, London: Sage.

Plummer, K. (1995) *Telling Sexual Stories: Power, Change and Social Worlds*, London: Routledge.

Plummer, K. (2004) 'Social Worlds, Social Change and the Rise of New Sexualities Theories' in B. Brooks-Gordon, L. Gelsthorpe, M. Johnson and A. Bainham (eds) (2004) *Sexuality Repositioned: Diversity and the Law*, London: Hart Publishing.

Pope, K. (1991) 'Dual Relationships in Psychotherapy', *Ethics and Behaviour* 1(1), 21–34.

Presbyterian Church of Wales (July 2003) 'Book of Order and Rules', www.ebcpcw.org.uk.

Register of Exercise Professionals (2003) 'Code of Ethical Practice' Sport and Recreation Industry Training Organisation.

Research Development and Statistics (2003), *Crime Statistics for England and Wales*, Home Office, www.crimestatistics.org.uk/output/Page27.asp.

Royal Berkshire Ambulance NHS Trust (November 2000) 'Harassment and Bullying at Work Policy PP/C15 Harassment and Bullying at Work', www.rbat.com

Russell, D.E.H. (1984) *Sexual Exploitation: Rape, Child Sexual Abuse and Workplace Harassment*, Beverly Hills, CA: Sage.

Russell, D.E.H. (1990) *Rape in Marriage*, Bloomington, IN: Indiana University Press.

Rutter, P. (1995) *Sex in the Forbidden Zone: when men in power abuse women's trust*, London: Aquarian.

Saks Berman, J. R. (1985) 'Ethical Feminist Perspectives on Dual Relationships with Clients' in L.B. Rosewater, and L.E.A. Walker, (eds) (1985) *Handbook of Feminist Therapy: Women's Issues in Psychotherapy*, New York: Springer Publishing Company.

Scottish and Southern Energy plc. (September 2000) 'Policy Against Harassment At Work', http://scottish-southern.com/.

Scouting Association (2003) Equal Opportunities Policy, www.scoutbase.org.uk.

Self, H. (2003) *Prostitution, Women and Misuse of the Law: the Fallen Daughters of Eve*, London: Cass Publishing.

Selfe, D. and Burke V. (2001) *Perspectives on Sex, Crime and Society*, London: Cavendish Publishing.

Shardlow, S. (1995) 'Confidentiality, accountability and the boundaries of client–worker relationships' in R. Hugman, and D. Smith, (eds) (1995) *Ethical Issues in Social Work*, London and New York: Routledge.

Sim, J. (1997) *Ethical Decision-Making in Therapy Practice*, Oxford: Butterworth-Heinemann.

Sion (1977) *Prostitution and the Law*, London: Faber and Faber.

Skogan, W. (1990) *Disorder and Decline*, New York: Free Press.

Smart, C. (1990) *Feminism and the Power of Law*, Routledge: London.

Social Exclusion Unit (1999) *Teenage Pregnancy*, London: The Stationery Office.

Spanner Trust (2003) Submission to Home Office Sexual Offences Review Board, www.spannertrust.org/documents/sexual offencesreview.asp.

Spongberg, M. (1997) *Feminising Venereal Disease: The Body of the Prostitute in Nineteenth Century Literature*, London: Macmillan Press.

Stone, J. (2002) *An Ethical Framework For Complementary and Alternative Therapists*, London and New York: Routledge.

Stop It Now! UK and Ireland (2004) 'Abuse Questions', www.stopitnow.org.uk//abuse_questions_3.htm.

Tadd, G. V. (1998) *Ethics and Values for Care Workers*, Oxford: Blackwells Science.

Telewest Broadband (2003) 'Nuisance Calls', www.telewest.co.uk/html/telephone/phonesecurity/unwantedcalls.htm

Temkin, J. (1987) *Rape and the Legal Process*, London: Sweet and Maxwell.

Temkin, J. (1995) *Rape and the Criminal Justice System*, London: Dartmouth Publishing.

Temkin, J. (1999) 'Reporting rape in London: a qualitative study', *Howard Journal of Criminal Justice*, Feb. 38(1), 17–41.

Temkin, J. (2000) 'Prosecuting and Defending Rape: Perspectives From the Bar', *Journal of Law and Society*, 27(2), 219–48.

Thames Valley Police (2003) 'Malicious and nuisance calls, messages and post', www.thamesvalley.police.uk/crime-reduction/mal-calls.htm.

Thomas, T. (2000) *Sex Crime: Sex Offending and Society*, Cullompton, Devon: Willan Publishing.

Toner, B. (1977) *The Facts of Rape*, London: Arrow Books.

UK Reiki Federation (2003) 'Codes of Ethics and Standards of Practice', www.reikifed.co.uk/codes.htm.

UK Council for Psychotherapy (1999) 'Codes of Ethics', www.psychotherapy.org.uk/downloads/CodeEthics.pdf.

University of Strathclyde (September 2003) 'Policies, Procedures and Codes of Practices', www.mis.strath.ac.uk/Personnel/site/policies/computing.html.

Vance, C. (ed.) (1989) *Pleasure and Danger: Exploring Female Sexuality*, London: Pandora Press.

Walklate, S. (1989) *Victimology*, London: Unwin Hyman.

Walkowitz, J. (1980) *Prostitution in Victorian Society: women, class and the state*, Cambridge: Cambridge University Press.

Weeks, J. (1981) *Sex, Politics and Society: the Regulation of Sexuality since 1800*, Harlow: Longmans.

West Country Ambulance Services NHS Trust (January 2003) 'Harassment and Bullying in the Workplace Policy' , www.was.co.uk.

West Midlands Fire Service (November 2003) 'Harassment and Bullying Policy', Equality and Diversity Section, Fire Brigade Headquarters, Birmingham.

Williams, B. (1979) *Report of the Committee on Obscenity and Film Censorship*, House of Commons Command Papers, No. 7772.

Wilson, J.Q. and Kelling, G. (1982) 'Broken Windows: The Police and Neighbourhood Safety', *Atlantic Monthly*, March, 29–35.

Younge, G. (2004) 'A Hierarchy of Suffering', *The Guardian*, 20th September 2004.

Index